Emerging Trends in Inclusive Education

Emerging Trends in Inclusive Education

Etash Ranjan

RANDOM

RANDOM PUBLICATIONS

NEW DELHI - 110 002 (INDIA)

Emerging Trends in Inclusive Education

ISBN 978-93-51112-99-0

Published in 2014 in India by

RANDOM PUBLICATIONS

4376-A/4B, Gali Murari Lal, Ansari Road
New Delhi-110 002
Phone: +9111-43580356, 23289044
E-mail: randomexports@gmail.com; sales@randompublications.com; info@randompublications.com

Reprinted 2026

Type Setting by: Friends Media, Delhi-110089

Preface

Inclusive education differs from previously held notions of integration and mainstreaming, which tended to be concerned principally with disability and 'special educational needs' and implied learners changing or becoming 'ready for' or deserving of accommodation by the mainstream. By contrast, inclusion is about the child's right to participate and the school's duty to accept the child. Inclusion rejects the use of special schools or classrooms to separate students with disabilities from students without disabilities. A premium is placed upon full participation by students with disabilities and upon respect for their social, civil, and educational rights. Inclusion gives students with disabilities skills they can use in and out of the classroom. Students in an inclusive classroom are generally placed with their chronological age-mates, regardless of whether the students are working above or below the typical academic level for their age. Also, to encourage a sense of belonging, emphasis is placed on the value of friendships. Teachers often nurture a relationship between a student with special needs and a same-age student without a special educational need. Another common practice is the assignment of a buddy to accompany a student with special needs at all times. This is used to show students that a diverse group of people make up a community, that no one type of student is better than another, and to remove any barriers to a friendship that may occur if a student is viewed as "helpless." Such practices reduce the chance for elitism among students in later grades and encourage cooperation among groups.

The proportion of students with disabilities who are included varies by place and by type of disability, but it is relatively common for students with milder disabilities and less common with certain kinds of severe disabilities. Educators generally say that some students with special needs are not good candidates for inclusion. Many schools expect a fully included student to be working at or near grade level, but more fundamental requirements exist: First, being included requires that the student is able to attend school. Students that are entirely excluded from school (for example, due to long-term hospitalization), or who are educated outside of schools cannot attempt inclusion. There are many positive effects of inclusions where both the students with special needs along with the other students in the classroom both benefit. Research has shown positive effects for children with disabilities in areas such as reaching individualized education program (IEP) goal, improving communication and social skills, increasing positive peer interactions, many educational outcomes, and post school adjustments. Positive effects on children without disabilities include the development of positive attitudes and perceptions of persons with disabilities and the enhancement of social status with nondisabled peers.

This is a practical guide to working with primary and secondary students who need extra attention because of disabilities or giftedness. The authors outline the principles behind educational diversity and inclusive policies, and discuss the range of different needs teachers can expect to encounter in an inclusive classroom.

I thank all members of my team who have helped in the preparation of the book. My special thanks go to "Random Publications" who have published the book.

—Etash Ranjan

Contents

1

Introduction

Inclusion in education is an approach to educating students with special educational needs. Under the inclusion model, students with special needs spend most or all of their time with non-disabled students. Implementation of these practices varies. Schools most frequently use them for selected students with mild to severe special needs.

Inclusive education differs from previously held notions of *integration* and *mainstreaming*, which tended to be concerned principally with disability and 'special educational needs' and implied learners changing or becoming 'ready for' or deserving of accommodation by the mainstream. By contrast, inclusion is about the child's right to participate and the school's duty to accept the child. Inclusion rejects the use of special schools or classrooms to separate students with disabilities from students without disabilities. A premium is placed upon full participation by students with disabilities and upon respect for their social, civil, and educational rights. Inclusion gives students with disabilities skills they can use in and out of the classroom.

Fully inclusive schools, which are rare, no longer distinguish between "general education" and "special education" programmes; instead, the school is restructured so that all students learn together.

Classification

Inclusion has two sub-types: the first is sometimes called regular inclusion or partial inclusion, and the other is full inclusion.

"Inclusive practice" is not always inclusive but is a form of integration. For example, students with special needs are educated in regular classes for nearly all of the day, or at least for more than half of the day. Whenever possible, the students receive any additional help or special instruction in the general classroom, and the student is treated like a full member of the class. However, most specialized services are provided outside a regular classroom, particularly if these services require special equipment or might be disruptive to the rest of the class (such as speech therapy), and students are pulled out of the regular classroom for these services. In this case, the student occasionally leaves the regular classroom to attend smaller, more intensive instructional sessions in a resource room, or to receive other related services, such as speech and language therapy, occupational and/or physical therapy, and social work. This approach can be very similar to many mainstreaming practices, and may differ in little more than the educational ideals behind it.

In the "full inclusion" setting, the students with special needs are always educated alongside students without special needs, as the first and desired option while maintaining appropriate supports and services. Some educators say this might be more effective for the students with special needs. At the extreme, full inclusion is the integration of all students, even those that require the most substantial educational and behavioural supports and services to be successful in regular classes and the elimination of special, segregated special education classes. Special education is considered a service, not a place and those services are integrated into the daily routines and classroom structure, environment, curriculum and strategies and brought to the student, instead of removing the student to meet his or her individual needs. However, this approach to full inclusion is somewhat controversial, and it is not widely understood or applied to date. Much more commonly, local educational agencies provide a variety of settings, from special classrooms to mainstreaming to inclusion, and assign students to the system that seems most likely to help the student achieve his or her individual educational goals. Students with mild or moderate disabilities, as well as disabilities that do not affect academic achievement, such as using wheelchair, are most likely to be fully included. However, students with all types of disabilities from all the different disability categories have been successfully included in general education classes, working and achieving their individual educational goals in regular school environments and activities.

Alternatives

Students with disabilities who are not included are typically either mainstreamed or segregated. A mainstreamed student attends some general education classes, typically for less than half the day, and often for less academically rigorous classes. For example, a young student with significant intellectual disabilities might be mainstreamed for physical education classes, art classes and storybook time, but spend reading and mathematics classes with other students that have similar disabilities. They may have access to a resource room for remediation of course content.

A segregated student attends no classes with non-disabled students. He or she might attend a special school that only enrolls other students with disabilities, or might be placed in a dedicated, self-contained classroom in a school that also enrolls general education students. Some students may be confined to a hospital due to a medical condition and are thus eligible for tutoring services provided by a school district. Less common alternatives include homeschooling and, particularly in developing countries, exclusion from education.

Legal Issues

The new anti-discriminatory climate has provided the basis for much change in policy and statute, nationally and internationally. Inclusion has been enshrined at the same time that segregation and discrimination have been rejected. Articulations of the new developments in ways of thinking, in policy and in law include:

- The UN Convention on the Rights of the Child (1989) which sets out children's rights in respect of freedom from discrimination and in respect of the representation of their wishes and views.
- The Convention against Discrimination in Education of UNESCO prohibits any dicrimination, exclusion or segregation in education.
- The UNESCO Salamanca Statement (1994) which calls on all governments to give the highest priority to inclusive education.
- The UN Convention on the Rights of Persons with Disabilities (2006) which calls on all States Parties to ensure an inclusive education system at all levels.

For schools in the United States, the federal requirement that students be educated in the least restrictive environment that is reasonable encourages the implementation of inclusion for some students.

Frequency of Use

The proportion of students with disabilities who are *included* varies by place and by type of disability, but it is relatively common for students with milder disabilities and less common with certain kinds of severe disabilities. In Denmark, 99% of students with learning disabilities like dyslexia are placed in general education classrooms. In the United States, three out of five students with learning disabilities spend the majority of their time in the general education classroom.

Necessary Resources

Although once hailed as a way to increase achievement while decreasing costs, full inclusion does not save money, reduce students' needs, or improve academic outcomes; in most cases, it merely moves the special education professionals out of their own classrooms and into a corner of the general classroom. To avoid harm to the academic education of students with disabilities, a full panoply of services and resources is required, including:

- Adequate supports and services for the student
- Well-designed individualized education programmes
- Professional development for all teachers involved, general and special educators alike
- Time for teachers to plan, meet, create, and evaluate the students together
- Reduced class size based on the severity of the student needs
- Professional skill development in the areas of cooperative learning, peer tutoring, adaptive curriculum
- Collaboration between parents or guardians, teachers or para educators, specialists, administration, and outside agencies.
- Sufficient funding so that schools will be able to develop programmes for students based on student need instead of the availability of funding.

In principle, several factors can determine the success of inclusive classrooms:

- Family-school partnerships
- Collaboration between general and special educators
- Well-constructed plans that identify specific accommodations, modifications, and goals for each student
- Coordinated planning and communication between "general" and "special needs" staff
- Integrated service delivery
- Ongoing training and staff development

Common Practices

Students in an inclusive classroom are generally placed with their chronological age-mates, regardless of whether the students are working above or below the typical academic level for their age. Also, to encourage a sense of belonging, emphasis is placed on the value of friendships. Teachers often nurture a relationship between a student with special needs and a same-age student without a special educational need. Another common practice is the assignment of a buddy to accompany a student with special needs at all times (for example in the cafeteria, on the playground, on the bus and so on). This is used to show students that a diverse group of people make up a community, that no one type of student is better than another, and to remove any barriers to a friendship that may occur if a student is viewed as "helpless." Such practices reduce the chance for elitism among students in later grades and encourage cooperation among groups.

Teachers use a number of techniques to help build classroom communities:

- Using games designed to build community
- Involving students in solving problems
- Sharing songs and books that teach community
- Openly dealing with individual differences by discussion
- Assigning classroom jobs that build community
- Teaching students to look for ways to help each other
- Utilizing physical therapy equipment such as standing frames, so students who typically use wheelchairs can stand when the other students are standing and more actively participate in activities
- Encouraging students to take the role of teacher and deliver instruction (e.g. read a portion of a book to a student with severe disabilities)
- Focusing on the strength of a student with special needs

Collaboration

Inclusion settings allow children with and without disabilities to play and interact every day, even when they are receiving therapeutic services. When a child displays fine motor difficulty, his ability to fully participate in common classroom activities, such as cutting, colouring, and zipping a jacket may be hindered. While occupational therapists are often called to assess and implement strategies outside of school, it is frequently left up to classroom teachers to implement strategies in school. Collaborating with occupational therapists will help classroom teachers use intervention strategies and increase teacher's awareness about student's needs within school settings and enhance teacher's independence in implementation of occupational therapy strategies.

As a result of the 1997 re-authorization of the Individuals With Disabilities Education Act (IDEA), greater emphasis has been placed on delivery of related services within inclusive, general education environments. [Nolan, 2004] The importance of inclusive, integrated models of service delivery for children with disabilities has been widely researched indicating positive benefits. [Case-Smith& Holland, 2009] In traditional "pull out" service delivery models, children typically work in isolated settings one on one with a therapist, Case-Smith and Holland(2009) argue that children working on skills once or twice a week are "less likely to produce learning that leads to new behaviours and increased competence." [Case Smith &Holland, 2009, pg.419]. In recent years, occupational therapy has shifted from the conventional model of "pull out" therapy to an integrated model where the therapy takes place within a school or classroom.

Selection of Students for Inclusion

Educators generally say that some students with special needs are not good candidates for inclusion. Many schools expect a fully included student to be working at or near grade level, but more fundamental requirements exist: First, being included requires that the student is able to attend school. Students that are entirely excluded from school (for example, due to long-term hospitalization), or who are educated outside of schools (for example, due to enrollment in a distance education programme) cannot attempt inclusion.

Additionally, some students with special needs are poor candidates for inclusion because of their effect on other students. For example, students with severe behavioural problems, such that they represent a serious physical danger to others, are poor candidates for inclusion, because the school has a duty to provide a safe environment to all students and staff.

Finally, some students are not good candidates for inclusion because the normal activities in a general education classroom will prevent them from learning. For example, a student with severe attention difficulties or extreme sensory processing disorders might be highly distracted or distressed by the presence of other students working at their desks. Inclusion needs to be appropriate to the child's unique needs. Most students with special needs do not fall into these extreme categories, as most students do attend school, are not violent, do not have severe sensory processing disorders, etc.

The students that are most commonly included are those with physical disabilities that have no or little effect on their academic work (diabetes mellitus, epilepsy, food allergies, paralysis), students with all types of mild disabilities, and students whose disabilities require relatively few specialized services.

Bowe says that regular inclusion, but not full inclusion, is a reasonable approach for a significant majority of students with special needs. He also says that for some students, notably those with severe autism spectrum disorders or mental retardation, as well as many who are deaf or have multiple disabilities, even regular inclusion may not offer an appropriate education. Teachers of students with autism spectrum disorders sometimes use antecedent procedures, delayed contingencies, self-management strategies, peer-mediated interventions, pivotal response training and naturalistic teaching strategies.

Relationship to Progressive Education

Some advocates of inclusion promote the adoption of progressive education practices. In the progressive education or inclusive classroom, everyone is exposed to a "rich set of activities," and each student does what he or she can do, or what he or she wishes to do and learns whatever comes from that experience. Maria Montessori's schools sometimes named as an example of inclusive education.

Inclusion requires some changes in how teachers teach, as well as changes in how students with and without special needs interact with and relate to one another. Inclusive education practices frequently rely on active learning, authentic assessment practices, applied curriculum, multi-level instructional approaches, and increased attention to diverse student needs and individualization.

Arguments for Full Inclusion

Advocates say that even partial non-inclusion is morally unacceptable. Proponents believe that non-inclusion reduces the disabled students' social importance and that maintaining their social visibility is more important than their academic achievement. Proponents say that society accords disabled people less human dignity when they are less visible in general education classrooms. Advocates say that even if typical students are harmed academically by the full inclusion of certain special needs students, that the non-inclusion of these students would still be morally unacceptable, as advocates believe that the harm to typical students' education is always less important than the social harm caused by making people with disabilities less visible in society.

A second key argument is that everybody benefits from inclusion. Advocates say that there are many children and young people who don't fit in (or feel as though they don't), and that a school that fully includes all disabled students feels welcoming to all. Moreover, at least one author has studied the impact a diversified student body has on the general education population and has concluded that students with mental retardation who spend time among their peers show an increase in social skills and academic proficiency.

Advocates for inclusion say that the long-term effects of typical students who are included with special needs students at a very young age have a heightened sensitivity to the challenges that others face, increased empathy and compassion, and improved leadership skills, which benefits all of society.

A combination of inclusion and pull-out (partial inclusion) services has been shown to be beneficial to students with learning disabilities in the area of reading comprehension, and preferential for the special education teachers delivering the services.

Inclusive education can be beneficial to all students in a class, not just students with special needs. Some research show that inclusion helps students understand the importance of working together, and fosters a sense of tolerance and empathy among the student body.

Positive Effects

There are many positive effects of inclusions where both the students with special needs along with the other students in the classroom both benefit. Research has shown positive effects for children with disabilities in areas such as reaching individualized education programme (IEP) goal, improving communication and social skills, increasing positive peer interactions, many educational outcomes, and post school adjustments. Positive effects on children without disabilities include the development of positive attitudes and perceptions of persons with disabilities and the enhancement of social status with nondisabled peers.

Several studies have been done on the effects of inclusion of children with disabilities in general education classrooms. A study on inclusion compared integrated and segregated (special education only) preschool students. The study determined that children in the integrated sites progressed in social skills development while the segregated children actually regressed.

Another study shows the effect on inclusion in grades 2 to 5. The study determined that students with specific learning disabilities made some academic and affective gains at a pace comparable to that of normal achieving students. Specific learning disabilities students also showed an improvement in self-esteem and in some cases improved motivation.

Criticism

Critics of full and partial inclusion include both educators, administrators and parents. Full and partial inclusion approaches neglect to acknowledge the fact most students with significant special needs require individualized instruction or highly controlled environments. Thus, general education classroom teachers often are teaching a curriculum while the special education teacher is remediating instruction at the same time. Similarly, a child with serious inattention problems may be unable to focus in a classroom that contains twenty or more active children. Although with the increase of incidence of disabilities in the student population, this is a circumstance all teachers must contend with, and is not a direct result of inclusion as a concept.

Full inclusion may in fact be a way for schools to placate parents and the general public, using the word as a phrase to garner attention for what are in fact illusive efforts to education students with special needs in the general education environment.

At least one study examined the lack of individualized services provided for students with IEPs when placed in an inclusive rather than mainstreamed environment.

Some researchers have maintained school districts neglect to prepare general education staff for students with special needs, thus preventing any achievement. Moreover, school districts often expound an inclusive philosophy for political reasons, and do away with any valuable pull-out services, all on behalf of the students who have no so say in the matter.

Inclusion is viewed by some as a practice philosophically attractive yet impractical. Studies have not corroborated the proposed advantages of full or partial inclusion. Moreover, "push in" servicing does not allow students with moderate to severe disabilities individualized instruction in a resource room, from which many show considerable benefit in both learning and emotional development.

Parents of disabled students may be cautious about placing their children in an inclusion programme because of fears that the children will be ridiculed by other students, or be unable to develop regular life skills in an academic classroom.

Some argue that inclusive schools are not a cost-effective response when compared to cheaper or more effective interventions, such as special education. They argue that special education helps "fix" the special needs students by providing individualized and personalized instruction to meet their unique needs. This is to help students with special needs adjust as quickly as possible to the mainstream of the school and community. Proponents counter that students with special needs are not fully into the mainstream of student life because they are secluded to special education. Some argue that isolating students with special needs may lower their self-esteem and may reduce their ability to deal with other people. In keeping these students in separate classrooms they aren't going to see the struggles and achievements that they can make together. However, at least one study indicated mainstreaming in education has long-term benefits for students as indicated by increased test scores, where the benefit of inclusion has not yet been proved.

Broader Approach: Social and Cultural Inclusion

As used by UNESCO, inclusion refers to far more than students with special educational needs. It is centred on the inclusion of marginalized groups, such as religious, racial, ethnic, and linguistic minorities, immigrants, girls, the poor, students with disabilities, HIV/AIDS patients, remote populations, and more. In some places, these people are not actively included in education and learning processes. In the U.S. this broader definition is also known as "culturally responsive" education, and is promoted among the ten equity assistance centres of the U.S. Department of Education, for example in Region IX (AZ, CA, NV), by the Equity Alliance at ASU. Gloria Ladson-Billings points out that teachers who are culturally responsive know how to base learning experiences on the cultural realities of the child (e.g. home life, community experiences, language background, belief systems). Proponents argue that culturally responsive pedagogy is good for all students because it builds a caring community where everyone's experiences and abilities are valued.

Proponents want to maximize the participation of all learners in the community schools of their choice and to rethink and restructure policies, curricula, cultures and practices in schools and learning environments so that diverse learning needs can be met, whatever the origin or nature of those needs. They say that all students can learn and benefit from education, and that schools should adapt to the physical, social, and cultural needs of students, rather than students adapting to the needs of the school. Proponents believe that individual differences between students are a source of richness and diversity, which should be supported through a wide and flexible range of responses. The challenge of rethinking and restructuring schools to become more culturally responsive calls for a complex systems view of the educational system, where one can extend the idea of strength through diversity to all participants in the educational system (e.g. parents, teachers, community members, staff).

Although inclusion is generally associated with elementary and secondary education, it is also applicable in postsecondary education. According to UNESCO, inclusion "is increasingly understood more broadly as a reform that supports and welcomes diversity amongst all learners." Under this broader definition of inclusion, steps should also be taken to eliminate discrimination and provide accommodations for all students who are at a disadvantage because of some reason other than disability.

Special Education

Special education or special needs education is the education of students with special needs in a way that addresses the students' individual differences and needs. Ideally, this process involves the individually planned and systematically monitored arrangement of teaching procedures, adapted equipment and materials, accessible settings, and other interventions designed to help learners with special needs achieve a higher level of personal self-sufficiency and success in school and community than would be available if the student were only given access to a typical classroom education.

Common special needs include challenges with learning, communication challenges, emotional and behavioural disorders, physical disabilities, and developmental disorders. Students with these kinds of special needs are likely to benefit from additional educational services such as different approaches to teaching, use of technology, a specifically adapted teaching area, or resource room.

Intellectual giftedness is a difference in learning and can also benefit from specialized teaching techniques or different educational programmes, but the term "special education" is generally used to specifically indicate instruction of students whose special needs reduce their ability to learn independently or in an ordinary classroom, and gifted education is handled separately.

In most developed countries, educators are modifying teaching methods and environments so that the maximum number of students are served in general education environments. Special education in developed countries is often regarded less as a "place" and more as "a range of services, available in every school." Integration can reduce social stigmas and improve academic achievement for many students.

The opposite of *special education* is *general education.* General education is the standard curriculum presented with standard teaching methods and without additional supports.

Identifying Students with Special Needs

Some children are easily identified as candidates for special needs from their medical history. They may have been diagnosed with a genetic condition that is associated with mental retardation, may have various forms of brain damage, may have a developmental disorder, may have visual or hearing disabilities, or other disabilities.

Among students whose identification is less obvious, such as students with learning difficulties, two primary methods have been used for identifying them: the discrepancy model and the response to intervention model. The discrepancy model depends on the teacher noticing that the students' achievements are noticeably below what is expected. The response to intervention model advocates earlier intervention.

In the discrepancy model, a student receives special educational services for a specific learning difficulty (SLD) if and only if the student has at least normal intelligence and the student's academic achievement is below what is expected of a student with his or her IQ. Although the discrepancy model has dominated the school system for many years, there has been substantial criticism of this approach (e.g., Aaron, 1995, Flanagan and Mascolo, 2005) among researchers. One reason for criticism is that diagnosing SLDs on the basis of the discrepancy between achievement and IQ does not predict the effectiveness of treatment. Low academic achievers who also have low IQ appear to benefit from treatment just as much as low academic achievers who have normal or high intelligence.

The alternative approach, response to intervention, identifies children who are having difficulties in school in their first or second year after starting school. They then receive additional assistance such as participating in a reading remediation programme. The response of the children to this intervention then determines whether they are designated as having a learning disability. Those few who still have trouble may then receive designation and further assistance. Sternberg (1999) has argued that early remediation can greatly reduce the number of children meeting diagnostic criteria for learning disabilities. He has also suggested that the focus on learning disabilities and the provision of accommodations in school fails to acknowledge that people have a range of strengths and weaknesses and places undue emphasis on academics by insisting that people should be propped up in this arena and not in music or sports.

Individual Needs

A special education programme should be customized to address each individual student's unique needs. Special educators provide a continuum of services, in which students with special needs receive services in varying degrees based on their individual needs. Special education programmes need to be individualized so that they address the unique combination of needs in a given student.

In the United States, Canada, and the UK, educational professionals used the initialism IEP when referring to a student's individualized education plan.

Students with special needs are assessed to determine their specific strengths and weaknesses. Placement, resources, and goals are determined on the basis of the student's needs. Accommodations and Modifications to the regular programme may include changes in curriculum, supplementary aides or equipment, and the provision of specialized physical adaptations that allow students to participate in the educational environment to the fullest extent possible. Students may need this help to access subject matter, to physically gain access to the school, or to meet their emotional needs. For example, if the assessment determines that the student cannot write by hand because of a physical disability, then the school might provide a computer for typing assignments, or allow the student to answer questions orally instead. If the school determines that the student is severely distracted by the normal activities in a large, busy classroom, then the student might be placed in a smaller classroom such as a resource room.

Methods of Provision

Schools use different approaches to providing special education services to identified students. These can be broadly grouped into four categories, according to whether and how much contact the student with special needs has with non-disabled students (using North American terminology):

- Inclusion: In this approach, students with special educational needs spend all, or at least more than half, of the school day with students who do not have special educational needs. Because inclusion can require substantial modification of the general curriculum, most schools use it only for selected students with mild to moderate special needs, for which is accepted as a best practice. Specialized services may be provided inside or outside the regular classroom, depending on the type of service. Students may occasionally leave the regular classroom to attend smaller, more intensive instructional sessions in a resource room, or to receive other related services that might require specialized equipment or might be disruptive to the rest of the class, such as speech and language therapy, occupational therapy, physical therapy, rehabilitation counselling, or might require greater privacy, such as counselling sessions with a social worker.
- Mainstreaming refers to the practice of educating students with special needs in classes with non-disabled students during specific time periods based on their skills. Students with special needs are segregated in separate classes exclusively for students with special needs for the rest of the school day.
- Segregation in a separate classroom or special school exclusively for students with special needs: In this model, students with special needs spend no time in classes with non-disabled students. Segregated students may attend the same school where regular classes are provided, but spend all instructional time exclusively in a separate classroom for students with special needs. If their special class is located in an ordinary school, they may be provided opportunities for social integration outside the classroom, e.g., by eating meals with non-disabled students. Alternatively, these students may attend a special school.
- Exclusion: A student who does not receive instruction in any school is excluded from school. Historically, most students

with special needs have been excluded from school. Such exclusion still affects about 23 million disabled children worldwide, particularly in poor, rural areas of developing countries. It may also occur when a student is in hospital, housebound, or detained by the criminal justice system. These students may receive one-on-one instruction or group instruction. Students who have been suspended or expelled are not considered excluded in this sense.

Special Schools

A *special school* is a school catering for students who have special educational needs due to severe learning difficulties, physical disabilities or behavioural problems. Special schools may be specifically designed, staffed and resourced to provide the appropriate special education for children with additional needs. Students attending special schools generally do not attend any classes in mainstream schools.

Special schools provide individualised education, addressing specific needs. Student:teacher ratios are kept low, often 6:1 or lower depending upon the needs of the children. Special schools will also have other facilities for the development of children with special needs, such as soft play areas, sensory rooms, or swimming pools, which are vital for the therapy of certain conditions.

In recent times, places available in special schools are declining as more children with special needs are educated in mainstream schools. There will always be some children, however, whose learning needs are not appropriately met in a regular classroom setting and will require specialised education and resources to provide the level of support they require. An example of a special need that may require the intensive services a special school provides is mental retardation. However this practice is often frowned upon by school districts in the USA in the light of Least Restrictive Environment as mandated in the Individuals with Disabilities Education Act.

An alternative is a special unit or special classroom, also called a self-contained classroom, which is a separate room or rooms dedicated solely to the education of students with special needs within a larger school that also provides general education. These classrooms are typically staffed by specially trained teachers, who provide specific, individualized instruction to individuals and small groups of students with special needs. Self-contained classrooms, because they are located in a general education school, may have students who remain in the self-contained classroom full-time, or students who are included in certain general education classes. In the United States a part-time alternative that is appropriate for some students is sometimes called a resource room.

History of Special Schools

One of the first special schools in the world was the Institut National des Jeunes Aveugles in Paris, which was founded in 1784. It was the first school in the world to teach blind students. The first school in U.K, for the Deaf was established 1760 in Edinburgh by Thomas Braidwood, with education for visually impaired people beginning in the Edinburgh and Bristol in 1765.

In the 19th Century, people with disabilities and the inhumane conditions where they were supposed to be housed and educated were addressed in the literature of Charles Dickens. Dickens characterized people with severe disabilities as having the same—if not more—compassion and insight in Bleak House and Little Dorrit.

Such attention to the downtrodden conditions of people with disabilities brought with it reforms in Europe including the re-evalutation of special schools. In the United States reform came slower. Throughout the mid half of the 20th century, special schools, termed institutions, were not only acceptable they were encouraged. Students with disabilites were housed with people with mental illness, and little if any education took place.

With the Amendments to the Individuals with Disabilities Act of 1997, school districts in the United States began to slowly integrate students with moderate and severe special needs into regular school systems. This changed the form and function of special education services in many school districts and special schools subsequently saw a steady decrease in enrollment as districts weighed the cost per student. It also posed general funding dilemmas to certain local schools and districts, changed how schools view assessments, and formally introduced the concept of inclusion to many educators, students and parents.

Instructional Strategies

Different instructional techniques are used for some students with special educational needs. Instructional strategies are classified as being either accommodations or modifications.

An *accommodation* is a reasonable adjustment to teaching practices so that the student learns the same material, but in a format that is accessible to the student. Accommodations may be classified by whether they change the presentation, response, setting, or scheduling. For example, the school may accommodate a student with visual impairments by providing a large-print textbook; this is a presentation accommodation.

A *modification* changes or adapts the material to make it simpler. Modifications may change what is learned, how difficult the material is, what level of mastery the student is expected to achieve, whether and how the student is assessed, or any another aspect of the curriculum. For example, the school may modify a reading assignment for a student with reading difficulties by substituting a shorter, easier book. A student may receive both accommodations and modifications.

Examples of modifications

- Skipping subjects: Students may be taught less information than typical students, skipping over material that the school deems inappropriate for the student's abilities or less important than other subjects. For example, students whose fine motor skills are weak may be taught to print block letters, but not cursive handwriting.
- Simplified assignments: Students may read the same literature as their peers but have a simpler version, for example Shakespeare with both the original text and a modern paraphrase available.
- Shorter assignments: Students may do shorter homework assignments or take shorter, more concentrated tests, e.g. 10 math problems instead of 30.
- Extra aids: If students have deficiencies in working memory, a list of vocabulary words, called a *word bank*, can be provided during tests, to reduce lack of recall and increase chances of comprehension. Students might use a calculator when other students are not.
- Extended time: Students with lower processing speed may benefit from extended time in assignments and/or tests in order to comprehend questions, recall information, and synthesize knowledge.

Examples of Accommodations

- Response accommodations: Typing homework assignments rather than hand-writing them (considered a modification if the subject is learning to write by hand). Having someone else write down answers given verbally.

- Presentation accommodations: Listening to audio books rather than reading printed books. Agencies like Recording for the Blind and Dyslexic in America and RNIB National Library Service in the UK offer a variety of titles on tape and CD. These may be used as substitutes for the text, or as supplements intended to bolster the students' reading fluency and phonetic skills. Similar options include designating a person to read text to the student, or providing text to speech software. (Considered a modification if the purpose of the assignment is reading skills acquisition). Designating a person to take notes during lectures. Using a talking calculator rather than one with only a visual display.
- Setting accommodations: Taking a test in a quieter room. Moving the class to a room that is physically accessible, e.g., on the first floor of a building or near an elevator. Arranging seating assignments to benefit the student, e.g., by sitting at the front of the classroom.
- Scheduling accommodations: Students may be given rest breaks or extended time on tests (may be considered a modification, if speed is a factor in the test).

All developed countries permit or require some degree of accommodation for students with special needs, and special provisions are usually made in examinations which take place at the end of formal schooling.

In addition to how the student is taught the academic curriculum, schools may provide non-academic services to the student. These are intended ultimately to increase the student's personal and academic abilities. Related services include developmental, corrective, and other supportive services as are required to assist a student with special needs and includes speech and language pathology, audiology, psychological services, physical therapy, occupational therapy, counselling services, including rehabilitation counselling, orientation and mobility services, medical services as defined by regulations, parent counselling and training, school health services, school social work, assistive technology services, other appropriate developmental or corrective support services, appropriate access to recreation and other appropriate support services. In some countries, most related services are provided by the schools; in others, they are provided by the normal healthcare and social services systems.

As an example, students who have autistic spectrum disorders, poor impulse control, or other behavioural challenges may learn self-management techniques, be kept closely on a comfortingly predictable schedule, or given extra cues to signal activities.

Issues

At-risk students (those with educational needs that are not associated with a disability) are often placed in classes with students who have disabilities. Critics assert that placing at-risk students in the same classes as students with disabilities may impede the educational progress of people with disabilities. Some special education classes have been criticized for a watered-down curriculum.

The practice of inclusion (in mainstream classrooms) has been criticized by advocates and some parents of children with special needs because some of these students require instructional methods that differ dramatically from typical classroom methods. Critics assert that it is not possible to deliver effectively two or more very different instructional methods in the same classroom. As a result, the educational progress of students who depend on different instructional methods to learn often fall even further behind their peers.

Parents of typically developing children sometimes fear that the special needs of a single "fully included" student will take critical levels of attention and energy away from the rest of the class and thereby impair the academic achievements of all students.

Some parents, advocates, and students have concerns about the eligibility criteria and their application. In some cases, parents and students protest the students' placement into special education programmes. For example, a student may be placed into the special education programmes due to a mental health condition such as obsessive compulsive disorder, depression, anxiety, panic attacks or ADHD, while the student and his parents believe that the condition is adequately managed through medication and outside therapy. In other cases, students whose parents believe they require the additional support of special education services are denied participation in the programme based on the eligibility criteria.

Whether it is useful and appropriate to attempt to educate the most severely disabled children, such as children who are in a persistent vegetative state, is debated. While many severely disabled children can learn simple tasks, such as pushing a buzzer when they want attention, some children may be incapable of learning. Some parents and advocates say that these children would be better served by substituting improved physical care for any academic programme. In other cases, they question whether teaching such non-academic subjects, such as pushing a buzzer, is properly the job of the school system, rather than the health care system.

Another large issue is the lack of resources enabling individuals with special needs to receive an education in the developing world. As a consequence, 98 percent of children with special needs in developing countries do not have access to education.

National Approaches

Africa

South Africa: White Papers in 1995 and 2001 discuss special education in the country. Local schools are given some independent authority.

Both modifications and accommodations are recommended, depending on the student's individual needs.

Asia

China: According to the latest census, there are 82.96 million disabled people in China, accounts for 6.34% of the overall population. There are various problems relating to the living conditions of these large group of people. Proper education plays a crucial role in solving such problems.

Current Situation

One of the biggest problems China faces related to disabled people is the education problem. Comparing with the large number of disabled population, there are quite few educational institutions for them. Up to 2008, there are only 1640 schools and institutions specifically for disabled people; and there are only 46 thousand teaching staffs in total.

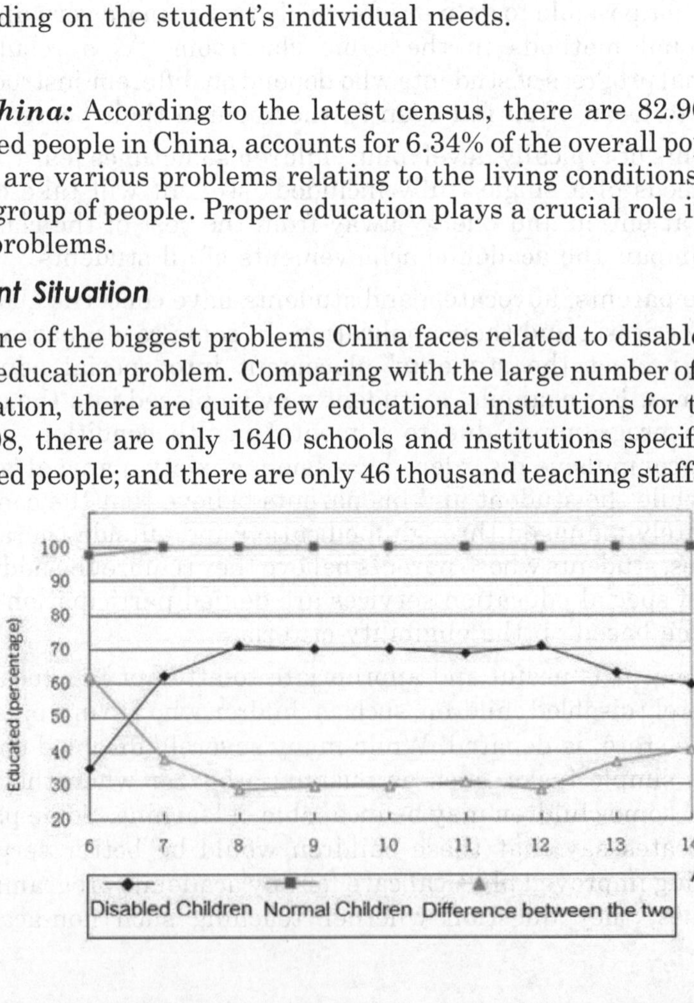

As the graph above indicates, only about 60% to 70% of the 6–14 years old school-aged children can receive proper education. For disabled people 15 years old and above, there are even larger differences in education level between normal people and disabled people. Most of the disabled people have very low education level. Only 25% of them have gone to high schools or higher educational institutions.

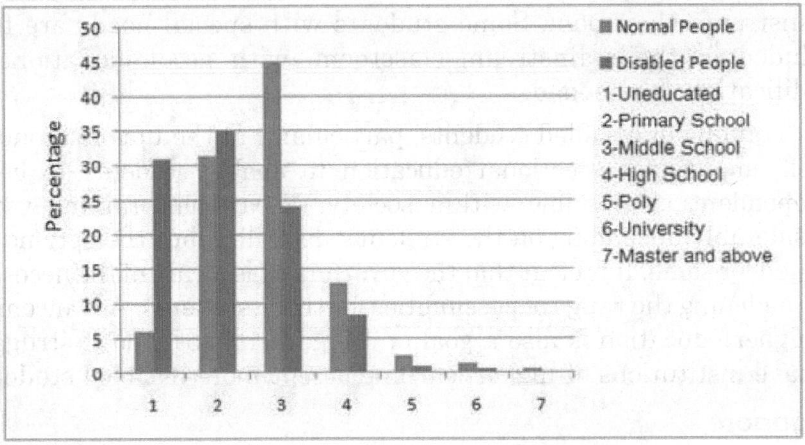

Another issue directly related to education is the employment rate. As some of the researchers report, more than 10% of the disabled people do not have adequate food and clothing; about 40% have very low income; and only 25% are employed on a full-time basis. Among those who are employed, 96.6% are manual workers, only 3.4% are mental workers. The main reason behind is more than clear, not well-educated disabled people can only take those manual works. Furthermore, employment status will directly affect peoples' income. Normal families will tend to have 23.26% higher family income than families with at least one disabled person.

Other than what is mentioned above, disabled people tend to need more psychological and mental help than normal people as well. There is a lot China could do to improve in the education related to disabled people.

Japan

Japanese students with special needs are placed in one of four different school arrangements: special schools, special classrooms with another school, in resource rooms (which are called *tsukyu*), or in regular classrooms.

Special schools are reserved for students whose severe disabilities cannot be accommodated in the local school. They do not use the same grading or marking systems as mainstream schools, but instead assess students according to their individualized plans.

Special classes are similar, and may vary the national curriculum as the teachers see fit. *Tsukyu* are resource rooms that students with milder problems use part-time for specialized instruction individually in small groups. These students spend the rest of the day in the mainstream classroom. Some students with special needs are fully included in the mainstream classroom, with accommodations or modifications as needed.

Training of disabled students, particularly at the upper-secondary level, emphasizes vocational education to enable students to be as independent as possible within society. Vocational training varies considerably depending on the student's disability, but the options are limited for some. It is clear that the government is aware of the necessity of broadening the range of possibilities for these students. Advancement to higher education is also a goal of the government, and it struggles to have institutions of higher learning accept more disabled students.

Singapore

Special education is regulated centrally by the Singapore Ministry of Education. Both special schools and integration into mainstream schools are options for students with special educational needs, but most students with disabilities are placed in special schools.

Students with special education who wish accommodations on national exams must provide appropriate documentation to prove that they are disabled. Accommodations, but not modifications (e.g., simpler questions) are normally approved if they are similar to the accommodations already being used in everyday schoolwork, with the goal of maintaining the exam's integrity while not having students unfairly disadvantaged by factors that are unrelated to what is being tested. The accommodations are listed on the Primary School Leaving Exam.

Australia

Australian Association of Special Education Inc (AASE)'s position is informed by the Disability Standards for Education 2005 which require that students with disabilities are treated on the same basis as other students in regards to enrolment and participation in education.

With respect to standardized tests, special consideration procedures are in place in all states for students who are disabled.

Students must provide documentation Not all desired forms of accommodations are available. For example, students who cannot read, even if the inability to read is due to a disability, cannot have the exam read to them, because the exam results should accurately show that the student is unable to read. Reports on matriculation exams do not mention whether the student received any accommodations in taking the test.

Europe

Each country in Europe has its own special education support structures.

Czech Republic

Schools must take students' special education needs into account when assessing their achievements.

Denmark

In Denmark, 99% of students with specific learning difficulties like dyslexia are educated alongside students without any learning challenges.

Finland

Schools adapt the national guidelines to the needs of individual students. Students with special educational needs are given an individualized plan.

They may be exempted from some parts of school examinations, such as students with hearing impairments not taking listening comprehension tests. If the student receives modifications to the school-leaving exams, this is noted on the certificate of achievement. If they are not following the national core curriculum, then they are tested according to the goals of their individual educational programme.

France

French students with disabilities are normally included in their neighbourhood school, although children may be placed in special schools if their personalized plan calls for it. Each student's personalized school plan describes teaching methods, psychological, medical and paramedical services that the school will provide to the student.

Germany

Most students with special needs in Germany attend a special school that serves only children with special needs. These include:

- *Förderschule für Lernbehinderte* (special school for learning disabilities): for children who have challenges that impair learning
- *Förderschule mit dem Förderschwerpunkt Geistige Entwicklung* (school for cognitive development): for children with very severe learning challenges
- *Förderschule Schwerpunkt emotionale und soziale Entwicklung* (school for emotional and social development): for children who have special emotional needs
- *Förderschule für Blinde* (school for the blind): for blind children
- *Förderschule für Sehbehinderte* (school for the visually impaired): for children who are visually challenged
- *Förderschule für Gehörlose* (school for the deaf): for deaf children
- *Förderschule für Schwerhörige* (school for the hearing impaired): for children who are hearing impaired
- *Förderschule für Körperbehinderte* (school for children with physical disabilities): for children with physical disabilities
- *Förderschule für Sprachbehinderte* (school for children with language disorders): for children with language disorders
- *Förderschule für Taubblinde* (school for the deafblind): for children who are deafblind
- *Schule für Kranke* (school for ill children): for children who are too ill to attend school or are hospitalized for a longer
- *Förderschule für schwer mehrfach Behinderte* (school for children with severe and multiple disabilities): for children with severe and multiple disabilities who needs very special care and attention. Sometimes these children are only susceptible for very basic emotional and sensory stimulation. Thus teachers at these school (as well as at schools for the deafblind) are highly specialized professionals.

One in 21 German students attends a special school. Teachers at those schools are specially trained professionals who have specialized in special needs education while in university. Special schools often have a very favourable student-teacher ratio and facilities other schools do not have.

Some special needs children in Germany do not attend a special school, but are educated in a mainstream school such as a Hauptschule or Gesamtschule (comprehensive school).

Students with special educational needs may be exempted from standardized tests or given modified tests.

Greece

Greek students with special needs may attend either mainstream schools or special schools.

Students whose disabilities have been certified may be exempted from some standardized tests or given alternative tests. Accommodations are responsive to students' needs; for example, students with visual impairments may take oral tests, and students with hearing impairments take written tests. Accommodations and modifications are noted on the certificate of achievement.

Hungary

Special Education is Regulated Centrally: According to the 1993 Act on Public Education, students with special educational needs may be exempted from standardized tests or given modified tests. They have a right to extra time, a choice of formats for the tests (e.g., oral rather than written), and any equipment that they normally use during the school day.

As of 2006, students with disabilities received a significant bonus (eight points) on the university entrance examination, which has been criticized as unfair.

The Netherlands

As a general rule, students with special educational needs are integrated into their regular, mainstream schools with appropriate support, under the "Going to School Together" policy (*Weer Samen Naar School*). Four types of disability-specific special schools exist. The national policy is moving towards "suitable education" (*passend onderwijs*), based on the individual's strengths and weakensses.

A strong emphasis is placed on the specific needs and positive capabilities of the individual, rather than on limitations. Disabilities are normally documented by experts.

Norway

The National Support System for Special Needs Education (Statped) is managed by the Norwegian Directorate for Education and Training. The general objective for Statped is to give guidance and support to those in charge of the education in municipalities and county administrations to ensure that children, young people and adults with major and special educational needs are secured well-advised educational and developmental provisions. The institutions affiliated with Statped offer a broad spectrum of services. Statped consists of 13 resource centres owned by the State, and 4 units for special education, where Statped buys services. These centres offer special educational guidance and support for local authorities and county administrations.

Portugal

Students with disabilities have a "guaranteed right" to appropriate accommodations on assessments. Schools are generally considered autonomous.

Slovenia

On national tests, the National Examination Centre normally grants most requests for accommodations that are supported by the local school's examination committee. Legislation opposes the use of modifications that would be unfair to non-disabled students.

Spain

Schools are required to provide services and resources to students with special educational needs so that they make progress and participate in school. If the local school is unable to provide appropriately for an individual student, then the student may be transferred to a special school. Spanish non-governmental organizations like ONCE have traditionally provided significant services to students with disabilities.

Sweden

Local schools have significant autonomy, based on national guidelines. Schools are expected to help students meet the goals that are set for them. There are special schools (Swedish:Särskola) for students with low abilities to attend normal education. There has in 2012-2013 been media criticism on the fact that students with light problems such as dyslexia have been placed in special schools, seriously hampering their chances on the labour market.

Switzerland

Education is controlled by the 26 cantons, and so special education programmes vary from place to place. However, integration is typical. Students are assessed according to their individual learning goals.

United Kingdom

Special Educational Needs' is an umbrella term for an aspect of UK school education focusing on students primarily with learning difficulties and/or disability. In school documents, it is abbreviated to 'SEN' / 'SEND' - it is also commonly interchanged with 'Inclusion' and 'Narrowing the Gap' as broad terminology. The term covers specific learning difficulties such as dyslexia and ADHD, pervasive disorders such as autism and physical disability such as visual impairment and hearing impairment.

SEN policy and provision is a devolved matter with each of the countries of the United Kingdom having separate systems under separate governments: the UK Government is responsible for education in England, the Scottish Government is responsible for education in Scotland, the Welsh Government is responsible for education in Wales and the Northern Ireland Executive is responsible for education in Northern Ireland.

Across the UK school education systems, provision for SEN is widely varied with a 'mixed economy' of 'learning support' teams based in mainstream schools, specialist schools offering permanent placements and pupil referral units offering temporary placements for students subject to formal exclusion and requiring further assessment.

However, there are common practices found across the country. All schools are legally obliged to maintain an SEN Coordinator post or equivalent position. It is the only mandatory position other than the headteacher / principal position. There is also an SEN Code of Practice, originally published in 2001, which provides non-binding guidance on how provision should be shaped and maintained. Most authorities operate a graduated approach based on the level of need and additional support required - typically using the terms 'School Action', 'School Action+' and 'Statement of Special Educational Need'.

Since the publishing of the SEND Green Paper in 2011, current common practices are being reviewed and reformed with a small number of authorities acting as 'pathfinders'.

Special Education in England

Special education in England is the responsibility of the Government of the United Kingdom and the term "special educational needs" is used to describe the needs of children who need additional provision in order to make progress. This includes children with moderate or severe learning difficulties and physical, neurological or sensory disabilities (such as hearing, motor and visual disabilities) as well as needs such as dyslexia, developmental coordination disorder, autism, Asperger syndrome and attention-deficit hyperactivity disorder (ADHD).

Special Educational Needs (SEN)

Children who face barriers to their learning will often require additional educational intervention to support their learning. This may include what is commonly referred to as Wave 2 or Wave 3 intervention. Wave 2 intervention consists of time limited support for a child, focusing on a particular area of difficulty. This support is provided, within the classroom, with the view to accelerate progress and address misconceptions that may have developed. Wave 3 intervention consists of more individualised support designed specifically for an individual child, again, with the view to accelerate progress.

If a child or young person has not made progress despite such differentiated teaching he or she would usually be supported by a staged method of support outlined in the 2001 SEN Revised Code of Practice. A meeting would usually be arranged between key school staff such as the child's class teacher and SENCo (special educational needs coordinator), parents and the child. Key learning objectives would be agreed and a plan made for the provision necessary to achieve these. The Code of Practice recommends an Individual Education Plan as a means of recording and reviewing this. That level of support is known as School Action and would usually result in additional support being made available for a child, such as a few hours working with an adult each week. If a child's needs are greater or (s)he has not made sufficient progress in response to a School Action level of support then a School Action Plus level may be appropriate. This is similar to School Action but usually includes a greater level of resource and additional advice from appropriate professionals from outside the school, such as an educational psychologist or speech and language therapist.

If a child or young person's parent(s) or educational setting believe that his or her needs cannot be met by the school's resources they can apply to their local authority to carry out a Statutory Assessment of Special Educational Needs. If this is agreed the Statutory Assessment can lead to a Statement of Special Educational Needs. This is a document which summarises the child or young person's needs; what learning objectives need to be addressed and what provision is necessary to achieve this. The local authority is responsible for the provision on the Statement and will provide funding and advice to the educational setting to ensure this happens. The number of children with Statements of SEN often varies according to location due to the different arrangements for supporting SEN in each authority. However the criteria for whether a statutory assessment is necessary are national and described in the 2001 SEN Revised Code of Practice and parents have a right to appeal to the First-tier Tribunal (formerly the Special Educational Needs and Disabilities Tribunal) if they do not agree with the local authority's decision. In most cases it is appropriate for children with statements of SEN to be educated in their local mainstream school with additional support. However it may be agreed that some children or young people with very significant needs will have their needs better met in a special school.

Figures published in 2009 showed that 17.8% of pupils in English schools have special educational needs (SEN), a proportion that has steadily grown over the last four years, from 14.9% in 2005.

The previous year, in January 2008, the Department for Children, Schools and Families (DCSF) stated that some 223,600 (or 2.8 per cent) of pupils across all schools in England had statements of SEN. The percentage of pupils with statements of SEN placed in mainstream schools (nursery, primary, secondary) was 56.6 per cent. The corresponding figures for the proportion of pupils with statements of SEN placed in maintained special schools was 36.9 per cent, with 3.6 per cent in independent schools.

In 2008 there were some 1,390,700 pupils with SEN without statements representing 17.2 per cent of pupils across all schools. This is an increase from 16.4 per cent from a year earlier. Contrary to the pattern for pupils with statements of SEN, the incidence of pupils with SEN without statements is greater in primary schools (18.1 per cent) than in secondary schools (17.8 per cent).

In spring of 2011, the Conservative - Liberal Democrat coalition released a new green paper entitled "Support and aspiration: a new approach to special educational needs and disability." It looks to change the way that special needs provision is assessed. The green paper proposes a new assessment that will take all areas of a child's needs into consideration, the 'education, health and care plan' would start from birth and until the age of 25. The paper also proposes that by 2014 parents would have option to have an independent budget. The consultation period is from March until June 2011 and can be completed online.

Procedures for SEN

The procedures for SEN in England (and Wales) were set in the Education Act 1996 (Part 4). The definition of SEN was amended in the Special Educational Needs and Disability Bill of 2001.

Support for Dyslexia

In the English law case of *Skipper v Calderdale Metropolitan Borough School* (2006) EWCA Civ 238, the Court of Appeal applied *Phelps v London Borough of Hillingdon* (2001) 2 AC 619 as the landmark case on the failure to diagnose dyslexia, in accordance with duty of care in English law, and to hold that the appellant could pursue her claim against her school for humiliation, lost confidence, lost self-esteem, and for loss of earnings following its failing to diagnose and treat her dyslexia. In England and Wales, the failure of schools to diagnose and provide remedial help for dyslexia following the House of Lords decision in the case of Pamela Phelps has created an entitlement for students with dyslexia in Higher education to receive support funded via the Disabled Students Allowance.

Special Education in Scotland

Special education in Scotland, being an aspect of education in Scotland, is a devolved matter with Scotland having its own arrangements. The Education (Additional Support for Learning) (Scotland) Act 2004 redefined the law in Scotland relating to the provision of special education to children with additional needs by establishing a framework for the policies of inclusion and generally practicing the "presumption of mainstreaming" in Scottish education. The Act is an attempt to broaden the narrow definition of Special Educational Needs (SEN) which has typically been used to define children with special needs.

North America

In North America, special education is commonly abbreviated as *special ed*, *SpecEd*, *SPED*, or *SpEd* in a professional context.

Canada: Education in Canada is the responsibility of the individual provinces and territories. As such, rules vary somewhat from place to place. However, inclusion is the dominant model.

For major exams, Canadian schools commonly use accommodations, such as specially printed examinations for students with visual impairments, when assessing the achievements of students with special needs. In other instances, alternative assessments or modifications that simplify tests are permitted, or students with disabilities may be exempted from the tests entirely.

United States

All special-needs students receive an Individualized Education Programme (IEP) that outlines how the school will meet the student's individual needs. The Individuals with Disabilities Education Act (IDEA) requires that students with special needs be provided with a Free Appropriate Public Education in the Least Restrictive Environment that is appropriate to the student's needs. Government-run schools provide special education in varying degrees from the least restrictive settings, such as full inclusion, to the most restrictive settings, such as segregation in a special school. The education offered by the school must be appropriate to the student's individual needs. Schools are not required to maximize the student's potential or to provide the best possible services. Unlike most of the developed world, American schools are also required to provide many medical services, such as speech therapy, if the student needs these services.

According to the Department of Education, approximately 6 million children (roughly 10 percent of all school-aged children) currently receive some type of special education services. As with most countries in the world, students who are poor, ethnic minorities, or do not speak the dominant language fluently are disproportionately identified as needing special education services. Poor, black and Latino urban schools are more likely to have limited resources and to employ inexperienced teachers that do not cope well with student behaviour problems, "thereby increasing the number of students they referred to special education."

During the 1960s, in some part due to the civil rights movement, some researchers began to study the disparity of education amongst people with disabilities. The landmark Brown v. Board of Education decision, which declared unconstitutional the "separate but equal" arrangements in public schools for students of different races, paved the way for PARC v. Commonwealth of Pennsylvania and Mills vs. Board of Education of District of Columbia, which challenged the segregation of students with special needs. Courts ruled that unnecessary and inappropriate segregation of students with disabilities was unconstitutional. Congress responded to these court rulings with the federal Education for All Handicapped Children Act in 1975 (since renamed the Individuals with Disabilities Education Act (IDEA)). This law required schools to provide services to students previously denied access to an appropriate education.

In US government-run schools, the dominant model is inclusion. In the United States, three out of five students with academic learning challenges spend the overwhelming majority of their time in the regular classroom.

Disability

Disability is the consequence of an impairment that may be physical, cognitive, mental, sensory, emotional, developmental, or some combination of these. A disability may be present from birth, or occur during a person's lifetime.

Disabilities is an umbrella term, covering impairments, activity limitations, and participation restrictions. An *impairment* is a problem in body function or structure; an *activity limitation* is a difficulty encountered by an individual in executing a task or action; while a *participation restriction* is a problem experienced by an individual in involvement in life situations. Thus disability is a complex phenomenon, reflecting an interaction between features of a person's body and features of the society in which he or she lives.

An individual may also qualify as disabled if he/she has had an impairment in the past or is seen as disabled based on a personal or group standard or norm. Such impairments may include physical, sensory, and cognitive or developmental disabilities. Mental disorders (also known as psychiatric or psychosocial disability) and various types of chronic disease may also qualify as disabilities.

Some advocates object to describing certain conditions (notably deafness and autism) as "disabilities", arguing that it is more appropriate to consider them developmental differences that have been unfairly stigmatized by society.

Types of Disability

The term "disability" broadly describes an impairment in a person's ability to function, caused by changes in various subsystems of the body, or to mental health. The degree of disability may range from mild to moderate, severe, or profound. A person may also have multiple disabilities.

Conditions causing disability are classified by the medical community as:

- inherited (genetically transmitted);
- congenital, meaning caused by a mother's infection or other disease during pregnancy, embryonic or fetal developmental irregularities, or by injury during or soon after birth;
- acquired, such as conditions caused by illness or injury; or
- of unknown origin.

Types of disability may also be categorized in the following way:

Physical Disability

Any impairment which limits the physical function of limbs, fine bones, or gross motor ability is a physical disability. Other physical disabilities include impairments which limit other facets of daily living, such as severe sleep apnea.

Sensory Disability

Sensory disability is impairment of one of the senses. The term is used primarily to refer to vision and hearing impairment, but other senses can be impaired.

Vision Impairment

Vision impairment (or incorrectly "visual impairment") is vision loss (of a person) to such a degree as to qualify as an additional support need through a significant limitation of visual capability resulting from either disease, trauma, or congenital or degenerative conditions that cannot be corrected by conventional means, such as refractive correction, medication, or surgery. This functional loss of vision is typically defined to manifest with

1. best corrected visual acuity of less than 20/60, or significant central field defect,
2. significant peripheral field defect including homonymous or heteronymous bilateral visual, field defect or generalized contraction or constriction of field, or
3. reduced peak contrast sensitivity with either of the above conditions.

Hearing Impairment

Hearing impairment or hard of hearing or deafness refers to conditions in which individuals are fully or partially unable to detect or perceive at least some frequencies of sound which can typically be heard by most people. Mild hearing loss may sometimes not be considered a disability.

Olfactory and Gustatory Impairment

Impairment of the sense of smell and taste are commonly associated with aging but can also occur in younger people due to a wide variety of causes.

There are various olfactory disorders:

- Anosmia – inability to smell
- Dysosmia – things smell different than they should

- Hyperosmia – an abnormally acute sense of smell.
- Hyposmia – decreased ability to smell
- Olfactory Reference Syndrome – psychological disorder which causes patients to imagine they have strong body odour
- Parosmia – things smell worse than they should
- Phantosmia – "hallucinated smell", often unpleasant in nature

Complete loss of the sense of taste is known as ageusia, while dysgeusia is persistent abnormal sense of taste,

Somatosensory Impairment

Insensitivity to stimuli such as touch, heat, cold, and pain are often an adjunct to a more general physical impairment involving neural pathways and is very commonly associated with paralysis (in which the motor neural circuits are also affected).

Balance Disorder

A balance disorder is a disturbance that causes an individual to feel unsteady, for example when standing or walking. It may be accompanied by symptoms of being giddy, woozy, or have a sensation of movement, spinning, or floating. Balance is the result of several body systems working together. The eyes (visual system), ears (vestibular system) and the body's sense of where it is in space (proprioception) need to be intact. The brain, which compiles this information, needs to be functioning effectively.

Intellectual Disability

Intellectual disability is a broad concept that ranges from mental retardation to cognitive deficits too mild or too specific (as in specific learning disability) to qualify as mental retardation. Intellectual disabilities may appear at any age. Mental retardation is a subtype of intellectual disability, and the term *intellectual disability* is now preferred by many advocates in most English-speaking countries as a euphemism for mental retardation.

Mental Health and Emotional Disabilities

A mental disorder or mental illness is a psychological or behavioural pattern generally associated with subjective distress or disability that occurs in an individual, and perceived by the majority of society as being outside of normal development or cultural expectations. The recognition and understanding of mental health conditions has changed over time and across cultures, and there are still variations in the definition, assessment, and classification of mental disorders, although standard guideline criteria are widely accepted.

Developmental Disability

Developmental disability is any disability that results in problems with growth and development. Although the term is often used as a synonym or euphemism for intellectual disability, the term also encompasses many congenital medical conditions that have no mental or intellectual components, for example *spina bifida.*

Nonvisible Disabilities

Several chronic disorders, such as diabetes, asthma, inflammatory bowel disease or epilepsy, would be counted as nonvisible disabilities, as opposed to disabilities which are clearly visible, such as those requiring the use of a wheelchair.

Sociology of Disability

Different terms have been used for people with disabilities in different times and places. The euphemism treadmill and changing fashions have caused terms to rise or fall in popularity.

At this time, *disability* or *impairment* are commonly used, as are more specific terms, such as *blind* (to describe having no vision at all) or *visually impaired* (to describe having limited vision).

Handicap has been disparaged as a result of false folk etymology that says it is a reference to begging. It is actually derived from an old game, Hand-i'-cap, in which two players trade possessions and a third, neutral person judges the difference of value between the possessions. The concept of a neutral person evening up the odds was extended to handicap racing in the mid-18th century. In handicap racing, horses carry different weights based on the umpire's estimation of what would make them run equally. The use of the term to describe a person with a disability—by extension from handicap racing, a person carrying a heavier burden than normal—appeared in the early 20th century.

Handicap replaced terms that are now considered insulting, such as *crippled.*

People-first Language

Many people would rather be referred to as a person with a disability instead of handicapped. "Cerebral Palsy: A Guide for Care" at the University of Delaware offers the following guidelines:

Impairment is the correct term to use to define a deviation from normal, such as not being able to make a muscle move or not being able to control an unwanted movement. Disability is the term used to define a restriction in the ability to perform a normal activity of daily living which someone of the same age is able to perform. For example, a three-year-old child who is not able to walk has a disability because a normal three-year-old can walk independently. Handicap is the term used to describe a child or adult who, because of the disability, is unable to achieve the normal role in society commensurate with his age and socio-cultural milieu. As an example, a sixteen-year-old who is unable to prepare his own meal or care for his own toileting or hygiene needs is handicapped. On the other hand, a sixteen-year-old who can walk only with the assistance of crutches but who attends a regular school and is fully independent in activities of daily living is disabled but not handicapped. All disabled people are impaired, and all handicapped people are disabled, but a person can be impaired and not necessarily be disabled, and a person can be disabled without being handicapped.

The American Psychological Association style guide states that, when identifying a person with an impairment, the person's name or pronoun should come first, and descriptions of the impairment/disability should be used so that the impairment is identified, but is not modifying the person. Improper examples are "a borderline", "a blind person", or "an autistic boy"; more acceptable terminology includes "a woman with Down syndrome" or "a man who has schizophrenia". It also states that a person's adaptive equipment should be described functionally as something that assists a person, not as something that limits a person, for example, "a woman who uses a wheelchair" rather than "a woman in/confined to a wheelchair."

A similar kind of "people-first" terminology is also used in the UK, but more often in the form "people with impairments" (such as "people with visual impairments"). However, in the UK, the term "disabled people" is generally preferred to "people with disabilities". It is argued under the social model that while someone's impairment (for example, having a spinal cord injury) is an individual property, "disability" is something created by external societal factors such as a lack of wheelchair access to the workplace. This distinction between the individual property of impairment and the social property of disability is central to the social model. The term "disabled people" as a political construction is also widely used by international organisations of disabled people, such as Disabled Peoples' International (DPI).

Literature

Masculinity: According to author Daniel J. Wilson, the characteristics of masculinity include strength, activeness, speed, endurance, and courage. These characteristics are often challenged when faced with a disability and the boy or man must reshape what it means to be masculine. For example, rather than define "being a man" through what one can physically do, one must re-define it by how one faces the world with a disability and all the obstacles and stereotypes that come with the disability.

In Leonard Kriegel's book, *Flying Solo*, he describes his fight with poliomyelitis and the process of accepting his disability in a world that values able-bodiedness. He writes, "I had to learn to be my own hero, my own role model – which is another way of saying that I had to learn to live with neither heroes nor role models" (pg. 40).

Femininity

Some note that women who are disabled face what is called a "double disability", meaning they must not only deal with the stereotypes and challenges posed by femininity, but they must also deal with those posed by being disabled. Culture also tends to view women as fragile and weaker than men, stereotypes which are only heightened when a woman has a disability.

According to the "Survey of Income and Programme Participation", as described in the book *Gendering Disability*, 74 percent of women participants and 90 percent of men participants without disabilities were employed. In comparison, of those with a form of disability, 41 percent of women and 51 percent of men were employed. Furthermore, the nondisabled women participants were paid approximately $4.00 less per hour than the nondisabled men participants. With a disability, women were paid approximately $1.00 less than the nondisabled women participants and the men were paid approximately $2.00 less than the nondisabled men participants. As these results suggest, women without disabilities face societal hardships as compared to men, but disability added to the equation increases the hardships.

Disability and Poverty

There is a global correlation between disability and poverty, produced by a variety of factors. Disability and poverty may form a vicious circle, in which physical barriers make it more difficult to get income, which in turn diminishes access to health care and other necessities for a healthy life.

Disability and Disasters

There is limited research knowledge, but many anecdotal reports, on what happens when disasters impact people with disabilities. Individuals with disabilities are greatly affected by disasters. Those with physical disabilities can be at risk when evacuating if assistance is not available. Individuals with cognitive impairments may struggle with understanding instructions that must be followed in the event a disaster occurs. Those who are blind, hearing impaired, etc. may have difficulty communicating during the emergency. All of these factors can increase the degree of variation of risk in disaster situations with disabled individuals.

Research studies have consistently found discrimination against individuals with disabilities during all phases of the disaster cycle. The most common limitation is that people cannot physically access buildings or transportation, as well as access disaster-related services. The exclusion of these individuals is caused in part by the lack of disability-related training provided to emergency planners and disaster relief personnel.

Theory

The International Classification of Functioning, Disability and Health (ICF), produced by the World Health Organization, distinguishes between body functions (physiological or psychological, such as vision) and body structures (anatomical parts, such as the eye and related structures). Impairment in bodily structure or function is defined as involving an anomaly, defect, loss or other significant deviation from certain generally accepted population standards, which may fluctuate over time. Activity is defined as the execution of a task or action. The ICF lists 9 broad domains of functioning which can be affected:

- Learning and applying knowledge
- General tasks and demands
- Communication
- Basic physical mobility, Domestic life, and Self-care (for example, activities of daily living)
- Interpersonal interactions and relationships
- Community, social and civic life, including employment
- Other major life areas

In concert with disability scholars, the introduction to the ICF states that a variety of conceptual models has been proposed to understand and explain disability and functioning, which it seeks to integrate. These models include the following:

The Medical Model

The medical model is presented as viewing disability as a problem of the person, directly caused by disease, trauma, or other health condition which therefore requires sustained medical care provided in the form of individual treatment by professionals. In the medical model, management of the disability is aimed at a "cure," or the individual's adjustment and behavioural change that would lead to an "almost-cure" or effective cure. In the medical model, medical care is viewed as the main issue, and at the political level, the principal response is that of modifying or reforming healthcare policy.

The Social Model

The social model of disability sees the issue of "disability" as a socially created problem and a matter of the full integration of individuals into society. In this model, disability is not an attribute of an individual, but rather a complex collection of conditions, many of which are created by the social environment. Hence, the management of the problem requires social action and it is the collective responsibility of society at large to make the environmental modifications necessary for the full participation of people with disabilities in all areas of social life. The issue is both cultural and ideological, requiring individual, community, and large-scale social change. From this perspective, equal access for someone with an impairment/disability is a human rights issue of major concern. Medical humanities can bridge the gap between medical and social model of disability.

Other Models

- The spectrum model refers to the range of visibility, audibility and sensibility under which people function. The model asserts that disability does not necessarily mean reduced spectrum of operations. Rather, disability is often defined according to thresholds set on a continuum of disability.
- The moral model refers to the attitude that people are *morally responsible* for their own disability. For example disability may be seen as a result of bad actions of parents if congenital, or as a result of practicing witchcraft if not. Echoes of this can be seen in the doctrine of karma in Indian religions. It also includes notions that a disability gives a person "special abilities to perceive, reflect, transcend, be spiritual".

- The expert/professional model has provided a traditional response to disability issues and can be seen as an offshoot of the medical model. Within its framework, professionals follow a process of identifying the impairment and its limitations (using the medical model), and taking the necessary action to improve the position of the disabled person. This has tended to produce a system in which an authoritarian, over-active service provider prescribes and acts for a passive client.
- The tragedy/charity model depicts disabled people as victims of circumstance who are deserving of pity. This, along with the medical model, are the models most used by non-disabled people to define and explain disability.
- The legitimacy model views disability as a value-based determination about which explanations for the atypical are legitimate for membership in the disability category. This viewpoint allows for multiple explanations and models to be considered as purposive and viable.
- The social adapted model states although a person's disability poses some limitations in an able-bodied society, oftentimes the surrounding society and environment are more limiting than the disability itself.
- The economic model defines disability in terms of reduced ability to work, the related loss of productivity and economic effects on the individual, employer and society in general. This model is directly related to the charity/tragedy model.
- The empowering model (also, customer model) allows for the person with a disability and his/her family to decide the course of their treatment and what services they wish to benefit from. This, in turn, turns the professional into a service provider whose role is to offer guidance and carry out the client's decisions. This model "empowers" the individual to pursue his/her own goals.
- The market model of disability is minority rights and consumerist model of disability that recognizing people with disabilities and their stakeholders as representing a large group of consumers, employees and voters. This model looks to personal identity to define disability and empowers people to chart their own destiny in everyday life, with a particular focus on economic empowerment. By this model, based on US Census data, there are 1.2 billion people in the world who

consider themselves to have a disability. An additional two billion people are considered stakeholders in disability (family/friends/employers), and when combined to the number of people without disabilities, represents 53% of the population. "This model states that, due to the size of the demographic, companies and governments will serve the desires, pushed by demand as the message becomes prevalent in the cultural mainstream."

- The consumer model of disability is based upon the "rights-based" model and claims that people with disabilities should have equal rights and access to products, goods and services offered by businesses. The consumer model extends the rights-based model by proposing that businesses, not only accommodate customers with disabilities under the requirements of legislation, but that businesses actively seek, market to, welcome and fully engage people with disabilities in all aspects of business service activities. The model suggests that all business operations, for example websites, policies and procedures, mission statements, emergency plans, programmes and services, should integrate access and inclusion practices. Furthermore, these access and inclusion practices should be based on established customer service access and inclusion standards that embrace and support the active engagement of people of all abilities in business offerings.

Management

Assistive Technology: Assistive Technology is a generic term for devices and modifications (for a person or within a society) that help overcome or remove a disability. The first recorded example of the use of a prosthesis dates to at least 1800 BC. The wheelchair dates from the 17th century. The curb cut is a related structural innovation. Other examples are standing frames, text telephones, accessible keyboards, large print, Braille, & speech recognition software. People with disabilities often develop personal or community adaptations, such as strategies to suppress tics in public (for example in Tourette's syndrome), or sign language in deaf communities.

As the personal computer has become more ubiquitous, various organizations have formed to develop software and hardware to make computers more accessible for people with disabilities. Some software and hardware, such as Voice Finger, Freedom Scientific's *JAWS*, the Free and Open Source alternative *Orca* etc. have been specifically designed for people with disabilities while other software and hardware, such as Nuance's Dragon Naturally Speaking, were not developed specifically for people with disabilities, but can be used to increase accessibility. The LOMAK keyboard was designed in New Zealand specifically for persons with disabilities. The World Wide Web consortium recognised a need for International Standards for Web Accessibility for persons with disabilities and created the Web Accessibility Initiative (WAI). As at Dec 2012 the standard is WCAG 2.0 (WCAG = Web Content Accessibility Guidelines).

Adapted Sports

The Paralympic Games (meaning "alongside the Olympics") are held after the (Summer and Winter) Olympics. The Paralympic Games include athletes with a wide range of physical disabilities. In member countries organizations exist to organize competition in the Paralympic sports on levels ranging from recreational to elite (for example, Disabled Sports USA and BlazeSports America in the United States).

The Paralympics developed from a rehabilitation programme for British war veterans with spinal injuries. In 1948, Sir Ludwig Guttman, a neurologist working with World War II veterans with spinal injuries at Stoke Mandeville Hospital in Aylesbury in the UK, began using sport as part of the rehabilitation programmes of his patients.

In 2006, the Extremity Games was formed for people with physical disabilities, specifically limb loss or limb difference, to be able to compete in extreme sports.

Ableism

Ableism is a form of discrimination or social prejudice against people with disabilities. It may also be referred to as disability discrimination, physicalism, handicapism, and disability oppression. It is also sometimes known as disablism, although there is some dispute as to whether ableism and disablism are synonymous, and some people within disability rights circles find the latter term's use inaccurate. Discrimination faced by those who have or are perceived to have a mental disorder is sometimes called mentalism rather than ableism.

Similar to many of the assumptions underlying the medical model of disability amongst many clinicians, the "ableist" societal world-view is that the able-bodied are the norm in society, and that people who have disabilities must either strive to become that norm or should keep their distance from able-bodied people. A disability is thus, inherently, a "bad" thing that must be overcome. The ableist worldview holds that disability is an error, a mistake, or a failing, rather than a simple consequence of human diversity, akin to race, ethnicity, sexual orientation or gender.

Campbell draws a distinction between disablism and ableism. Disablism, she notes, has been the traditional focus of study within the field of disability studies. Disablism promotes the unequal treatment of the (physically) disabled versus the able-bodied. It marks the disabled as the Other, and works from the perspective of the able-bodied.

Campbell acknowledges that the concept of ableism is, as of 2009, not clearly defined in the literature and has "limited definitional or conceptual specifity". She herself distinguishes between ableism and disablism, defining the former as:

A network of beliefs, processes and practices that produces a particular kind of self and body (the corporeal standard) that is projected as the perfect, species-typical, and therefore essential and fully human. Disability is then cast as a diminished state of being human.

Other definitions of ableism include those of Chouinard, who defines it as "ideas, practices, institutions, and social relations that presume able-bodiedness, and by so doing, construct persons with disabilities as marginalized and largely invisible 'others'" and Amundson and Taira, who define it as "a doctrine that falsely treats impairments as inherently and naturally horrible and blames the impairments themselves for the problems experienced by the people who have them".

Harpur argues that the term ableism is a powerful label that has the capacity to ameliorate the use of negative stereotypes and facilitate cultural change by focusing attention on the discriminator rather than on the victim or impairment.

United Kingdom

In the UK, disability discrimination became unlawful as a result of the Disability Discrimination Act 1995 and, later, the Disability Discrimination Act 2005. These were later repealed but the substantive law is replicated in the Equality Act 2010. Under the Equality Act 2010 there are several types of discrimination that are prohibited. These are direct discrimination (s.13(1) Equality Act 2010), indirect discrimination (s.6 and s.19 Equality Act 2010, harassment (s.26 Equality Act 2010), victimisation (s.27(2) Equality Act 2010), discrimination arising from disability (s.15(1) Equality Act 2010) and failure to make reasonable adjustments (s.20 Equality Act 2010).

The Legal Definition of Disability is: *"A person (P) has a disability if P has a physical or mental impairment, and the impairment has a substantial and long-term adverse effect on his ability to carry out normal day-to-day activities".*

Some conditions (such as blindness, AIDS and cancer) are expressly included; others (such as drug and alcohol addictions) are expressly excluded.

Legal experts have suggested that this definition of disability may change as a result of a Danish case currently before the European Court of Justice.

USA

Until the 1970s, ableism in the United States was often codified into law. For example, in many jurisdictions, so-called "ugly laws" barred people from appearing in public if they had diseases or disfigurements that were considered unsightly.

Section 504 and other sections of the Rehabilitation Act of 1973 and the Americans with Disabilities Act of 1990 (ADA) enacted into law certain civil penalties for failing to make public places comply with access codes known as the ADA Access Guidelines (ADAAG); this law also helped expand the use of certain adaptive devices, such as TTYs (phone systems for the hearing/speech impaired), some computer-related hardware and software, wheelchair ramps or lifts on public transportation and curb-cuts at intersections which allow wheelchairs and their users to safely move between sidewalks and crosswalks. In addition these laws prohibit direct discrimination against disabled people in government programmes, employment, public transit and public accommodations like stores and restaurants.

The building modification provisions of these directives apply to three general categories of buildings: existing government administration buildings and structures regardless of age; all newly constructed buildings and structures intended for use as public accommodations like stores and restaurants; significantly renovated and/or refurbished buildings and structures and any public accommodation where the cost of modification is slight when compared with the income it generates. The US government also offered significant tax incentives to businesses to make these modifications.

The federal Fair Housing Amendments Act of 1988 prohibits housing discrimination on the basis of disability and requires that newly constructed multi-family housing meet certain access guidelines while requiring landlords to allow disabled persons to modify existing dwellings for accessibility. The Telecommunications Act, Individuals with Disabilities Education Act, Air Carriers Access Act, Voting Accessibility Act and others have codified the notion that persons with disabilities have some of the same rights and privileges as other citizens.

California

In addition to the federal protections provided by the ADA, California's Fair Employment and Housing Act (FEHA) provides additional protections to California employees. Notably, FEHA applies to employers with 5 or more employees and offers more extensive protection than the ADA.

Discrimination, Government Policies, and Support

United Nations: On December 13, 2006, the United Nations formally agreed on the Convention on the Rights of Persons with Disabilities, the first human rights treaty of the 21st century, to protect and enhance the rights and opportunities of the world's estimated 650 million disabled people. As of April 2011, 99 of the 147 signatories had ratified the Convention. Countries that sign the convention are required to adopt national laws, and remove old ones, so that persons with disabilities will, for example, have equal rights to education, employment, and cultural life; to the right to own and inherit property; to not be discriminated against in marriage, etc.; to not be unwilling subjects in medical experiments. In 1976, the United Nations launched its International Year for Disabled Persons (1981), later renamed the International Year of Disabled Persons. The UN Decade of Disabled Persons (1983–1993) featured a World Programme of Action Concerning Disabled Persons. In 1979, Frank Bowe was the only person with a disability representing any country in the planning of IYDP-1981. Today, many countries have named representatives who are themselves individuals with disabilities. The decade was closed in an address before the General Assembly by Robert Davila. Both Bowe and Davila are deaf. In 1984, UNESCO accepted sign language for use in education of deaf children and youth.

Costa Rica

Under the *Ley de Igualdad de Opportunidades* (Law of Equal Opportunities), no person can be discriminated by their disabilities if they are equally capable as another person. This law also promotes that public places and transport should have facilities that enable people with disabilities to access them.

May 28 is the *Día Nacional de la Persona con Discapacidad* (National Disabled People Day) to promote respect for this population.

Currently the political party *Partido de Acceso Sin Exclusión* (Access Without Exclusion Party) fights for the rights of disabled persons, and one congressman, Oscar López, is blind.

United Kingdom

Under the Disability Discrimination Act (DDA) (1995, extended in 2005), it is unlawful for organisations to discriminate (treat a disabled person less favourably, for reasons related to the person's disability, without justification) in employment; access to goods, facilities, services; managing, buying or renting land or property; education. Businesses must make "reasonable adjustments" to their policies or practices, or physical aspects of their premises, to avoid indirect discrimination.

Since 2010 the Disability Discrimination Act has been replaced with the Equality Act 2010. This act still protects disabled people against discrimination but also encompasses a number of other characteristics including age, disability, gender reassignment, marriage, pregnancy, race, religion, sex and sexual orientation.

A number of financial and care support services are available.

Employment

The Business Disability Forum (BDF), formerly the Employers' Forum on Disability, is a membership organisation of UK businesses. Following the introduction of the DDA the membership of BDF recognised the need for a tool with which they could measure their performance on disability year on year.

In 2005 eighty organisations took part in the Disability Standard benchmark providing the first statistics highlighting the UK's performance as a nation of employers.

Following the success of the first benchmark Disability Standard 2007 saw the introduction of the Chief Executives' Diamond Awards for outstanding performance and 116 organisations taking the opportunity to compare trends across a large group of UK employers and monitor the progress they had made on disability. 2009 saw the introduction of the third benchmark, Disability Standard 2009.

In 2012 BDF had a number of initiatives to assist businesses in meeting and including the needs of disabled customers and employees. These consisted of The Technology Taskforce (a Business Disability Forum partner initiative which brings together some of the world's largest procurers and suppliers of ICT); Accessible Technology Charter (launched nov 2011) in which the 'Accessibility Maturity Model' (AMM) is a self-assessment tool to enable businesses to identify and plan key policies for accessible and usable technologies.

United States

Discrimination in Employment: The US Rehabilitation Act of 1973 requires all organizations that receive government funding to provide accessibility programmes and services. A more recent law, the Americans with Disabilities Act of 1990 (ADA), which came into effect in 1992, prohibits private employers, state and local governments, employment agencies and labour unions from discriminating against qualified individuals with disabilities in job application procedures, hiring, firing, advancement, compensation, job training, or in the terms, conditions and privileges of employment. This includes organizations like retail businesses, movie theaters, and restaurants. They must make "reasonable accommodation" to people with different needs. Protection is extended to anyone with (A) a physical or mental impairment that substantially limits one or more of the major life activities of an individual, (B) a record of such an impairment, or (C) being regarded as having such an impairment. The second and third criteria are seen as ensuring protection from unjust discrimination based on a perception of risk, just because someone has a record of impairment or appears to have a disability or illness (e.g. features which may be erroneously taken as signs of an illness).

African Americans and Disability

According to the 2000 U.S. Census, the African American community has the highest rate of disability in the United States at 20.8 percent, slightly higher than the overall disability rate of 19.4%. Although people have come to better understand and accept different types of disability, there still remains a stigma attached to the disabled community.

Social Security Administration

The US Social Security Administration defines disability in terms of inability to perform substantial gainful activity (SGA), by which it means "work paying minimum wage or better". The agency pairs

SGA with a "listing" of medical conditions that qualify individuals for disability benefits.

Education

Before the Individuals with Disabilities Education Act was passed, children with disabilities were segregated into seperate schools designed to meet their needs. These programmes were on a fixed continuum that placed the child into the desired programme based on the results of an assessment. Disabled children were kept seperate from other children. In these special schools, children were treated like disabled children but not included in activities in which other children were able to participate. Under the Individuals with Disabilities Education Act, special educational support is limited to children and youth falling into one of a dozen disability categories (e.g., specific learning disability) and adds that, to be eligible, students may require both special education (modified instruction) and related services (supports such as speech and language pathology).

Insurance

It is illegal for California insurers to refuse to provide car insurance to properly licensed drivers solely because they have a disability. It is also illegal for them to refuse to provide car insurance "on the basis that the owner of the motor vehicle to be insured is blind," but they are allowed to exclude coverage for injuries and damages incurred while a blind unlicensed owner is actually operating the vehicle (the law is apparently structured to allow blind people to buy and insure cars which their friends, family, and caretakers can drive for them).

Demographics

Estimates Worldwide

Estimates of worldwide and country-wide numbers of individuals with disabilities are problematic. The varying approaches taken to defining disability notwithstanding, demographers agree that the world population of individuals with disabilities is very large. For example, in 2004, the World Health Organization estimated a world population of 6.5 billion people, of those nearly 100 million people were estimated to be moderately or severely disabled. In the United States, Americans with disabilities constitute the third-largest minority (after persons of Hispanic origin and African Americans); all three of those minority groups number in the 30-some millions in America. According to the U.S. Bureau of the Census, as of 2004, there were some 32 million disabled adults (aged 18 or over) in the United States, plus another 5 million children and youth (under age 18). If one were to add impairments—or limitations that fall short of being disabilities—Census estimates put the figure at 51 million.

There is also widespread agreement among experts in the field that disability is more common in developing than in developed nations. The connection between disability and poverty is thought to be part of a "vicious cycle" in which these constructs are mutually reinforcing.

Nearly eight million men in Europe returned from the World War I permanently disabled by injury or disease. About 150,000 Vietnam veterans came home wounded, and at least 21,000 were permanently disabled. Increased US military involvement has resulted in a significant increase of disabled military personnel since 2001. According to Fox News, this is a '25 percent' rise, with more than '2.9 million' total veterans now disabled. After years of war in Afghanistan, there are more than one million disabled people. Afghanistan has one of the highest incidences of people with disabilities in the world. An estimated 80,000 Afghans have lost limbs, mainly as a result of landmines.

In Australia, 18.5% of the population reported having a disability in a 2009 survey.

Political Issues

Political rights, social inclusion and citizenship have come to the fore in developed and some developing countries. The debate has moved beyond a concern about the perceived cost of maintaining dependent people with disabilities to an effort of finding effective ways to ensure that people with disabilities can participate in and contribute to society in all spheres of life. Many are concerned, however, that the greatest need is in developing nations—where the vast bulk of the estimated 650 million people with disabilities reside. A great deal of work is needed to address concerns ranging from accessibility and education to self-empowerment and self-supporting employment and beyond.

In the past few years, disability rights activists have also focused on obtaining full citizenship for the disabled. However obstacles reside in some countries in getting full employment, also public perception of disabled people may vary in areas.

Disability Abuse

Disability abuse is where disabled people are abused physically, financially, verbally or mentally due to the person having a disability. As many disabilities are not visible (for example, asthma, learning disabilities) some abusers cannot rationalise the non-physical disability with a need for understanding, support, and so on.

As the prevalence of disability and the cost of supporting disability increases with medical advancement and longevity in general this aspect of society becomes of greater political importance and how political parties treat their disabled constituents may/will become a measure of a political parties true understanding of disability, particularly in the "social" measure of disability.

Disability Rights Movement

The disability rights movement is the movement to secure equal opportunities and equal rights for people with disabilities. The specific goals and demands of the movement are: accessibility and safety in transportation, architecture, and the physical environment, equal opportunities in independent living, employment, education, and housing, and freedom from abuse, neglect, and violations of patients' rights. Effective civil rights legislation is sought in order to secure these opportunities and rights.

Disability Insurance

Disability benefit, or disability pension, is a major kind of disability insurance, and is provided by government agencies to people who are temporarily or permanently unable to work due to a disability. In the U.S., disability benefit is provided within the category of Supplemental Security Income, and in Canada, within the Canada Pension Plan. In other countries, disability benefit may be provided under Social security systems.

Costs of disability pensions are steadily growing in Western countries, mainly European and the United States. It was reported that in the UK, expenditure on disability pensions accounted for 0.9% of Gross Domestic Product (GDP) in 1980, but two decades later had reached 2.6% of GDP. Several studies have reported a link between increased absence from work due to sickness and elevated risk of future disability pension.

A study by researchers in Denmark suggests that information on self-reported days of absence due to sickness can be used to effectively identify future potential groups for disability pension. These studies may provide useful information for policy makers, case managing authorities, employers, and physicians.

Private, for-profit disability insurance plays a role in providing incomes to disabled people, but the nationalized programmes are the safety net that catch most claimants.

2

Awareness Towards Inclusion

There is a form of prejudice in our society that surrounds disability — a discomfort, a subtle fear of that which is different and unfamiliar. It manifests as pity, avoidance or mockery. When we see someone with a profound disability, a fleeting thought occurs: "What if that were me?" from which we quickly turn with a shudder.

Naturally, many people, especially young people, tend to avoid those who make us feel uncomfortable or guilty. Not knowing how to act or respond to someone very different can be scary, especially for a young person.

Bringing students with disabilities into general education classrooms should result in true, long-term acceptance. How inclusion happens varies with every school. The approaches range from including students with disability on every level with no separation to maintaining self-contained classrooms with only periodic mingling of students. Only when attitudes are inclusive, however, will classrooms naturally follow.

Disability education brings attitudes to the surface, where they can be examined consciously, rather than putting students together and hoping for the best. It's not surprising that, despite the best of intentions, students with disabilities who participate in inclusion programmes may continue to feel left out.

Educator Attitudes Towards the Implementation of Inclusive Education

Within the contemporary inclusive classrooms, teachers face increased pressure as their roles diversify, compared to previous generations. Teachers have varied in their responses to these challenges. Mainstream teachers are now called upon to be sensitive to the variety of modern classrooms and to be able to rise to the challenge by adjusting their teaching styles in accordance with the multiplicity of learning styles they face. They are further required to be psychologically and practically prepared to take on the dynamic role of inclusive educator, while being aware that making physical provision for students with disabilities is not as important as making attitudinal changes resulting in the removal of barriers to physical and educational access.

Several mainstream educators view the philosophy of inclusive education as an exciting challenge, the stresses associated with its introduction being seen as life-sustaining, enjoyable and beneficial; on the other hand, it has been noted that the experience of being an inclusive educator is challenging enough to cause teachers to become physiologically and psychologically stressed. Fritz and Miller (1995) found that inclusion was an impossible obstacle for some teachers; however, others have seen it as an opportunity for personal and professional growth while contributing to the dynamic field of education. It would appear that the attitudes of educators towards the inclusion of students with disabilities are multidimensional and complex. Positive attitudes are considered to encourage the inclusion of students with disabilities into regular classrooms, while negative attitudes support low achievement and poor acceptance of students with disabilities into mainstream settings.

Legislative Measures for Persons with Disabilities

Human Rights is the first universally accepted ideology. Although most observers regard the formation of the United Nations and the promulgation of the universal Declaration of Human Rights as the beginning of the modern struggle to protect human rights, one can trace the origins of human rights back to early philosophical and legal theories of the 'natural law', a law higher than positive laws of states. According to these theories, individuals were entitled to certain immutable rights as human beings. The establishment of United Nations after the Second World War is an unambigous manifestation of recognition of these rights as every government undertakes to promote 'Universal respect for and observance of, human rights and fundamental freedoms without distinction as to race, sex, language, or religion'.

No doubt universal declaration of Human Rights adopted by UN Genaral Assembly by resolution No.217A(111) of 10th December 1948, which recognised the freedom of individuals as well as their rights to equality, is a milestone in this area, but people with disabilities were not specifically covered by this important international declaration. In spite of the fact that this segment of society constitutes 10 to 12 percent of the world's population, this declaration did not include the prohibition of discrimination on the ground of disability specifically. This reflects insensitivity and apathy of policy makers towards the people with disabilities. In fact, all initial policies and programmes were focused on the institutionalisation, giving passive community care and providing some welfare measures for them. All this resulted into denial of opportunities in different spheres of life, discrimination on the ground of disability and their social and cultural isolation. They were also not allowed in the process of planning, implementation and monitoring of policies and programmes designed for them even in the organisations working for them. Gradually, people with disabilities organised themselves in almost every part of the world and undertook their struggles for ensuring their fundamental human rights of equality and life with dignity.

Probably, it was for the first time in 1958 that an international covenant included the needs of disabled persons in Article 5 of discrimination (Employment and occupation) convention adopted by ILO. Under this article, the convention declared special measures in favour of various disadvantaged groups including people with disabilities to meet the specific needs to be an acceptation to forms of discrimination envisaged and prohibited by it. Later on, UN general Assembly vide its resolutions no. 2865(XXVI) of 20th December, 1971 made the first International Proclamation on the Rights of Mentally Retarded Persons, one category of disabilities. This declaration recognises that mentally retarded persons have the same rights as other citizens. In addition, it also recognised their rights to development in all spheres of life as well as medical care and physical therapy. Four years later, UN General Assembly adopted a declaration on the rights of disabled persons through resolution no. 3447(XXX) of 9th December, 1975 which might be regarded as the most important document containing international commitment on the protection of the following human rights of disabled persons:

1. Right to respect for their human dignity (Para 3 of declaration)
2. Right to enjoy some civil and political rights as other human beings (Para 4 of the declaration of human rights)
3. Their entitlements to the measures designed to enable them to become as self-reliant as possible (Para 5 of the declaration)

4. Right to medical, psychological and functional treatment, including prosthetic and orthetic applicances , to medical and social rehabilitation, education, vocational training and rehabilitation aid, counselling, placement service, and other services which will enable them to develop their capabilities and skills to the maximum and will hasten the processes of their social integration or reintegration (Para 6 of declaration)
5. Right to 'economic and social security' and to a decent level of living (Para 7 of declaration)
6. Right to get their specific needs considered at all stages of social and economic planning (Para 8 of the declaration)
7. Right to live with their families or foster parents and to participate in all social, and cultural activities (Para 9 of declaration)
8. Right to be protected against exploitation or discrimination of any form (Para 10 of declaration)
9. Right to have legal aid for the protection of their persons and properties (Para 10 of declaration)
10. Right of organisations of disabled persons to be consulted in matters concerning them (Para 12 of the declaration)

Thus, it may be noticed that rights of people with disabilities were recognised by the member government of United Nations in the year 1975. But national action was imperative to guarantee these rights to them. There are two other major UN initiatives which helped the organisations of people with disabilities to persuade their respective governments for granting of fundamental human rights to this segment of society. While UN decade for disabled persons 1983-92 created an awareness among policy makers for promoting equality and participation of disabled persons, the Asian and Pacific Decade of Disabled Persons 1993-2002 proclaimed by UN concrete actions by the Governments in the region of the achievement of these goals. Adoption of the Standard Rules on the Equalisation of Opportunities for Persons with Disabilities by UN General Assembly in December, 1993 is yet another important international instrument in support of advocacy and realisation of these rights.

India being one of the most populous countries in ESCAP region has undergone similar challenges in the area of recognition and grant of human rights to disabled persons.

The region is experiencing rapid social and economic changes which have made marginalised groups such as disabled persons particularly vulnerable. In this changing scenario, there is a need to ensure that they have full access to their entitlements and to protect them for some of the consequences of rapid changes. Legislative support is one of the most important means of achieving this objective. We, therefore, start lobbying in India for the following three actions to get protection for the rights of people with disabilities:-

1. Inclusion of people with disabilities in the part relating to the fundamental rights of the Indian constitution guarantees fundamental rights to its citizens which include rights to equality, enjoy various forms of freedoms, rights against exploitation etc.. All these rights are justifiable but so far people with disabilities have not been specifically mentioned in this part of constitution which makes it difficult to get proper policies framed and measures adopted for the protection of these fundamental rights of people with disabilities.

So far constitutional provisions have not been suitably amended to include disabled persons in this part of the constitution. Though three committees constituted by the Government of India of legislative support to people with disabilities have made positive recommendations on this demand of organisations of people with disabilities.

2. A comprehensive legislation on the rights and measures for persons with disabilities: In this year, we are proud to have succeeded in getting a comprehensive legislation passed and brought into force on 7th February, 1996 after a long and historic struggles by self-help organisations of people with disabilities in general and National Federation of the Blind, and apex self-help organisation in particular. This legislation is a fine example of combination of right based legislation and service as well as welfare legislation.

During the process of its enactment, there had been wide consultations with NGOs working in the area of disability. It seeks to promote equality in all areas of life. It also prohibits discrimination on the ground of disability in every sphere. Some of the important rights guaranteed by it are as follows:

1. Right to have free education up to the age of 18 years.
2. Right to have preferential treatment in the matter of employment by reservation of 3 percent vacancies for them in Government and Public Sectors.
3. Right to have preferential treatment in allotment of land and housing.

4. Prohibition of discrimination on the ground of disability in any area of life, education, training and employment, etc..
5. Right to have access to buildings, roads and transport, and other public services.

Owing to unique federal structure of India, this central legislation has the challenging task involving provincial governments in its implementation. In order to meet this challenge, it provides the following implementing authorities:

1. Central Co-ordination Committee at central level and State Co-ordination Committees at provincial levels. NGOs working in the field of disabilities have been given adequate representation in these committees. These committees have been envisaged to serve as bodies responsible for planning and formulating policies and programmes for persons with disabilities.
2. Chief Commissioners at central level and State Commissioners at provincial levels - These Commissioners would be responsible for implementation of various schemes in different sectors of life envisaged by this law and monitor its work.

Since the violation of any provision of this law has been made. Violation of human rights of disabled persons guaranteed under this law as well as under Indian Constitution would be an offence.

3. Another important concern is in the area of identification of discriminatory provisions in the existing public laws on different subjects as well as inclusion of enabling provision in those law to enable people with disabilities to enjoy the rights guaranteed to them by the Constitution in the same manner as enjoyed by the non-disabled citizens. The self-help organisations have succeeded in getting the process initiated for such identification of legal provisions.

To conclude, campaign for the protection of human right of disabled persons is quite recent as the case in many countries in the Asia & Pacific region. Very few countries of ESCAP Region such as Australia, Hong Kong, the Peoples Republic of China, New Zealand, the Republic of Korea, Japan, Thailand, Pakistan and the Philippines have some legislations for the protection of rights of disabled persons. These legislations mark a welcome beginning for the elimination of discrimination on the ground of disability and their social, economic and cultural isolations. But there is a long journey ahead in our efforts to work for a society which is sensitive and caring for persons with disabilities. At this juncture, organisations both national and international in the area of disability should introspect and commit themselves to allow disabled persons to participate at all levels including decision making process which will have a favourable impact on the Government to promote equality and participation.

As a member of self-help organisation, may I therefore call upon the service provider to join this long struggle nationally and internationally with us on equal terms respecting the rights of self-help organisations for a new societal order for disabled persons based on equality in place of discrimination, opportunity in place of deprivation and participation in place of exclusion.

Disability Discrimination Act

In the late 20th and early 21st centuries, a number of countries have passed laws aimed at reducing discrimination against people with disabilities. These laws have begun to appear as the notion of civil rights has become more influential globally, and follow other forms of anti-discrimination and equal opportunity legislation aimed at preventing racial discrimination and sexism which began to emerge in the second half of the 20th century.

List of Disability Discrimination Acts

Australia: Disability Discrimination Act 1992

Canada: Ontarians with Disabilities Act (2002) (only in Ontario, no other province has disability protection)

United Kingdom: Equality Act 2010 (prior to October 2010 the relevant legislation was the Disability Discrimination Act 1995 as amended)

United States of America: Americans with Disabilities Act of 1990

Pakistan: National Policy for Persons with Disablilities 2002

Equal Opportunity

Equal opportunity is a stipulation that all people should be treated similarly, unhampered by artificial barriers or prejudices or preferences, except when particular distinctions can be explicitly justified. The aim according to this often complex and contested concept is that important jobs should go to those "most qualified" – persons most likely to perform ably in a given task – and not go to persons for arbitrary or irrelevant reasons, such as circumstances of birth, upbringing, friendship ties to whoever is in power, religion, sex, ethnicity, race, caste, or involuntary personal attributes such as disability, age, or sexual orientation. Chances for advancement should be open to everybody interested such that they have "an equal chance to compete within the framework of goals and the structure of rules established." The idea is to remove arbitrariness from the selection process and base it on some "pre-agreed basis of fairness, with the assessment process being related to the type of position," and emphasizing procedural and legal means. Individuals should succeed or fail based on their own efforts and not extraneous circumstances such as having well-connected parents. It is opposed to nepotism and plays a role in whether a social structure is seen as legitimate.

Existential Challenges for Disabled Women in the Abled Society

People with disabilities face many obstacles in their struggle for equality. Although men and women with disabilities are subject to discrimination because of their disabilities, women with disabilities are at a further disadvantage because of the combined discrimination based on gender and discrimination based on disability. This paper examines the lives of women with disabilities and explores the effects of this double discrimination. It demonstrates how women with disabilities have been neglected by the disability field and the feminist movement alike and reviews the existing literature on women with disabilities, most of which has been written within the last decade. The paper will also examine three major areas of life and how women with disabilities fare within these areas, compared to women without disabilities and men with disabilities. These three areas are (1) the traditional female sphere of reproduction and nurturing; (2) education; and (3) employment.

Women with disabilities have historically been neglected by disability studies and feminist scholarship alike and issues of importance to women with disabilities have, for the most part, been ignored by the disability rights movement as well as the women's movement.

The Disability Field

Almost all research on people with disabilities has assumed the irrelevance of gender as well as other social dimensions such as social class, race, ethnicity, and sexual orientation. "Having a disability presumably eclipses these dimensions of social experience. Even sensitive students of disability...have focused on disability as a unitary concept and have taken it to be not merely the "master" status, but apparently the exclusive status for disabled people".

Disability studies have traditionally used a gender blind approach to examine the lives of people with disabilities and have neglected to explore the influence of gender in the lives of men and women with disabilities. The field of disability has not yet recognized the combined discrimination of gender and disability experienced by women who have disabilities, and policies and practices in the field have not been designed to meet the specific needs of women with disabilities.

The disability rights movement has also ignored issues of importance to women with disabilities and many feminists with disabilities have complained about its male domination and male orientation. Deegan and Brooks have criticized the disability rights movement for directing most of its attention to male concerns while women's issues, such as child-bearing problems, have received little attention. They point out that, "Like many other social change movements, the disability movement has often directed its energies towards primarily male experiences." This makes many feminists with disabilities uneasy members of the disability rights movements, for example, Israel and McPherson, who describe how "Disabled feminists...feel uncomfortable in the disability movement because it is often male dominated and at times blatantly sexist."

Education

Access to education still remains a major problem for people with disabilities, not least for women with disabilities. When it comes to education, women with disabilities are likely to report less education than both non-disabled women and men with disabilities. Women with disabilities are five times as likely as women without disabilities to have less than eight years of formal education; 17.4% of all women with disabilities have less than 8 years of formal education as compared to 3.5% of non-disabled women. Only 16% of all women with disabilities are likely to have any college education compared to 31% of non-disabled women and 28% of men with disabilities.

Special Education Placement and Gender

Children with disabilities have traditionally been educated in segregated special schools or segregated classes within regular schools and their education has been vastly inferior to the mainstream regular education. Past decades have seen progress towards integrated education for students with disabilities, mostly due to a federal initiative in the form of the Education of All Handicapped Children Act, also known as PL 94-142. This law was enacted in 1975 to guarantee children with disabilities free and appropriate education in the least restrictive environment. Despite the progress most students with disabilities are still educated in segregation from their non-handicapped peers.

Most studies indicate that boys are more likely to be identified as needing special education than girls. While boys count for 51% of all students in elementary and secondary schools, they can count for up to 75% of students in special education classes. Researchers have speculated why boys are more readily identified as needing special education. Some authors have suggested that this reflects discrimination against boys with disabilities and deprives them from the benefits of regular education. They suggest that boys are more readily labelled as having a disability and channelled into special education on the grounds of disruptive behaviours. Others have suggested that the over representation of boys in special education reflects the view that educating boys with disabilities is regarded as a priority; they are seen as in need of special education services in order to develop the skills to be able to support themselves and a family later on.

Research also indicates that boys labelled as having mental retardation have higher IQs than girls with the same label. Gillespie-Silver and Heshusius (1981) have suggested that the reason for this may be that the stereotypes of a female and a person with mental retardation are very similar, both are seen as illogical, dependent, emotional, and needing protection. Girls may therefore not be labelled as having mental retardation unless they have significantly low intelligence.

Although the over representation of boys in special education is one of the best documented gender-influence on special education placement, at least one study has reported girls as over represented in certain types of special educational programmes. In their study of 8,000 people with disabilities, the Disability Rights Education and Defense Fund (1983) found among other things that girls with physical disabilities were more likely to be placed in segregated special schools than boys with physical disabilities. The authors suggest that these differences stem from the assumption that males must support themselves and a family and therefore need a better education.

The influence of gender on labelling and special education placement is further complicated by the influence of race and class. It has been documented that children, especially boys, of minority races are grossly over represented in special education programmes, especially programmes for students with mild mental retardation.

A Complicated Picture

Research clearly indicates that boys and girls with the same disability often receive different kinds of education. This suggests that gender may play a significant role in how students are identified for educational services. At the same time, studies that have examined the relationship between gender and special educational placement seem to report conflicting findings. We do know that gender can influence special educational placement but we do not know how. Some of the research seems to indicate that the influence of gender may vary between disability groups. In addition, the interaction between gender, disability, and race complicates the picture. It seems safe to conclude that there is a need for more research in this area in order to understand the relationship between special education placement, disability, gender, class, and race.

Special Education and Sex-Role Stereotyping

While all students, males and females, with and without disabilities are subject to sex-biased assumptions in most schools and curriculum, research seems to indicate that sex-role stereotyping may be even more pervasive when students have disabilities. For example, Gillespie and Fink (1974) found that sex-role stereotyping seemed to be especially pervasive for children who have mental retardation or behavioural problems. They report that these students tended to be taught traditional sex-role modes of behaviour because that would supposedly enable them to better adjust to society. The authors also found that schoolbooks for children with disabilities tended to include stories and illustrations that were deliberately sex-role stereotypical in order to foster this adjustment.

Higher Education

Higher education continues to be a challenge for women with disabilities. Like men with disabilities, they face accessibility problems; unwillingness on behalf of educational institutions to provide accommodations for disabilities; and lack of special services such as readers for blind students. In addition to the problems women with disabilities share with their male counterparts, they face additional barriers. Like non-disabled women, women with disabilities are channelled into traditional female fields by school counsellors and they are likely to encounter even greater obstacles than non-disabled women if they attempt to pursue a career in male-dominated professions. In addition to being channelled into traditional female fields by educational and career counsellors, women with disabilities often receive pressure from such counsellors to pursue a career in disability related fields such as rehabilitation counselling or special education. Russo and Jansen suggest that the combined effects of gender and disability stereotyping tracks women with disabilities into the most traditional female roles. As a result, women with disabilities are unlikely to have the educational opportunities that will allow them access to highly valued, well-paying professional positions.

Marriage, Nurturance, Sexuality, Reproduction

Women's traditional roles as nurturers, mothers, wives, homemakers, and lovers are usually not seen as appropriate for women with disabilities. While the ability to acquire women's most traditional roles is usually not regarded as the best measure of women's social success, examining the limitations women with disabilities face within this traditional women's sphere provides valuable insights into the restricted social options available to them.

Intimacy and Marriage

Compared to both men with disabilities and non-disabled women, women with disabilities are more likely to never marry, marry later, and be divorced if they do get married. While 60% of non-disabled women and men with disabilities are married, only 49% of women with disabilities are married. Comparison of divorce rates of women and men with disabilities seem to suggest that women with disabilities are more likely to be left alone than men and when disability occurs after marriage men are much more likely to divorce their wives who become disabled, while the marriage rarely breaks down if it is the man who becomes disabled (Hannaford, 1989). These realities are reflected in the writings where women with disabilities describe their lives. For example, only five of the forty-five women interviewed by Matthews (1983) were married and there is hardly a mention of marriage in a collection of first-person accounts written by more than sixty women. Asch and Fine (1988: 15) report only one group of women with disabilities that is more likely to be married than men of the same disability group. This group is women with mental retardation.

Non-disabled women often feel trapped in unfulfilling or abusive relationships because they cannot imagine how they will survive economically on their own. Hannaford (1989) suggests that this may be even more true of women with disabilities who often may have to put up with abusive or exploitative relationships because of their limited social and economical means or because the only other alternative may be a life in an institution. In addition, Asch and Fine

(1988) report that women with disabilities may return to abusive relationships because it may be the only intimate relationship they ever had and they may judge it better to have a bad relationship than no relationship at all.

Although non-disabled lesbians have been reported to be more accepting of women with disabilities within their meetings and conferences (Israel & McPherson, 1983), the literature seems to indicate that lesbians with disabilities have the same difficulties as heterosexual women with disabilities in establishing intimate, long-lasting relationships with a partner.

Many women may not see marriage as a preferred status, nor may they regard the most traditional female roles as desirable. At the same time, non-disabled women are more likely than women with disabilities to have the possibilities to choose between traditional and nontraditional life-styles. Women with disabilities rarely have the same options and their access to even the most traditional female roles is very restricted.

Motherhood and Nurturance

Although the traditional image of the mother as the sole caretaker and nurturer of her child is in the process of change, it is still the image society uses as its reference point. Since women with disabilities are seen as dependent and in need of being taken care of, it is difficult for many to imagine how a mother with a disability can fill the caring and nurturing mothering role. The widespread belief that women with disabilities cannot and should not bear and raise children has made it difficult for pregnant women with disabilities to find doctors who will accept them. They have also found it problematic to gain access to information and services related to their special needs. When women with disabilities do become mothers they encounter many difficulties because the non-disabled world assumes that the disability makes them unfit to be mothers. Many lose custody of their children in divorce while others may have their children removed from their care by social welfare agencies, solely on the grounds that they have a disability. Not only have women with disabilities reported difficulties in becoming biological mothers and keeping custody of their own children, they have also encountered discrimination if they have attempted to adopt children or become foster mothers. If they manage to keep their children they may encounter further difficulties in dealing with early childhood programmes that traditionally have neglected and ignored the needs of mothers with disabilities.

There are only scattered accounts of motherhood as experienced by women with disabilities. These accounts have mostly been written by women who have physical disabilities, or based on interviews with this group of mothers. Mothers with mental retardation have not been represented in this literature, and as a result these mothers are even more invisible than other mothers with disabilities and very little is known about their lives and struggles. The limited information available has been written by professionals who tend to discuss mothers with mental retardation in terms of the problems they pose for the social welfare services that encounter them. Few, if any, resources are available that presents their own point of view and how they experience motherhood. One of the few resources available about this group of mothers found that 25% of them had had their children removed from their care.

Although society's fears that women with disabilities will produce defective children are for the most part groundless, because the vast majority of disabilities are not hereditary, these fears have resulted in severe discrimination against women with disabilities in general and women with mental retardation in particular. Around the turn of the century what was referred to as "feeble-mindedness" was considered a major threat to society. As reflected in the following quotation from 1908, it was generally believed that feeble-mindedness was hereditary: "No feeble-minded mother will ever have a child absolutely normal in every respect". More important, these women were thought to lack moral restraints concerning sexual activities and it was believed that as a consequence they would produce a large number of illegitimate and deficient children. The preventative measures taken against this threat included large scale forced sterilization and institutions for "feeble minded women of child-bearing age" were established, where women with mental retardation were segregated from society as well as from men with mental retardation. In 1960, 26 states still had sterilization laws and as late as 1980, 33 states still had laws that prohibited people with mental retardation from marrying. No group of women with disabilities has been as severely discriminated against in terms of their reproductive rights as women with mental retardation and some of the myths surrounding women with mental retardation, such as the myth of their uncontrollable sexuality, are unfortunately still very much alive today.

Sexuality and Sexual Abuse

It is widely documented that women with disabilities are typically seen as asexual. This is true of society in general as well as of most professionals with whom women with disabilities come into contact. Because women with disabilities are seen as asexual they are not seen as in need of information about birth control or what is possible in terms of having a sex life and children. Some women with disabilities have criticized the disability rights movement for not addressing sexuality as a political issue similar to housing and transportation. For example, Waxman (1989: 2) claims that many people with disabilities consider sexuality to be the area of greatest oppression: "We are more concerned with being loved and finding sexual fulfillment than getting on a bus." Some authors have speculated about the pervasive stereotype of women with disabilities as asexual, for example Finger (1985), who suggests that at least part of this stereotyping stems from seeing people with disabilities as eternal children. Others have suggested that people without disabilities tend to view sex as an acrobatic activity which makes it difficult for them to imagine how people with physical impairments can be sexually active.

Sexual abuse of women and children with disabilities is an area that has received growing attention in recent years (Watson, 1984). Much of the literature in this area is based on studies which show that women with disabilities are at a much greater risk of being sexually abused than other women. This is true in society in general, and within residential facilities in particular. One author reports that sexual assault and battering may be two or three times higher for women with disabilities than for other women (O'Toole, 1990). Others report that women in institutions are at a much greater risk of being sexually abused than other women with disabilities.

It may seem like a contradiction that women with disabilities are not seen as sexual beings and at the same time they are at a much greater risk of being sexually abused. Those who have studied sexual abuse, for example Cole (1984), have documented that sexual abuse has more to do with oppressive use of power than it has to do with sex. Based on their work with sex offenders, Longo and Gochenour (1981) report that sexual abuse is more related to issues of control and power than to sex. They claim that abusers look for and use vulnerability to create the opportunity to rape. This vulnerability is increased in people who are marginalized, dependent, and in need of affection. Thus, the more vulnerable and powerless people are, the more they are at risk of being sexually abused. Existing studies have documented that women with disabilities are at a greater risk than any other group of women of being sexually abused. Yet, professionals within the human service system continue to ignore this widespread abuse. These chilling realities have led Asch and Fine (1988: 23) to wonder "...how many of these same women have been sterilized to keep the effects of rape from the public eye."

Reproductive Rights and Disability Rights

The area of reproductive rights has been problematic for many women with disabilities and has been a source of tension between feminists with disabilities and the women's movement. Feminists with disabilities have criticized the reproductive rights movement for ignoring the forced sterilization of women with disabilities; for failing to address the denial of reproductive rights to women with disabilities; and for exploiting fears of disability when it argues for abortion. Many of those who struggle with the moral dilemma between disability rights and reproductive rights are feminists with disabilities who are pro-choice, but argue against selective abortion of "defective" fetuses. They argue that the disability rights movement and the reproductive rights movement share a tradition of commitment to women's control over their lives and bodies. They see the battles of these two movements as intertwined; one movement should not try to further its cause at the cost of the other and women's equality with men should not be obtained by subverting the equality and potentiality of people with disabilities. The current trend of prenatal screening and abortion of fetuses identified as disabled has also been criticized, and feminists with disabilities challenge the assumptions about disabilities that underlie these practices. They have demonstrated how oppressive attitudes against disability dominate the counselling given to pregnant women and have challenged the assumption that the world would be a better place without people born with disabilities. While the vast majority of writings on the moral dilemma between disability rights and reproductive rights have argued that these are compatible rights, at least one author has taken a different standpoint. Davis (1987) argues that disability rights and reproductive rights are incompatible and that abortion is far from being a right. Instead, abortion underlines women's oppression and is counter-productive to women in general and to women with disabilities in particular.

Comparing Men and Women with Disabilities

While men with disabilities have serious employment problems, women with disabilities are significantly worse off and this seems to be true for all types and levels of disabilities. Men with disabilities are almost twice as likely to have jobs than women with disabilities. Almost 42% of men with disabilities are in the labour force (meaning that they either work or are actively seeking work), compared to 24% of women. In addition, while more than 30% of men with disabilities work full-time jobs, only 12% of women with disabilities have full time employment. Women with disabilities are also significantly poorer than men with disabilities, partly due to the fact that they are more likely to be unemployed and partly due to the fact that when they work they receive considerably lower wages than men with disabilities. Women with disabilities who work full-time earn only 56% of what full-time employed men with disabilities do (Bowe, 1984).

Gender-Biases in Rehabilitation Services

A handful of studies have been conducted to examine and explain the unequal employment status of women with disabilities as compared to men with disabilities. In a study of gender equity in access to rehabilitation services, Menz, et al., (1989) found that nationally, women represent less than one-third of the population in rehabilitation programmes. They also found that women were more likely to be "successfully rehabilitated" into part-time jobs or to a homemaker status, while men were more likely to enter full-time jobs in the labour force. These attitudes seem to be shared by the general public and rehabilitation counsellors, the result being that women with disabilities are less likely to be referred to vocational training; have a harder time gaining access to rehabilitation programmes; are less likely to get quality training; and are more likely to be "successfully rehabilitated" into non-employment.

Women with Disabilities and Disability Policy

The impact of disability policy on women with disabilities has been the focus of a small number of studies. For example, Kutza examined the impact of current U.S. disability policy on women with disabilities. She demonstrates how the major programmes designed to assist people with disabilities, such as supplemental security income, disability insurance, workers' compensation, and vocational rehabilitation, disadvantage women because of their relationship to labour market participation. The study found that not only did women receive fewer benefits than men, they also received lower benefits. Thus, these programmes do not protect women with disabilities from the economic threats associated with disability to the same extent they protect men.

A similar study of the influence of income support on the lives of women with disabilities was conducted by Mudrick (1988). She found that compared to men with disabilities, women with disabilities received less from public income support programmes, despite their often greater need. Mudrick demonstrates how crucial income support is to the livelihood of women with disabilities. At the same time, income support is usually both less accessible and smaller for women with disabilities than for men with disabilities. Mudrick suggests the reason for this is partly due to the misfit between women's work patterns and the design of the programmes, and partly rooted in the stereotypical attitudes towards women's economic roles and women's family roles, as well as attitudes towards people with disabilities.

Women with Developmental Disabilities

The studies reviewed above have mostly been conducted with women who have physical impairments. Women with mental retardation and other developmental disabilities have traditionally been neglected by those who have examined the employment situation of women with disabilities. The developmental disability field has recently devoted increasing attention to the importance of employment and a new federal initiative, supported employment, has been developed to assist even those with the most severe disabilities to get and hold a job. The newly found emphasis on employment in the field of developmental disabilities recognizes the importance of productive work as a means to achieve social equality and financial independence, and supported employment programmes are now being developed across the country. Despite a wealth of recent writings on employment for people with developmental disabilities, the specific barriers women with developmental disabilities face have basically been ignored. It appears as though those who write about employment for people with mental retardation assume that gender, as well as class, race and other social dimensions, are irrelevant. Having mental retardation is seen as such an overpowering characteristic that it makes all other social dimensions irrelevant. A search through the literature on employment for people with developmental disabilities only brought two resources that mention sex differences. In their study of employment outcomes for young adults with mental retardation Kregel and Wehman (1989) make a passing remark about sex-differences. The study focused on a group of 186 adolescents with mental retardation, between the age of 18 and 22, who had been placed in competitive jobs through supported employment programmes. Among other things, they found a "...disproportionate representation of males (68 percent male to 32 percent female) in the population of placed consumers". In an earlier study Hill, et al (1985) found a similar trend among a group of 155 people with mental retardation between the age of 16 and 66. This was a long term study of people who had been placed in various competitive jobs by one supported employment programme and focused on, "client and family demographic characteristics in relation to a successful vocational outcome defined as retention in employment six months after the date of first placement". Among the findings of the study were that the majority of people being placed through the programme were males, or 66%, while females represented only 34% of those who received jobs through the programme. The study also showed that males were more likely to reach the successful retention rate of 6 months, or 70%, compared to 55% of the females. A significant number of the 155 people in this study had a secondary handicap, in addition to the label of mental retardation. Thus, 24% are reported to have had behaviour disorders; 10% had cerebral palsy; 12% had mobility impairments; 5% had impaired hearing; 10% had visual impairment; nearly 10% had limited use of arms or hands; and 5% had schizophrenia. One of the interesting findings of this study is that, except for the people who were identified as having schizophrenia, the secondary handicap did not seem to influence the retention rate. That is, people with secondary handicaps, in addition to the label of mental retardation, had either the same retention rate, or slightly higher retention rate than the general mental retardation population. These findings seem to indicate that, when it comes to employment of people with mental retardation, being a woman may be a greater handicap than having physical, sensory, or behavioural handicaps. Only schizophrenia seems to be as severe a handicap in terms of getting and keeping a job as being female.

Comparing Women With and Without Disabilities

A comparison between women with disabilities and non-disabled women also reveals the disadvantage of women with disabilities. The past few decades have seen a revolutionary increase of women's participation in the paid labour force. Especially noticeable has been the increased number of working mothers. In 1970, 45% of non-disabled women were in the labour force, while by 1982, 64% of women participated in the labour force and more than 51% of mothers with preschool children were working. Women with disabilities have not been a part of the women's employment revolution. In 1982 only 20% of women with disabilities had jobs. Employment policies have devoted little attention to the disadvantaged employment status of women with disabilities. This seems to hold true of both the generic state and federal employment policies as well as the employment policies directed specifically towards people with disabilities.

The evidence available to date leads to the conclusion that the economy in general, and the specialized services in particular, restrict the employment opportunities and lives of women with disabilities.

Women, Work, and Mental Health

The increase in women's labour force participation, and especially the dramatic increase of working mothers, has led to some speculation about the possible negative effect on women's mental health because of the added stress employment may bring to women who already have the primary responsibility for childrearing and other demands within the family. In a study of the relationship between women's work and women's mental health, Sales and Frieze found that the influence of women's increased employment participation is primarily positive and very few negative effects have been found. Their study indicates that work is a source of self-esteem and satisfaction for most women and, as a central contributor to adult adjustment, participation in the labour force may be health enhancing for women. They also report that the group of women who is most at risk of having mental health problems are non-white, non-married, non-employed women, and women who live in social isolation with limited social roles. This suggests that women with disabilities may be at greater risk than most other women of having mental health problems as a result of their social isolation and the limited social roles available to them, including their limited access to labour force participation.

An Artificial Ear for Real Hear Education with Hearing Aids

Sound offers us a powerful means of communication. Our sense of hearing enables us to experience the world around us through sound. Because our sense of hearing allows us to gather, process, and interpret sounds continuously and without conscious effort, we may take this special sense of communication for granted. But, did you know that

- Human communication is multisensory, involving visual, tactile, and sound cues?
- The range of human hearing, from just audible to painful, is over 100-trillion-fold?
- Tiny specialized cells in the inner ear, known as hair cells, are responsible for converting the vibrational waves of sound into electrical signals that can be interpreted by the brain?
- Tinnitus, commonly known as "ringing in the ears," is actually a problem that originates in the brain?

- A recent study showed that men who hunt experience an increased risk of high-pitched hearing loss of 7 percent for every five years that they hunt? Nearly all (95 percent) of these same hunters report that they do not use hearing protection while hunting.

Contemporary hearing research is guided by lessons learned from sensory research, namely that specialized nerve cells respond to different forms of energy—mechanical, chemical, or electromagnetic—and convert this energy into electrochemical impulses that can be processed by the brain. The brain then works as the central processor of sensory impulses. It perceives and interprets them using a "computational" approach that involves several regions of the brain interacting all at once. This notion is different from the long-held view that the brain processes information one step at a time in a single brain region. Over the past decade, scientists have begun to understand the intricate mechanisms that enable the ear to convert the mechanical vibrations of sound to electrical energy, thereby allowing the brain to process and interpret these signals.

Hearing Aid

A hearing aid is an electroacoustic device which is designed to amplify sound for the wearer, usually with the aim of making speech more intelligible, and to correct impaired hearing as measured by audiometry. In the United States, Hearing aids are considered medical devices and are regulated by the Food and Drug Administration (FDA). Ordinary small audio amplifiers or other plain sound reinforcing systems cannot be sold as "hearing aids".

Earlier devices, known as ear trumpets or ear horns, were passive funnel-like amplification cones designed to gather sound energy and direct it into the ear canal. Similar devices include the bone anchored hearing aid, and cochlear implant.

Cochlear Implants

Cochlear implants improve outcomes in people with hearing loss in either one or both ears. Cochlear implants artificially stimulate the cochlear nerve by providing an electric impulse substitution for the firing of hair cells. Cochlear implants are expensive, and require sophisticated programming in conjunction with extensive training for effectiveness. Cochlear implant recipients may be at higher risk for bacterial meningitis. Thus, meningitis vaccination is recommended for those with cochlear implant. People who have hearing impairments, especially those who develop a hearing problem in childhood or old age, may need support and technical adaptations as part of the rehabilitation process. Recent research shows variations in efficacy but some studies show that if implanted at a very young age, some profoundly impaired children can acquire effective hearing and speech, particularly if supported by appropriate rehabilitation.

Classroom

Inside the classroom, children with hearing impairments may also benefit from interventions. These include providing favourable seating for the child. This can be achieved by having the student sit as close to the teacher as possible so that they will be able to hear the teacher, or read their lips more easily. When lecturing, teachers should try to look at the student as much as possible and limit unnecessary noise in the classroom. If a student has a hearing aid, they are likely to hear a lot of unwanted noises.

Pairing hearing impaired students with hearing students is a common technique, allowing the non-hearing student to ask the hearing student questions about concepts that they have not understood. When teaching students with hearing impairments, overheads are commonly used, allowing the teacher to write, as well as maintain visual focus on the hearing impaired student. For those students who are completely deaf, one of the most common interventions is having the child communicate with others through an interpreter using sign language.

Government Policies

Those who are hearing disabled do have access to a free and appropriate public education. If a child does qualify as being hearing impaired and receives an individualized education plan, the IEP team must consider, "the child's language and communication needs. The IEP must include opportunities for direct communication with peers and professionals. It must also include the student's academic level, and finally must include the students full range of needs" The government also distinguishes between deafness from hearing loss. The U.S. Department of Education states that deafness is hearing loss that is so severe that a person cannot process any type of oral information even if they have some sort of hearing-enhancing device. The U.S. Department of Education states that a hearing impairment is when a person's education is affected by how much that person is able to hear. This definition is not included under the term deafness. In order for a person to qualify for special services, they have to hear more than 20 decibels and their educational performance must be affected by their hearing loss. This is what the government has to say about governmental policies and individualized services.

Inclusion vs. Pullout

There are mixed opinions on the subject between those who live in deaf communities, and those who have deaf family members who do not live in deaf communities. Deaf communities are those communities where only sign languages are typically used.

Many parents who have a child with a hearing impairment prefer their child to be in the least restrictive environment of their school. This may be because most children with hearing loss are born to hearing parents. This can also be because of the recent push for inclusion in the public schools.

It is commonly misunderstood that least restrictive environment means mainstreaming or inclusion. Sometimes the resources available at the public schools do not match up to the resources at a residential school for the deaf. Many hearing parents choose to have their deaf child educated in the general education classroom as much as possible because they are told that mainstreaming is the least restrictive environment, which is not always the case. However, there are parents that live in Deaf communities who feel that the general education classroom is not the least restrictive environment for their child. These parents feel that placing their child in a residential school where all children are deaf may be more appropriate for their child because the staff tend to be more aware of the needs and struggles of deaf children. Another reason that these parents feel a residential school may be more appropriate is because in a general education classroom, the student will not be able to communicate with their classmates due to the language barrier.

In a residential school where all the children use the same language (whether it be a school using ASL, Total Communication or Oralism), students will be able to interact normally with other students, without having to worry about being criticized. An argument supporting inclusion, on the other hand, exposes the student to people who aren't just like them, preparing them for adult life. Through interacting, children with hearing disabilities can expose themselves to other cultures which in the future may be beneficial for them when it comes to finding jobs and living on their own in a society where their disability may put them in the minority. These are some reasons why a person may or may not want to put their child in an inclusion classroom.

3

Vocational Education for Children with Disabilities

Students and their families look forward to graduation from high school and the possibilities the future holds. The shift to adulthood doesn't magically happen following the commencement ceremony. Careful planning takes place prior to graduation to ensure a successful transition. Starting at 16 years of age, the student's Individualized Education Programme (IEP) addresses his/her vocational interests.

Individualized Education Programme

A coordinated team of educators, service providers, school counsellors, and agencies assist the student and his/her family to explore training opportunities. The student's needs are assessed and team members assume a variety of roles to help the student reach his/her goals. Post-secondary education, vocational training, employment options, adult social services, independent living skills, financial planning, and community participation are all transition topics the team considers.

Vocational Education

The IEP addresses individual strengths and needs. Academic classes, work place skills aligned with the Arizona Standards, vocational programmes, and job training experiences tailored to his/her needs help the student prepare for the transition to adulthood. Vocational education—education for employment—is critical for the student who wants to enter the work force following high school. Job Corps, EVIT, CAVIT and NAVIT courses offered for junior and senior students through high schools should be considered. Career exploration, decision making, learning appropriate ways of interacting in social and work situations, finding and maintaining employment, and learning self-advocacy skills should be a part of the programme. Services may start during high school and continue after graduation. That's why it is crucial for the IEP team to involve agency representatives who can offer support services beyond high school.

Employment

Vocational options range from competitive jobs to supported employment environments. As needed, services offered by Vocational Rehabilitation may include: evaluation, help in finding employment, job skills training, job shadowing opportunities, disability specific accommodations and/or modifications in the work setting, assistive technology, and access to additional resources. Individuals with disabilities may also be eligible for services from the Division of Developmental Disabilities or financial assistance from the Social Security Administration.

Community Participation

High school activities and community programmes prepare the special education student for inclusion in adult social pastimes. Students should be included in extracurricular sports and clubs. They may also be interested in participating in city recreation programmes to foster interest in other activities and to form new friendships. Young adults, who have a variety of hobbies and special interests, such as independent and group involvement in sports, clubs, and civic activities, tend to be more satisfied with their transition after high school.

Independent Living Skills

Independent living skills should be included in the transition planning process. The student should be prepared to the best of his/her ability to manage personal care, income and finances, transportation needs, medical care and living arrangements.

Some students will be capable of living independently. Other students may need assistance. In any case, the student with a disability should have options and assistance to reach his/her full potential. IEP team participants can use their knowledge and resources to make transition from high school to adulthood as meaningful and successful as possible.

The Efficacy of Vocational Education for Students with Disabilities

Transition from school to adult life for students with disabilities has dominated the field of special education for well over a decade.

Students with disabilities are defined as those identified with one or more of the 13 disability categories specified in the Individuals with Disabilities Education Act (IDEA) and served by an individualized educational programme (IEP) (IDEA P.L. 105-17). The central theme in special education transition has been an emphasis on productive post-school outcomes, primarily focused in the area of employment. The interest in transition is multi-faceted, but the most compelling reason is economic. Being gainfully employed and functionally independent is the "expected" post-school adult outcome in American society. The challenges associated with successful independence may be more problematic for individuals with disabilities. This highlights the importance of successful transitional planning and programming for students with disabilities at the secondary level.

Education is a powerful instrument of social change, and often initiates upward movement in the social structure. Thereby, helping to bridge the gap between the different sections of society. The educational scene in the country has undergone major change over the years, resulting in better provision of education and better educational practices. In 1944, the Central Advisory Board of Education (CABE) published a comprehensive report called the Sergeant Report on the post-war educational development of the country.

As per the report, provisions for the education of the handicapped 2, were to form an essential part of the national system of education, which was to be administered by the Education Department. According to this report, handicapped children were to be sent to special schools only when the nature and extent of their defects made this necessary. The Kothari Commission (1964–66), the first education commission of independent India, observed: "the education of the handicapped children should be an inseparable part of the education system." The comission recommended experimentation with integrated programmes in order to bring as many children as possible into these programmes.

Learners With Special Educational Needs (Sen)

In India a learner with SEN is defined variously in different documents. For example, a child with SEN in a District Primary Education Programme (DPEP) document is defined as a child with disability, namely, visual, hearing, locomotor, and intellectual (DPEP, 2001). However, the country report in the NCERT-UNESCO regional workshop report titled Assessment of needs for Inclusive Education: Report of the First Regional Workshop for SAARC Countries (2000) states that SEN goes beyond physical disability.

Special schools have been set up in the past and provisions have been made for integrated education.

In 1947, India had a total of 32 such schools for the blind, 30 for the deaf, and three for the mentally retarded.

The number of such schools increased to around 3000 by the year 2000 (NCERT-UNESCO Regional Workshop Report, 2000). Thus India at present has "two tracks". In other words, it has parallel but separate policies on segregation and integration.

Special schools for children with visual impairment, hearing impairment, and locomotor disabilities are streamlined to follow a curriculum that is almost in line with the general education curriculum. The plus curriculum and the adaptation of instructional methodologies are followed where necessary. Children with mental retardation on the other hand require a specialised curriculum to meet their specific educational needs.

Over time, however, there has been growing awareness that special education in special schools may be overlay restrictive, and instead of working outside the mainstream classrooms, the special schools can work with, and provide support to, regular schools.

Early in 1992, the Programme of Action, while promoting integrated education, had also suggested a Pragmatic Placement Principle. It postulated that learners with disabilities who can be educated in general schools should be educated in general schools, and those studying in special schools should be transferred to general schools once they are ready to make the shift (MHRD, Programme of Action, 1992). This was endorsed in 1994 by the Salamanca Statement recommendations for an alternative role for special schools. Hence, special schools in their newfound identity would become a far more flexible resource, by working in partnership with and creating a response to special needs, not only in the alternative form of provision and intervention, but within the mainstream classroom, curricula, and pedagogies.

Special and general education, in other words, are gearing for a significant move to come closer together.

Special Needs Education in India

Many international schools cater to the needs of children with special needs and learning difficulties such as dyslexia, attention deficit disorder, attention deficit hyperactivity disorder and cognitive disabilities. Efforts are made to integrate these children into the mainstream school environment. Under India's Disability Act (1995), children with disabilities have the right to free education up to the age of 18. Other rights include provisions such as transportation, scholarships, and free uniforms, books and teaching materials.

Children with special needs have access to special schools providing non-formal education and vocational training. To gain access to these, a "disability certificate" is required. They are issued by the Office of the Commissioner for Disabilities and can be obtained from any government hospital.

There are more than 2,500 schools for children with special needs in India. Some are run or supported by the government, while many are registered NGOs or private institutions. Children resident in India can apply to these schools.

Technology in Inclusive Education

Every child has the right to education regardless of race, religion, colour, creed, or ability or disability. Learners with disability experienced great difficulty in gaining access to education. It is therefore imperative that such inequalities be amended and the process of 'education for all" accelerated. In a foreign country such as the USA for example, "Calls for educational reform" and "school restructuring" within the educational community are echoed in media, in state legislatures and in local schools. Questions regarding the effectiveness of current educational systems approaches to educating an increasing diverse student population are raised. The concept of "inclusive school practices" is discussed as a philosophical basis for reconstructing the manner in which schools are organized to meet the needs of all learners". As teachers alter their instructional methods in response to student diversity in South Africa, they also need to change their practices in response to other social, political and economic conditions. Information Technology (IT) has expanded both the amount of information we access and the ways we access it. Changes in the world necessitate changes in what and how students are taught.

Assistive Technology

Assistive technology is any device that helps a person with a disability complete an everyday task. If you break your leg, a remote control for the TV can be assistive technology. If someone has poor eyesight, a pair of glasses or a magnifier is assistive technology.

Assistive technology includes many specialized devices as well, like typing telephones for people who are deaf and motorized wheelchairs for people who cannot walk. Assistive technology can be "low-tech" (something very simple and low-cost, like a pencil grip), or "high-tech" (something sophisticated, like a computer). Assistive technology can be critical for the person using it – if you wear glasses, think how hard it would be to get through the day without them!

IDEA states that school districts must consider assistive technology for any child in special education. That means that for any child receiving special education services, the educational team must ask if there is a device that will "increase, maintain, or improve functional capabilities" of that child. If the answer is yes, the school district must provide certain services:

- a qualified evaluator must complete an assistive technology evaluation;
- if the evaluator recommends a device, it must be acquired;
- and if you, your child or the staff in your child's school need training to use the device, that training must be provided, too.

Re Engineering of ODL System Through ICT Venture

The Open Distance Learning (ODL) system is an open concept education system that offers an opportunity for everyone to study and attain a Degree credentials irrespective of age, qualification, race, creed or colour. This system is distinct from traditional education system as learners do not necessarily have to start their studies at very young age. The ODL system does not favour those from better economic families as it is always "Open" to everyone who has dogged determination to pursue higher education.

Costly academic studies fee is always the main hurdle for tertiary education. Most of the earnest learners prevented by financial constraint do not have the opportunity for further studies. The ODL system affords conscientious learners the chance to study further; it is widely regarded as an inexpensive path to quality education in terms of cost and time.

A tremendous flexibility is one of the most outstanding elements of the ODL system. Students embark on the academic career of this system are actually learning at self-paced. They take responsibility for what they learn, where they learn, when they learn, how quickly they learn and how they have their learning assessed. The ODL system helps students to instill self-confidence and awareness, as learning need not necessarily take place at the same time of teaching.

The ODL system is having excellent administration systems and gives their students access to accreditation and qualifications. It has been perceived as not an inferior quality of education but even better than contact education, and can meet the same rigorous academic standards. Today, the qualification of ODL graduates are gradually recognized and respected by world-wide, especially the large-scale private industries.

Learning under the ODL system can be done synchronously or asynchronously. This helps to create a virtual learning community, good for all learners, and especially helpful for students of distance learning. By taking advantage of advanced technologies and mixed-media courseware, such as the Internet, video and audio cassettes, computer-based learning materials and telecommunication, students are able to develop their learning at own pace, and foster an independent disposition.

The ODL system is overwhelmingly appealing to working adults as it has dramatically expanded with the growth of the World Wide Web, always accessible and absolutely accommodates the special needs of majority and minority groups. Separation of teaching and learning enables working adults to get rid of constraint of place and time because not everyone will be free at the same time, or will able to physically meet each other in designated place.

ICT in Open Distance Learning

In distance learning system, learners are remote to the institution and are in large scale. It is difficult for a learner to visit the institution every day to get a service/support as available in a conventional system and at same time, it is even difficult to the institution itself to provide various services to the learners at different phases of a student learning life cycle, due to limited human resource available. Information and Communication Technology (ICT) is a prime resource to overcome such limitations.

Information and communication technology is group of technologies by which various support services shall be provided at different phases of student learning life cycle in distance learning. The various phases are the admission phase (progamme details, fee structure, admission procedure and registration & re-registration), the learning phase (learning schedule, programme delivery(lectures through video conferencing, webinars, audio & video programmes, multimedia presentations and case studies), the evaluation phase (examination schedule, internal &external assessment, examinations, improvement, valuation, revaluation and result declaration) and the certification phase (marks/grades updates, certificate printing & issuing and convocation schedule).

In conventional system, learners are able to interact with one another face-to-face, which is a prerequisite to more meaningful social intercourse. Since, there is no such facility in the distance learning, web-based student learning and support system shall be developed and implemented using ICT to provide services at all different phases in student learning life cycle and also for knowledge and information sharing as done in a conventional system of education.

Ict Infrastructure in Open Distance Learning

Open distance learning system requires ICT infrastructure to provide various services effectively at different phases of a student life cycle. The ICT infrastructure include the network infrastructure, the computing infrastructure, the system and application software, the Internet Service Provider(ISP), the bandwidth, the policy framework and the security infrastructure.

The Network Infrastructure

The institution, that provides education in open distance learning mode requires a structured network at all its operational nodes (headquarters, the regional and study centres in case of IGNOU) and interconnected each other through a dedicated network so that all student services can be accessed easily by all operational nodes, students and other public. The network shall include adequate and standard network components that are used at gateway and other parts of the structured network. The standard network components are the router, the network switches, the standard network cable (fibre and UTP). Wireless connectivity (Wifi/Wi-max) shall also be used, where ever needed.

The Computing Infrastructure

The standard computing infrastructure include standard computer hardware such as servers(database servers, web servers, backup/ recovery servers and application servers) to host various student learning and support services and personal computers (desktop computers, laptops and net books) to access and use services.

The Stable System and Application Software

The system and application software is required to develop software for various student learning and support services that are needed at various phases of student learning life cycle. The software is a main component in open distance learning by which various support services shall be provided to students and other public in large scale. The present Web technologies support to develop web-based software for various services that can be accessed any where and any time. Web technologies broadly categorized as LAMP (Linux, Apache, MySQL and PHP) and WAMP(Windows, Apache, MySQL and PHP). There are several learning management systems (LMS) available and MOODLE is one of popular LMSs. LMS is a complete system that covers all phases of a student learning life cycle.

The Internet Service Provider(ISP) and Internet Bandwidth

Internet bandwidth is needed to access web-based student learning and support services. The amount of internet bandwidth required is directly proportional to the number of users, who access the service(s) and is one of the parametres to access a service easily with no time. The accessibility of a service depends on the availability of internet bandwidth reserved in a particular institution, where service is hosted. The internet service provider is an organization who provides internet bandwidth.

The Security Infrastructure

Security infrastructure is essentially required to protect the systems(servers and personal computers), software, applications and the data that are being used in an institution, where student learning and support services are made available in open distance learning system. Security infrastructure enhance the security of a System/ Application/data and are intended to counter security attacks. The gateway(the starting and ending point for inbound and outbound traffic) of systems shall be protected with security devices. The standard security devices are the firewall, intrusion detection system(IDS), intrusion prevention system(IPS), the antivirus software and other monitoring systems. Security for a service shall be ensured by protecting its network domain where service is running, its system domain on which the service is hosted and the service/application itself. Each security device shall be configured with proper access controls.

The Challenging Issues of Ict Infrastructure Setup & Usage In Odl

Information and communication technologies playing a prime role in supporting various services in open distance learning in large scale and at same time there are many issues and challenges in setup and usage of ICT infrastructure. The following are various issues and challenges:

Application/service Compatibility with Respect to the Computer Hardware and Software

Technology is changing very frequently, but it is difficult every time to develop application software for various services using such technology. New technology has always flexible features that are needed in ODL system to meet the demands of the learners in large scale, but it is a challenging task to choose ideal hardware and software that have compatibility with existing application software. Application compatibility with respect to hardware and software can be achieved by placing platform independent infrastructure(the hardware, software and application).

Scalability Issues

Open distance learning is a more flexible education system than any other conventional education system. Due to this, the student enrollment is very high and at same time expectations from learners also high. As learners are more in scale and remote to the institution, most of the activities being performed remotely through the online services that are provided by the institution. Since, the learners and their usage is increasing progressively, time to time ,it is a challenging issue to maintain always scalable resources in terms of memory space, handle number of users and their transactions. This issue can be addressed by anticipating the scalable load at network level, system level, application/service level and data storage level at least for a period of 5 to 7 years and place an adequate computing, storage and network infrastructure.

Ensure Data Compatibility

As database technology is changing time to time, ensuring data compatibility with changing database technology is a challenging task. If the old data is not compatible with new database technology, it is very difficult to use and access data through various services/ applications. Data compatibility problem can be achieved by encouraging data migration process in various stages time to time so that the data is always compatible to new database technology to use and access it all the times.

Dynamic Allocation of Internet Bandwidth

Dynamic allocation of internet bandwidth to a specific service is a challenging issue. The accessibility of a service shall be ensured only with the availability of internet bandwidth as it is one of the prime parametres. As allocation of internet bandwidth to a specific service is directly proportional to the amount of usage of that service, there is a need of dynamically allocation of bandwidth time to time to that service. The problem can be achieved by introducing bandwidth management and load balancing system to ensure availability of a service. As online services are essential in ODL, it is ideal to have more than one ISP so that the availability of a service can be ensured always.

Policy Updates

Due to flexibility in open distance learning system, there will be frequent changes in admission criteria, evaluation criteria and even in learning procedure and policies to be adopted accordingly. As there is a frequent change in policies, it is a difficult task to update the policies every time, but if policy updation has not been done in time, it leads to many other operational problems. This issue can be addressed by introducing dynamic policy updation and enforcement approach in open distance learning system.

Dedicated Network Connectivity Among Various Operational Nodes

In open distance learning system, learners are remote to the institution in many ways and getting services through one of its operational nodes. It is a difficult to have proper network connectivity among various operational nodes to provide/access services due to non availability of technical manpower. This problem can be achieved by establishing dedicated network connectivity among various operational nodes in form of intranet by using MPLS/VPN technology.

Support Services

In open distance learning system, learners are remote to the institution many ways and require various online support services to perform their activities. Since ODL is a flexible system, the operational policies need to be changed frequently and is difficult to provide updated support services in time due to laps at various levels in the system. This problem can be addressed by involving all related personnel at the time of initiation of an activity so that its impact, if any on existing services can be discussed and find timeframe to provide support services in time.

Manpower Inline with Change in Technology

As technology is frequently changing time to time, it is a difficult task to have updated manpower inline with change in technology. It is even very difficult to have such manpower in government organizations. This problem can be achieved by introducing brainstorming and counselling sessions time to time and also to impart training/workshops on change in technology time to time.

Security in Open Distance Learning

In open distance learning, many online learning and support services are made available to its learners and other public. As usage of services is increasing day by day, at same time hackers/attackers are playing a vital role to deny the service and damage system resources. Security is essential to protect the resources from hackers and in turn protect the sensitive information and data.

Hackers take advantage of different security flaws in a network service, hosting infrastructure and exploit the vulnerability to compromise the system. The following are various security flaws by which a hacker will play a role:

- Lack of proper hardening of Servers
- Insufficient network boundary security controls
- Flaws or bugs in application/service software
- Insecure design and coding of hosted software (OS, application, etc.)
- Weak passwords
- Social engineering
- Lack of operational control

Security of a system/service/data shall be ensured by protecting the sensitive resources at network, system and the application/service domains. Some of the security parametres are authentication, access control, availability, confidentiality, integrity and non-repudiation. Violation in any of the parametre leads a breach in security. All these security parametres to be enforced along with security policy on the ICT infrastructure being used in open distance learning. The following are some of the policies to be framed and implemented for smooth functioning of ICT infrastructure in open distance learning system:

- Network security policy
- Host/ Server security policy
- Application software security
- Database security
- Content management policy

- Web server logging policy
- Backup a policy
- Password management policy
- Encryption policy
- Audit, Incident handling and Recovery policy
- Physical security policy

ICT in Distance Education Challenges and Opportunities in Higher Education

Information and Communication Technologies (ICTs) have pervaded every level of education around the world. Higher Education, particularly, has seen an unprecedented growth in the use of ICTs in teaching, research and extension activities.

Participation in higher education today is at a record high. Analysts of current educational trends estimate that by 2020, 40% of the global workforce will be knowledge workers, with a need for tertiary qualifications.

The World Bank is of the view that for countries to achieve sustainable economic development, the Age Participation Rates (APRs) in higher education must be in the region of 40 to 50%, but APRs are less than 10% of the relevant age group in most of South Asia and Sub Saharan Africa.

Many developing countries have extraordinary ambitions for growth. Malaysia plans to raise its APRs to 40% by 2010, while Jamaica, wants to raise it to 30% by 2015. India has set an ambitious target of lifting the APR to 15% by 2012.

But can the existing institutions cater to the rising demand? Dhaka University, Bangladesh, could only enroll 10,000 of the 80,000 applicants in 2000, while in Kenya only 9,000 of the 40,000 qualified students could be accommodated in the public university system. Building more brick and mortar institutions to cope with such demand is not a viable option for most countries. Open and distance learning emerges as a viable option as countries struggle to improve access, enhance the quality and cut the costs of higher education.

Forty years ago, the British Open University was launched to bring education to the homes of people in the UK. The success of the British Open University led to a huge expansion in open universities, particularly in the developing world.

In 1994, there were eleven mega-universities in the world with a collective enrolment of about 3 million students. Today the number of mega-universities has doubled and student enrolments have tripled.

If we look just at the Commonwealth, we can see a phenomenal growth in the number of open universities between 1988 and today. Asia alone has over 70 open universities and the largest number of adult distance learners in the world.[1]

Governments have always faced the challenge of breaking the iron triangle of quality, access and cost. If access is increased, there is the danger of lowering quality. If this is to be avoided, then the costs would have to be raised. Distance education allows us, through division of labour, specialization, and economies of scale, to reconfigure the access-quality-cost triangle.[2]

Liberalization, privatization, and globalization constitute the current social, economic, technological and political space within which television and all other media have to exist, survive, and function.

Revolutions in information and communication technologies have reduced national boundaries to meaningless lines drawn on maps. And in the new scenarios, education has been identified as one of the twelve main services, which need to be opened up for free flow of trade between countries. The form of this flow will become clear only when GATS comes into full force after rounds of negotiations among participating countries. Then, more than now, knowledge is expected to become a tradable commodity; and it will be essential that Indian educators keep pace with the change, or else perish in the face of competition from multinational forces in all fields of education and learning, including adult learning.

At the same time, changes in the capabilities, needs, and interests of the user; changes in the medium and its content, the close interdependence of the media and the competition of each medium to survive, and changes in the availability and attractiveness of accessible alternatives; interact freely with social, economic and political and technological contexts.

The learner community: India's demographic mosaic consists of an increasing demand for education for a population, half of which is below 15 years of age, 75 per cent rural, a literacy rate of about 60 per cent; and a linguistic break-up of 15 different major languages. The demand for education far outstrips the conventional system's ability to provide it, leaving no alternative to the use of technology in education.

We are at a critical junction, when the new technologies of communication from the individualized computer assisted learning systems to the more mass directed radio and television today offer an unparalled opportunity to reconsider conventional educational and learning practices and institutions. The notion that teaching and learning can be taken out of the confines of existing schools and colleges, that teaching can be individualized and insensitive to geoclimatic distances is one which has emerged out of the telecommunications revolution sweeping across the world in the 1980s and 1990s. And yet, the urban-rural divide in terms of access, equity, and resources will continue to be the main issues that Indian educators, particularly adult educators will have to address as the needs of the learning community in the new social, economic and political contexts will change.

In the new educational system, there are likely to be four levels of learners. The first level will consist of students, who, able to afford the high cost of education, will obtain it from either public or private institutions of higher education. They will be getting the best of the facilities, and will soon form educational elites. The second level of learners will consist of intelligent and competent students, who unable to afford the cost of education, will obtain it from existing public institutions and will soon be competing with the first level for membership in the educational elite. A third level of students will consist of the academically and financially poor students, who will seek access to education from lower quality institutions of higher learning. And the last group of learners would be most of the illiterate and the poor, whom you will be addressing as part of your work.

Current ways of imparting adult education use extensive ground work in the field and require both large numbers of trained personnel as well as committed individuals working in a world where access to technology is going to determine the gap between the haves and the have-nots.

Information and communication technology application constitutes an absolute necessity, given huge dispersed populations in a sub continent; inadequate resources and mind boggling needs. The new technologies offer us the chance to telescope decades of infrastructure building and development activities by providing us with the advantage of high speed delivery with no dilution in quality; wide reach; individualization of learning in a anytime, anywhere situation; and interactivity, a low per unit cost. These technologies and facilities can be equally used for language teaching, for literacy and adult learning.

This brings the role of the teachers or educators into focus. The adult educator is a key person in the whole process of learning and transacting education and a gateway to the learner.

The responsibilities of the teachers or adult educators are many, and very often they feel threatened and further challenged when told that they have to use ICTs, sometimes even feeling that they may well lose their jobs or be replaced by the ICTs.

ICT and Inclusive Education From Need to Responsibility

Students with disabilities who receive Integrated Co-Teaching services are educated with age appropriate peers in the general education classroom. ICT provides students the opportunity to be educated alongside their non-disabled peers with the full or part-time support of a special education teacher to assist in adapting and modifying instruction.

As described in the NYC *Continuum of Services for Students with Disabilities*, Integrated Co-Teaching "ensures that students master specific skills and concepts in the general education curriculum, as well as ensuring that their special education needs are being met, including meeting alternate curriculum goals."

The title of the services was changed from Collaborative Team Teaching to Integrated Co-Teaching when the service was incorporated in the New York State continuum of services. The state requires all school districts to use the terminology "Integrated Co-Teaching" so that the level of services being provided to a student is clear and consistent among school districts.

Inclusive education (or "inclusion") is not a place. Inclusive education refers to those educational practices enabling students with disabilities to remain at their home school and receive appropriate, specially designed instruction within general education classrooms in the same curriculum as typically developing peers. This can be accomplished in a great many different ways depending upon the needs of students. That is why we don't talk about a single type of "inclusion" classroom. All classes are inclusive by relying upon different configurations of accommodations, adaptations, instructional differentiation, related services, and special programmes. Descriptions of the district's different programmes and services appear in the following pages. Key to maximizing opportunities within general education classrooms in all situations is the appropriate design and delivery of instruction for individual students with disabilities.

It is important for faculty to maintain records of instruction provided outside the classroom, and to frequently review with colleagues, building administrators, and parents the instructional need requiring removal from a class. If special education instruction outside the classroom is determined to be necessary on a regular basis due to the unique needs of an individual student with a disability, IEP recommendations should reflect this.

Accessibility and Use of Graphics and Illustrations in the Learning Environment

The decision to adopt online technology (defined here as predominantly Internet-based delivery, with provision for interaction throughout the process), even on a limited basis, is always complex and can be risky, especially if the adopting organization lacks structural, cultural, or financial prerequisites.

Before applying Fleming's typology, it might be useful to determine how this conception of learning relates to some well-known pre-online learning models and standards. The correspondence of Fleming's categories to those of Bloom's alterable variables of learning, Chickering and Gamson's (1989) seven principles of good practice, and Moore's needs of distance learners. The point to note is that most of the attention in the three pre-online learning models is focused on direct teaching and student involvement tasks, while pre-learning tasks, such as attention, perception, and recall, are not specifically addressed. The task of organization and sequencing (which assumes that instructional materials and activities may vary in response to individual needs and circumstances) is found only in two of the models.

Figure suggests that older models of learning, which the above represent, may not address all of the elements necessary for efficient learning. Fleming's (1987) framework is more complete, addressing as it does the pre-learning elements of attention, perception, and recall. For designers and users of online learning, Fleming's model also draws attention to key learning activities which media might help to accommodate and monitor.

Attention

Given the importance of attention in learning, it is surprising that the learning models displayed do not mention it specifically. (To be fair, gaining the attention of the learner may simply be assumed to be an outcome of other activities, an element of quality learning materials, or an outcome of contact with the instructor or other learners, for example. The message of Figure is more the importance of the task and the possible usefulness of media, than a critique of these models, which are used here because they have otherwise proven useful, even classic, in their scope and influence.)

A key learning principle, according to Fleming (1987), is that attention by the learner to appropriate instructional stimuli is fundamental to learning. To be effective, training must attract and hold the learner's attention. Instruction must also recognize that attention tends to be

- individual—the capacity to be attentive varies among individuals, and it varies for any individual at different times (e.g., fatigue or lack of background can cause attention to wander sooner than usual).
- selective—at any one time, a learner's attention can be focused on only a small part of the learning content.
- fluid—as a teaching topic changes, the learner must know when and how to shift attention; however, some learners may become distracted, confused, or otherwise lose the main point during shifts in attention.
- especially attracted to novelty, to moderate levels of complexity, and to the contents of more focused, less complex displays.

Perception and Recall

Perception requires that the learner selectively focus on and make sense of stimulation in the environment, including the learner's own internal states and responses (thoughts, feelings, and physiological states). In a sense, all education and training is intended to make learners capable of finer and more articulate perceptions and distinctions. Recall involves the ability to remember and make use of relevant prior learning, as well as of the learning acquired in a given situation.

Perception and recall in teaching draw on principles such as those below.

- Organization affects perception; that is, events, ideas, words, concepts, and other stimuli that are not organized in some meaningful way are more difficult to understand and remember than those that are.
- Perception and recall can be aided by comparison and contrast; similarity and grouping also assist recall.
- Presentations that focus on differences are distinguished better by learners, and their contents may be easier to recall.

Organization and Sequencing

Organization and sequencing are present in the learning models. In Chickering and Gamson's (1987) model, responding to diversity in learners' needs suggests the possibility of reorganizing and resequencing materials and activities. In regard to Moore's (in Garrison, 1989) model, providing guidance and support has direct implications for organization and sequence.

For Fleming (1987), the organization and sequencing of materials is an important task in instructional planning. The general principles listed below particularly apply to media design.

- The first and last items in a sequence are especially important; introductions and summaries represent key learning opportunities.
- Modelling and demonstrations can result in learning. While learners eventually must become active in the process of acquiring skills and knowledge, students can also learn while watching. Active internal states produce intellectual engagement, just as psychomotor activity accompanies the learning of physical skills.
- Repetition and review increase learning up to a point. Repetition can be used to increase skill, automaticity, and speed; however, power (depth of understanding, breadth of proficiency) is usually not increased by repetition alone.

Instruction and Feedback

While learners require skilful instruction, they also require feedback to enable them to monitor their progress, to discover errors or misconceptions, and to recognize what they should do differently (or continue to do) to gain further proficiency. Not all feedback is equally useful, however, and not all learners require the same kind of feedback (Fleming, 1987). Principles applicable to media design and use include those listed below.

- The more mature the learner, the more informative the feedback should be.
- With mature learners, correct answers should simply be marked "correct." Mature learners tend to dislike excessively demonstrative praise.
- Feedback should be prompt, but it does not have to be immediate. Learners should know how much delay to expect in test results and marking.

- Exceptions to the above point occur when feedback on previous steps is needed before subsequent ones can be taken; when there is a safety concern (i.e., previous steps must be correct or later ones could result in a dangerous situation); or when the task is highly complex.
- Feedback can be reduced as the learner becomes more experienced and more proficient. Initially, feedback should be frequent for most learners, to ensure that they have a positive initial experience.

All of the models recognize that quality instruction includes the presentation to the learner of appropriate explanations, with the option for additional feedback. Chickering and Gamson's (1987) reference to student-instructor "contact" implies this element in their model. Importantly for this discussion of media-based learning, none of the models assumes that contact or interaction need be face-to-face to be effective.

Learner Participation

Learning requires engagement with the subject matter, and engagement often implies some kind of performance. In the case of psychomotor skills, the activity is usually physical, with evaluation dependent on observable outcomes. Occasionally, however, an activity may be completely or largely mental, according to the following principles.

- Activities that encourage the formation in the learner of mental images increase learning. Activities that require the learner first to process and then to reproduce a version of the original information do more to encourage learning than do rote reproduction and imitation alone.
- Language use accompanying or providing context for newly learned concepts increases learning; for example, composing a verbal narrative while learning complex or abstract material assists in retention. This principle can even extend to psychomotor skills, which is the reasoning behind "visualization" exercises in sports.

The use of experience and practice in learning requires willing learner participation and the conscientious application of new skills and knowledge for proficiency to develop. Peter Garrison (2001) quotes Galison's observation that moving from declarative knowledge (knowing that something is true, or how something might theoretically be done), through procedural knowledge (knowing how an activity is performed), to craft knowledge (being able to perform a procedure or to use knowledge with expert proficiency) requires practice, feedback, and application. Craft knowledge, the distinction between the novice and the expert, is the objective of many kinds of academic learning, and all higher-level skill training.

As are the tasks of instruction and feedback, learner involvement is common to all three learning models under discussion here. Time on task is added to show that participation must be purposive and relevant. The noun "cooperation" and the adjective "active" in Chickering and Gamson's (1987) model add the notion that the learner's involvement should be more than passive observation of others' efforts or conclusions, a position with definite implications for media implementation.

Concept Formation and Higher-order Thinking

The learning of concepts or principles is often intended to be part of a process leading to engagement with other, related concepts. In formulations such as Gagne's (1970), below, the learning sequence is hierarchical, and as the learner moves up the sequence, more complex orders of reasoning are required:

1. *signal learning*—involuntary responses; for example, the startle response, or removing a hand from heat.
2. *stimulus-response learning*—voluntary, selective responses; for example, signalling in response to a specific cue, or imitating an action.
3. *motor-chain learning*—performing a sequence of actions in a certain order; for example, dancing, parallel parking, or replacing a light bulb.
4. *verbal association or verbal chaining*—reciting correct responses to cues; for example, singing the lyrics of a song, reciting the alphabet, or translating a word from one language to another.
5. *multiple discrimination*—responding differently to similar stimuli; for example, distinguishing individual but related members of a group, or giving an appropriate English equivalent for a foreign word.
6. *concept learning*—responding to new stimuli according to properties they share with previously encountered stimuli, or comparing properties of phenomena; for example, estimating the characteristics of similar objects based on knowledge about

their composition (a large rock vs. a large pillow), identifying members of a group (saltwater vs. freshwater fish), and distinguishing examples and non-examples of a class or phenomenon (vegetables vs. non-vegetables).

7. *principle learning*—putting two or more concepts together in a relationship (without necessarily being able to explain the underlying rule governing the relationship); for example, applying physical laws ("matter expands when heated") or mathematical theorems.
8. *problem-solving*—recalling previously learned principles and using them in combination to achieve a goal; for example, selecting and combining facts in an essay to persuade, analyzing a problem to determine its cause, or solving a complex problem by selecting and applying previously learned facts and principles.

Higher-order thinking skills (HOTS) are a challenge in technology-based learning. A persistent criticism of computer-assisted learning (CAL) and case-based learning using intelligent agents and artificial intelligence algorithms has been their failure to move beyond the mere identification and use of facts, to creative and synergistic linking of concepts.

HOTS are present by implication in two of the models, in references to improved reading and study skills (Bloom, 1984), and in the objective of communicating high expectations to learners. However, the lack of specific reference to concept formation or higher-order thinking in these models, and the other apparent gaps in the resulting table, may be less a lapse than a reminder in this discussion that *somehow* these tasks must be addressed in media-based learning. The developers of the pre-online models undoubtedly accept that higher-order outcomes are preferred. The challenge to media developers is to make this objective specific and achievable, as discussed below.

Implications

The implications of the above observations for the design and use of technology in general teaching include the following.

Attention

- Change and variety can help to create and sustain attention.
- Skill in interpreting cues embedded in materials, and in shifting focus appropriately within the instructional environment, should be taught.

- In graphics, captions increase learning by focusing attention on appropriate elements of illustrations.
- Learner expectations can be increased and attention focused by instructional design, including pre-reading questions and cognitive organizers, embedded cues and questions, skimming and scanning exercises, advance instructions, knowledge of objectives of an activity, pre-testing, and summaries.
- Mental sets are associated with some learning media or activities. For example, TV can be associated with trivial content or passivity, and the Internet with nonlinearity, or a "surfing" mentality. The learner's attention may be distracted if mental sets differ from the intention of the instruction.
- Mental sets may, on the other hand, assist learning: the expectation that a CAL programme will contain useful information, or that a simulation will be intense and realistic, can be an advantage.
- Moderate uncertainty about what will happen in instruction, or about the eventual outcome of a presentation, may increase and help maintain attention.

Merrill's (1996) caution about the use of attention-getting strategies, especially on the computer, continues to be relevant. He notes that screen motion and animated movement are very powerful in attracting attention. The programme should be careful about asking a user to do more than one thing at a time, such as requiring reading during an animated display. Audio, however, might be used effectively with animation, since listening should not distract from watching the graphic display (Mayer, 2001).

Perception and Recall

- Captions aid recall.
- To make distinctions easier to perceive, displays should especially highlight differences (ideally moving from more obvious differences to finer ones).
- Vision and hearing comprise perception. Vision is most acute in the centre of the spectrum of visible light (yellow and yellow-green are the most visible colours, especially in dim light); and hearing is most acute in the centre of the range of audible sound.
- Similarity, predictability, and routine aid the process of perception. The use of familiar designs and displays with new

material permits learners to use previously learned perceptual skills when focusing on salient elements of new material.

Organization and Sequencing

- In organizing and structuring opportunities for learning and practice, the designer or teacher should consider, and where possible accommodate, individual differences. If the information or skill is new to the individual learner, they will usually need more time to acquire it and to bring it to proficiency and automaticity. Novice performance is typically slow, self-conscious, and awkward; with proficiency, execution becomes more fluid, automatic, and natural ("craft knowledge).
- Practice is effective in facilitating long-term memory; if long-term retention is desired, practice should be spaced rather than massed. "Cramming" does not promote long-term retention.
- Repetition with variety (paraphrasing, rephrasing, and other forms of learner processing of information) is more effective for long-term retention than rote reproduction. Regurgitation of information is less likely to produce learning than reworking and rephrasing it.

Feedback

- With fully mature learners, all incorrect responses should be accompanied by some explanatory feedback, not simply a "wrong" mark.
- For mature learners, correct responses should not be indicated by sound effects or other displays; a simple "OK" is sufficient.
- If feedback is to be delayed (for any reason, deliberate or otherwise), trainees should be told how long the delay will be.

Learner Participation

- Participation in learning may take many forms, limited chiefly by the creativity of the participants, the resources, and the technologies available. Possible examples include questions, activities, seminars, learning teams, small-group discussions, case studies, team learning, peer and cohort groups, written assignments, tests, field trips, labs, oral presentations of written reports, debates, expert panels, etc..

Higher-order Thinking and Concept Formation

- In any discipline, the solving of authentic problems is the best test of a learner's mastery of facts, data sources, reasoning processes, and fundamental principles.

- In Bloom's terms, concept formation occurs at the higher levels of the taxonomy, specifically in activities that call for analysis, synthesis, and evaluation.
- Non-examples are helpful in enabling learners to develop concepts. They illustrate the differences between a concept and others that are similar. Similarly, non-examples can help learners to distinguish and clarify examples. When using examples and non-examples, the contrast between them should initially be large, and should be made progressively smaller as the learner demonstrates the ability to discriminate.
- Concrete concepts are generally easier to grasp than abstract ones, and thus may be useful in illustrating abstractions. It is easier to learn abstract (or concrete) concepts when constructs such as examples, models, analogies, descriptions, synonyms, and definitions are used.

Constructivism and Media

The use of media for teaching assumes that learning, as both an individual and a social activity, may be facilitated by intentional interaction. *Constructivism* is a general term for the view that the world is often too complex for general principles to be useful in teaching, and that the best learning results when the learner processes and integrates new experiences into his or her existing constructs. Constructivist teaching tends to be more holistic, more collaborative in method, and more encouraging and accepting of learner initiatives, including greater freedom and variety in assignments and assessments. The role of the instructor also changes in constructivist teaching from "sage on the stage" to "guide on the side," or coach.

In relation to Figure , constructivist teaching addresses the teaching tasks shown by emphasizing the learners' unique background and consequent preparedness. Constructivist learning outcomes strive to apply real-world standards, and to assure that learning outcomes are applicable beyond a merely academic context. "Higher-order" constructivist outcomes have the potential to be relevant in daily life to real problems or situations.

The uses of technology may vary, too, in different constructivist environments. *Social* and *radical* constructivists view interaction as of greater importance to learning than mere access to information, while *information processing* and *interactive* constructivists view information, facts, and contact with a wide circle of informed people as critical to the student's development of a fully adequate construction of the world (Henriques, 1997). In common, constructivists tend to use technologies for purposes such as those identified by Jonassen (1998):

- acquainting and involving students with real-world problems and situations.
- modelling the analytic and thinking skills of the instructor and other experts, which learners then apply, with appropriate feedback, to their own problems and constructs.
- working within an authentic problem context that reflects as much as possible the problem's real context and characteristics.

Overall, the contribution online media often make to constructivist teaching is in expanding the range and variety of experiences usually available in classroom-based learning. Because online media are by definition linked to networks of external resources, they can provide access to people, ideas, and information beyond those found in the classroom. Whether the result is a nearly self-sufficient *collaborative learning environment*, or, more simply, a forum for problem-based learning (Bridges, 1992), the result is an opening-up of the learning space to a wider variety of ideas and points of view.

Media, Modes, and Learning

Technologies, as *channels* through which *modes* (symbols acting as stimuli) pass, differ in the responses they evoke in users. For example, text is a mode of presentation. Print-on-paper is one possible *medium* (channel) for text, but there are others: a computer monitor, an overhead projection, a television screen, film (moving or still), etc. Wherever it is used, text remains text, and must be read to be comprehended.

Despite their different characteristics, useful online training technologies have in common the effect of somehow bringing students into contact with their tutors, the content, and their peers (Moore, 1989). In this way, media may help to reduce "transactional distance" in learning—the communication gap or psychological distance between participants which may open in a teaching-learning situation. Although similar in producing these outcomes, the differences in how various technologies accomplish their effects are important to their potential usefulness.

Human and Technology-based Teaching

Technologies differ from one another, and instruction delivered online differs from human-delivered teaching. Consider, in the analysis below, the effects of media-based training compared with training done by stand-up, face-to-face instructors.

A conclusion is that, as in most instructional design decisions, there are trade-offs related to the needs of the users and the resources available. An analysis such as that presented above may assist in identifying the trade-offs involved in the choice of one online technology over another approach.

Interestingly, it appears that human trainers are superior in exactly those activities shown to be overlooked: planning and preparation, and feedback and performance tracking (in relation to higher-order outcomes). Human trainers can deftly detect and respond to unexpected needs, if disposed and permitted to do so, while technology-based training programmes must be specially designed to assess and respond to unanticipated outcomes. Fleming's (1987) framework again appears to be superior for analysis of media's design needs.

Media Characteristics and Impacts on Learning

Five types of media, from print to multimedia (defined as "the integration of video, audio, graphics, and data within a single computer workstation), are discussed below. The intention is to make distinctions among media in relation to modes of delivery and presentation commonly used in teaching and training. The argument here is that, as technologies continue to evolve, it will be increasingly possible, technically, to use ever more complex media, including multimedia as defined above, to deliver instruction. Criteria will be needed, therefore, for making wise choices among the options, and for designing and supporting instruction based not only on the capabilities of the technology to deliver it, but also on the ability of learners to make effective use of the tools.

Print and Text

There is no medium more ubiquitous than print, and no mode more familiar than text in its many forms. Print was part of the first teaching machine—the book—and books were the first mass-produced commodity. Print has been the dominant medium to date in distance education, and distance students have traditionally spent most of their time studying alone, often using print materials only. The question is whether this situation is likely to continue.

The answer requires consideration of the strengths and weaknesses of text and print. The chief strengths of print and text have traditionally included:

- cost—Bates reports that print is one of the lowest cost one-way technologies.
- flexibility and robustness—print scores highest on these features.
- portability and ease of production—with desktop publishing hardware and software, printing has become enormously simpler and its quality much higher. In addition, costs can be reduced with local production.
- stability—organization and sequencing are positively affected, since text-only printed and online materials can be reorganized and resequenced with relative ease by cut-and-paste operations, using word-processors and HTML editors.
- convenience, familiarity, and economy—instruction and feedback are facilitated by the medium's familiarity, as, for adept learners and the highly literate, are higher-order thinking and concept formation.

Ironically, the major disadvantages of print are related to some of its advantages, and include those listed below.

- Print is static, and may fail to gain adequate involvement from low-functioning readers. Attention, perception and recall, and active learner participation may thus be lower for less able learners.
- Print is relatively non-interactive, or at least non-responsive, and may lead to passive, rote learning.
- Print often requires substantial literacy levels.

Print is accessible (to the literate), and comparatively low in cost; furthermore, online text is easy to produce, translates well across various platforms and operating systems, and in some of its forms, may be manipulated by the user if desired. However, print may be seen by some as the "slightly seedy poor relation" (Pittman, 1987) of other instructional media. Text's lack of appeal is exacerbated by the alternatives to reading which are increasingly appearing, and which use multimedia (especially audio and graphics) and improvements in voice recognition and reproduction technologies to make reading less critical for users. As a result, non-print multimedia-based technologies could come to be regarded as cost-effective, especially in cultures or industries where high levels of literacy cannot be assumed, or where the costs of reading inefficiencies are high. Developments such as instant text messaging and e-paper could reverse this trend, giving print and print-based materials new life, at least until e-paper-based multimedia evolve to make text less important once more.

Still Graphics and Static Displays

A wide and growing selection of graphic technologies is available to online programmers, from older technologies, such as overhead projectors and 35mm slide projectors, broadcast TV, and pre-produced videotapes, to various forms of digital video (interactive and non-interactive), computer-generated video, and interpersonal communications tools such as group and desktop video-conferencing using Voice over Internet Protocol (VoIP).

Graphics can increase the motivation of users to attend, prompt perception, and aid recall, and assist in the development of higher-order thinking and concept formation. Furthermore, still graphics combine high information content (they can illustrate abstract or unfamiliar concepts) with relatively low production and distribution costs. Online compression formats, such as .jpg, permit low-bandwidth distribution of high quality graphics. Screen resolution can be an issue in the use of graphics. The size at which a graphic is captured is key: capture at a high resolution and display at a lower resolution will result in a much larger image, which, depending upon the monitor's settings, may not be completely visible on the viewer's screen; conversely, an image captured at a lower resolution than that at which it is displayed will appear smaller. The end-users' likely technology platform should be the standard, to ensure that graphics will be viewed as intended. Online users should always be advised about which settings are optimal.

Online static visual displays which draw upon established design principles, including those listed below, are more likely to be successful.

- Visuals that emphasize the critical details relevant to learning are most effective. Unnecessary visuals may be distracting, especially to learners with limited attention spans or discrimination skills.
- The addition of detail and realism to displays does not increase learning. Unnecessary detail can add to learning time without increasing achievement, and in online situations can increase transfer times dramatically. Depending on the relevance of the cues to the learning task, simple line drawings tend to be superior to photographs or more realistic drawings.
- Winn cautions that diagrams, charts, and graphs should not be assumed to be self-explanatory, but may require the learner

to process the information given and to understand certain conventions. He suggests that graphics should routinely include supporting captions.

With the exception of instruction that directly employs colour for teaching (e.g., identifying colour-coded elements), there is little evidence that colour enhances learning. Colour may even distract some learners. Some other generalizations about colour are given below.

- Colour may increase the speed at which lists can be searched.
- The use of too many colours may reduce the legibility of a presentation. A maximum of four colours was suggested in one study, but up to eleven colours in screen displays were found to be acceptable in another.
- The most highly recommended colours are vivid versions of green, cyan, white, and yellow.
- The heavy use of colour may degrade performance of some older microcomputers and monitors, or may be displayed differently on various systems.

Based on his review of the data, Szabo concluded that "The disparity between effectiveness and perceived effectiveness is nowhere as great as it is in the realm of colour".

Some further advice on the use of colour in media production is presented below (Rockley, 1997).

- End-users should control the colour of displays, given the prevalence of colour-blindness (found to some degree in 8% of men and 0.5% of women).
- The best colour display combinations are blue, black, or red on a white background, or white, yellow, or green on a black background.

For online uses of still graphics, the following characteristics of the computer as a delivery medium must be accommodated by developers.

- A PC screen is about 1/3 of a piece of paper in display area, and most monitors are less sharp than the best laser printers or photographic reproductions. Screen positioning is critical: important information should go to the top-left; the lower-left is the least noticed area of the page/screen. What works on paper may not work, without translation or redesign, on a computer screen. (Designers should not assume users have superior equipment; design should be for displays of mid-range quality and size.)

- Single-colour backgrounds, with a high contrast ratio between the background and the text, are easiest for readers; white or off-white is best for the background.
- Textured backgrounds display differently on various systems, and should be used with care, if at all.
- Sans serif fonts, with mixed upper and lower case, are best for legibility and reading ease.
- The size of the font depends on the purpose. For extended reading, smaller (12-point) fonts are suitable; for presenting information that will be skimmed or scanned, larger fonts may be more appropriate.
- Font changes can be effective for emphasis (size and type), as can capitals, underlining, and especially the use of bolding. The use of colour alone should be avoided for emphasis, as systems handle colour differently. All of the above techniques should be used sparingly, to preserve their impact.

Sound and Music

The principal issues in online audio are technical (storage and bandwidth) and pedagogical. For maximum effect, materials must not simply be a recorded version of another medium (e.g., a lecture), but should be rescripted to incorporate and interrelate with other modes of presentation.

Online audio (including, when file sizes are large, distribution by CD and DVD) can be particularly useful in teaching for several technical reasons, presented below.

- An audio summary of previous material can aid recall, help retention, and lead to concept formation and higher-order thinking.
- Although CDs and DVDs are one-way technologies (non-interactive, like a lecture), they have the great advantage of learner control.
- CDs and DVDs are easy and cheap to produce and ship, and so reduce cost and improve accessibility.
- The technology of discs is easy to use and familiar. Operating systems (Windows, Apple OS, and Linux) now usually offer built-in sound reproduction technologies for both streamed and static sound files.
- The mode of presentation most often found on this medium, the human voice, is a familiar and powerful teaching tool.

- Audio may be more motivating than print alone, and together with print may form a powerful alternative and aid to reading alone.

A key issue in selecting a mix of other technologies to be used with audioconferencing is the relative importance of *relationship building* vs. *information exchange.* Picard (1999) sees audioconferencing's key contribution in its ability to promote relationship building in work or learning. The need for other technologies, according to Picard, is dependent upon the degree to which there is also a need to exchange information (for which, she warns, audio is not particularly effective). The schema presented emerges from Picard's analysis.

In Picard's (1999) analysis, when relationship building and information exchange needs are both low, audioconferencing alone may suffice. When both needs are high, however, audio-conferencing, video, and data (including text) should all be present. Relationship building can be enhanced by combining audio-conferencing and video together with data, especially text. (Text has formidable relationship building capabilities, as anyone who has ever had a pen-pal knows, but it assumes considerable skill on the user's part.) Video increases the likelihood that interaction will promote relationships, but audio alone is less capable of promoting this outcome. Data exchange alone seems to do little to promote relationships among those with access to other forms of interaction.

As technological evolutions permit more audio-based delivery, both interactive (e.g., VoIP) and one-way (streaming audio clips), research findings about audio's teaching capabilities become applicable.

- Learning gains from one-way audio alone are at best weak.
- Learners possessing higher verbal skills usually do not benefit from audio added to text.
- There are few or no apparent significant immediate recall effects between text-only and text plus audio presentation, except that sometimes audio may lengthen the time required to complete instruction.
- Audio may limit the ability of learners to proceed through material at their own individual rate.
- The quality and utility of digitized speech depends upon the amount of compression, the sampling rate, and the bandwidth available to the user.
- Users may relatively quickly become accustomed to synthetic speech; however, more cognitive effort is needed, and increased

demands on short-term memory may reduce retention. (Synthesized speech may be more useful in reading back a learner's work, for example from a word processor, than in presenting unfamiliar learning content.)

- For general audiences, the possible benefits of audio must be weighed against the increased costs. Exceptions include uses such as language training, music instruction, and as an aid to the visually impaired.
- Where possible, the learner should be able to decide whether or not to use available audio.

The key limitation to the use of synchronous (live) audio on the Internet continues to be bandwidth, but impressive advances in VoIP audio programmes are reducing the limitations. Some VoIP packages permit only point-to-point voice communications between two computers, while others permit point-to-multipoint group interaction, much like a teleconference, and require as little bandwidth as 56 Kbps. This online technology is expanding rapidly in business: in 2001, the proportion of companies of 100 employees or more using VoIP for business communications rose from 7% to 26%.

Video and Animation

Video suffers from the same kinds of limitations as audio, but to an even greater degree; bandwidth is the primary limitation to greater video use online. According to Roberts, video

- adds a sense of direct involvement and physical presence among geographically dispersed learners.
- provides quality learning opportunities (as good as or better than those offered by other methods and technologies).
- gives distant sites live, interactive learning opportunities.
- enables the delivery of global expertise to remote learners.
- eliminates or reduces travel time and time away from jobs and family.

The following strengths of video for learning and teaching can be exploited, with appropriate instructional strategies.

- The social presence and cohesion that video fosters among users is often valued, especially by participants new to distance education, and may improve motivation.
- The technology permits the sharing of various visual resources.

- Group-based learning activities may be more attractive and feasible with video technology support.
- Well-designed and appropriately implemented uses of video can help in the teaching of abstract, time-protracted, hazardous, or unfamiliar concepts.

The advantages in actual practice of various forms of video continue to be debated. In some studies, animation has been shown to result in a reduction in study time, "suggesting that animation results in more efficient learning", with learning effects persisting over time. There is, however, also some indication that, when compared with "highly imaginative examples and illustrations," the advantages of animated simulations were less obvious. Szabo concluded from his analysis that "any widespread belief in the superiority of animation over non-animated instruction within the context of computer-based instruction is at odds with the research".

According to Roberts, critical issues in the delivery of video-based training include those listed below.

1. Proper training of instructors.
2. User self-consciousness.
3. Integration of other media into video presentations.
4. Optimum length of sessions and size of groups.
5. Session variety.
6. Technical design and support.
7. Professional quality visual elements.

Obviously, video delivery is complex, potentially costly, and of uncertain benefit for some teaching tasks over simpler, more economical media. A clear pedagogic and business case is obviously needed for its use.

Multimedia

As Oliver notes, the term *multimedia* has not always designated computer-based media, as it does now, but originally referred to combinations of audio, visual, and print materials delivered by various media. Now, however, "the term has been adopted by the computer industry and re-defined to mean 'the integration of video, audio, graphics, and data within a single computer workstation'. Roblyer and Schwier note that the term has become "too slippery" to define easily, that consensus about its characteristics is rare, and that as a concept it is converging with others, including hypermedia.

While multimedia applications offer advantages and benefits, these do not come without costs, awareness of which may help users to make informed decisions about the true advantages of the medium. The key concerns include unnecessary duplication of existing instructional materials; teachers untrained in design becoming bogged down in the production of low-quality multimedia; problems of assessment using multimedia materials, which occur because learners using hyperlinks in multimedia do not always cover the same material in the same sequence; and high technical demands, with technical difficulties arising because of the complexity of some multimedia applications.

Obstacles to the widespread use of multimedia are myriad, and arise in part from the fact that multimedia applications, even if instituted carefully and with the intention of altering the learners' experiences, are an example of change and innovation, and so may provoke resistance, including such obstacles as:

- reluctance on the part of teachers to see materials transformed.
- the fear felt by users (staff and learners) over the level of technical knowledge required to get involved.
- the need of many tutors for special training (which may or may not be conveniently available) to use multimedia effectively.
- the significant challenge and expense of "adapting and transforming material intended for traditional delivery methods into new media".
- the desire to tinker endlessly and mindlessly on presentations, with negative results for productivity. This effect, called "the futz factor", has been estimated to cost US $5600 yearly for every corporate computer. Futzing may be a "revenge effect" of technology, an unexpected and troubling result of the interaction of computer technology with the "real world".

Despite these potential limitations and weaknesses, multimedia also has potential strengths when used appropriately. Newby et al. list the following advantages of multimedia for instruction:

- multiple, active learning modalities.
- accommodation of different learning styles and preferences, including disabilities.
- effective instruction across learning domains, including affective and psychomotor (with simulations, case studies, and other representational and interactive uses), promoting development of higher-order thinking skills, and concept formation.

- realism, especially when coupled with graphics and video.
- potential interactivity.
- individualization, with use of computer branching capabilities and CML (computer-managed learning).
- consistent experiences, compared with group-based face-to-face instruction.
- potential for high levels of learner control.

The impact of multimedia in teaching is ultimately dependent upon the incorporation of certain principles that govern its usefulness and effects. Mayer has suggested seven such principles, based on empirical evidence from his ongoing research on multimedia and actual learning. These principles not only describe the various impacts of multimedia on learning, they also constitute a good basic primer for instructional designers working with media generally.

1. *Multimedia principle:* Students learn better from words and graphics or pictures than from words alone.
2. *Spatial contiguity principle:* Students learn better when corresponding words and pictures are presented near rather than far from each other on the page or screen.
3. *Temporal contiguity principle:* Students learn better when corresponding words and pictures are presented simultaneously rather than successively.
4. *Coherence principle:* Students learn better when extraneous words, pictures, and sounds are excluded rather than included.
5. *Modality principle:* Students learn better from animation and audible narration than from animation and on-screen text.
6. *Redundancy principle:* People have only limited capacity to process visual and auditory material presented simultaneously; therefore, students learn better from animation and narration than from a combination of animation, generation, and onscreen text.
7. *Individual differences principle:* Design effects are stronger for low-knowledge learners than for high-knowledge learners, and for high-spatial-ability learners than for low-spatial-ability learners. (*Spatial ability* is the ability mentally to generate, maintain, and manipulate visual images).

The Internet

"Online learning" almost always denotes learning "on the Internet." The Internet offers both advantages and challenges to educators and trainers. The advantages arise from the Internet's enormous capacity to link participants with information and with each other. But problems with navigation, structure, interactivity, complexity, security, and sheer consumption of time must be addressed.

The Internet is potentially a powerful linking and communication vehicle. Heinich, Molenda, Russell, and Smaldino suggest that the Internet's power lies in its capacity for providing numerous connections to engrossing, multi-sensory experiences, suited to individual needs. The fact that these can be constructed by teachers themselves, and can incorporate knowledge of their students' needs and feature meaningful student-student collaboration and student-teacher interaction, also makes the Internet a revolutionary learning tool. At the same time, the Web's inherent lack of structure may result in some users getting unintentionally "lost in cyberspace," or making poor use of time ("surfing," or exploring interesting but irrelevant minutiae). Also, Internet materials often fail to exploit the medium's potential for interactivity, consisting of one-way presentations of information. The reliability of online information may also be suspect, unless its provenance is known. And successful use of the Internet currently demands proficient literacy and computer skills. (As noted earlier, this may change as bandwidth availability makes supplemental audio and video more available.)

In relation to Figure , the Internet offers a means for gaining the attention of learners, and of presenting opportunities for focusing perceptions and prompting recall. Learner participation can also be supported, especially with CMC and use of collaborative learning projects. Providing instruction, and assuring appropriate organization, sequencing, and higher-order outcomes are less easily accomplished with the Internet, for reasons discussed here.

Limitations such as those mentioned above may account for some of the increasing class of former users called "Internet dropouts." Of those who have stopped using the Internet, only 28% expect to return, having concluded that they have "no need" for the Web. While other reasons include cost (cited by 17% of dropouts) and lack of convenient access to a computer (14%), the fact that lack of utility is the most common reason indicates a serious potential problem for future Internet growth: unless a tool has a perceived legitimate purpose, it may not prosper, or even survive.

Two related Internet-based media show particular instructional promise for those with the skill and discipline to use them well, especially in relation to organization and sequencing challenges presented by the Internet: *hypermedia* and *hypertext.* Hypermedia is the linking of multimedia documents, while hypertext is the linking of words or phrases to other words or phrases in the same or another document. Internet delivery may be hyperlinked or linear. As a technology, hypermedia has existed for decades, but with advances in hardware, software, and human-computer interfaces, it is now technically feasible to incorporate hypermedia systems routinely in teaching, and dozens of hypertext and hypermedia development systems now exist.

While hypermedia permit huge amounts of information from a variety of media to be stored in a compact and easily accessible form, the sheer amount of available information may also overwhelm learners, especially if they are unable to refine a search or conduct an exploration successfully (with focus). Users require skills (some technical, others related to organization and self-discipline) to make efficient use of hypermedia materials. Although the results of hypertext use in teaching have previously been somewhat mixed, the promise is in the potential to offer self-directed learners the option to control the details of their own learning to a much greater extent than is possible in group instruction. With emerging online communications capabilities, the ability for teachers to oversee and monitor this kind of learning also increases. The problem, as in many of these new implementations, is to overcome the users' tendency only to "focus on facilitating access to information," and not on actual learning outcomes.

Commencing Computer Education Challenges and Opportunities

A broad approach has been taken in considering adult education in the field of intellectual and developmental disabilities, for the range and variability in performance amongst people with such disabilities is very wide indeed. Intellectual disability is regarded as a condition of arrested cognitive growth commencing in the developmental years of early and young childhood. It is not just associated with cognitive disability, but with a wide range of social limitations in areas known as social or adaptive skills

Providing Access to Technology

People with disabilities meet barriers of all types. However, technology is helping to lower many of these barriers. By using computing technology for tasks such as reading and writing documents, communicating with others, and searching for information on the Internet, students and employees with disabilities are capable of handling a wider range of activities independently. Still, people with disabilities face a variety of barriers to computer use. These barriers can be grouped into three functional categories: barriers to providing computer input, interpreting output, and reading supporting documentation. Hardware and software tools (known as adaptive or assistive technologies) have been developed to provide functional alternatives to these standard operations.

Mobility Impairments

Some wheelchairs may not fit under standard height computer tables and some computer users do not have enough use of their hands and arms to operate a standard keyboard or mouse.

Input

Equipment which provides flexibility in the positioning of monitors, keyboards, documentation, and tabletops is useful for many individuals with disabilities. Plugging all computer components into power outlet strips with accessible on and off switches makes it possible for some individuals to turn equipment on and off independently.

Some technology assists individuals with little or no use of their hands in using a standard keyboard. Individuals who have use of one finger, or have access to a mouth- or head-stick or some other pointing device, can control the computer by pressing keys with the pointing device. Software utilities can create "sticky keys" that electronically latch the SHIFT, CONTROL, and other keys to allow sequential keystrokes to input commands that normally require two or more keys to be pressed simultaneously. The key repeat function can be disabled for those who cannot release a key quickly enough to avoid multiple selections. Keyboard guards (solid templates with holes over each key to assist precise selection) can be used by those with limited fine motor control.

Sometimes repositioning the keyboard and monitor can enhance accessibility. For example, mounting keyboards perpendicular to tables or wheelchair trays at head-height can assist individuals with limited mobility who use pointing devices to press keys. Other simple hardware modifications can assist individuals with mobility impairments. For instance, disk guides can assist with inserting and removing diskettes; a dedicated hard disk or computer network access can eliminate or reduce the necessity to do so.

For individuals who need to operate the computer with one hand, left- and right-handed keyboards are available. They provide more efficient key arrangements than standard keyboards designed for two-handed users.

Some hardware modifications completely replace the keyboard or mouse for individuals who cannot operate these standard devices. Expanded keyboards (larger keys spaced far apart) can replace standard keyboards for those with limited fine motor control. Mini-keyboards provide access to those who have fine motor control but lack a range of motion great enough to use a standard keyboard. Track balls and specialized input devices can replace a mouse.

For those with more severe mobility impairments keyboard emulation is available, including scanning and Morse code input. In each case, special switches make use of at least one muscle over which the individual has voluntary control (e.g., head, finger, knee, mouth). In scanning input, lights or cursors scan letters and symbols displayed on computer screens or external devices. To make selections, individuals use switches activated by movement of the head, finger, foot, breath, etc. Hundreds of switches tailor input devices to individual needs. In Morse code input, users input Morse code by activating switches (e.g., a sip-and-puff switch registers dot with a sip and dash with a puff). Special adaptive hardware and software translate Morse code into a form that computers understand so that standard software can be used.

Speech input provides another option for individuals with disabilities. Speech recognition systems allow users to control computers by speaking words and letters. A particular system is "trained" to recognize specific voices.

Special software can further aid those with mobility impairments. Abbreviation expansion (macro) and word prediction software can reduce input demands for commonly used text and keyboard commands. For example, word prediction software anticipates entire words after several keystrokes and increases input speed.

Output

Screen output does not present a challenge, but individuals with mobility impairments who have difficulty obtaining output from printers may need assistance from others.

Documentation

On-screen help provides efficient access to user guides for individuals who are unable to turn pages in books.

Blindness

Individuals who are blind cannot access visual material presented on the computer screen or in printed materials.

Input

Most individuals who are blind use standard keyboards, however, Braille input devices are available. Braille key labels can assist with keyboard use.

Output

Speech output systems can be used to read screen text to computer users who are blind. Special software programmes (called screen readers) "read" computer screens and speech synthesizers "speak" the text. The availability of earphones for individuals using speech output systems can reduce the distractions for others nearby. Refreshable Braille displays allow line-by-line translation of screen text into Braille on a display area where vertical pins move into Braille configurations as screen text is scanned. Braille displays can be read quickly by those with advanced Braille skills, are good for detailed editing (e.g., programming and final editing of papers), and do not disrupt others in work areas because they are quiet. Braille printers provide "hard copy" output for users who are blind.

Documentation

Scanners with optical character recognition can read printed material and store it electronically on computers, where it can be read using speech synthesis or printed using Braille translation software and Braille printers. Such systems provide independent access to journals, syllabi, and homework assignments for students who are blind. Electronic versions of documentation can support computer users who are blind if it is delivered in an accessible format.

Low Vision

For some people with visual impairments the standard size of letters on the screen or printed in documents are too small for them to read. Some people cannot distinguish one colour from another.

Input

Most individuals who have visual impairments can use standard keyboards, but large print keytop labels are sometimes useful.

Output

Special equipment for individuals who are visually impaired can modify display or printer output. Computer-generated symbols, both text and graphics, can be enlarged on the monitor or printer, thereby allowing individuals with low vision to use standard word processing, spreadsheet, electronic mail, and other software applications. For individuals with some visual impairments, the ability to adjust the colour of the monitor or change the foreground and background colours is also of value. For example, special software can reverse the screen from black on white to white on black for people who are light sensitive. Anti-glare screens can make screens easier to read. Voice output systems are also used by people with low vision.

Documentation

Scanners with optical character recognition can read printed material and store it electronically on computers, where it can be read using speech synthesis or printed in large print.

Hearing or Speech Impairments

Speech and hearing disorders alone do not generally interfere with computer use. However, advanced speech synthesizers are close enough to human quality to act as substitute voices and thus provide a compensatory tool for students who cannot communicate verbally. Students with portable systems can participate in class discussions once adapted computers provide them with intelligible speaking voices. Word processing and educational software may also help students who are hearing impaired develop writing skills.

Input

Students with hearing or speech impairments typically use a standard keyboard and mouse.

Output

Alternatives to audio output can assist the computer user who is hearing impaired. For example, if the sound volume is turned to zero, a computer may flash the menu bar when audio output is normally used.

Documentation

Individuals with hearing or speech impairments typically do not have difficulty using standard written or on-screen documentation.

Specific Learning Disabilities

Educational software where the computer provides multi-sensory experiences, interaction, positive reinforcement, individualized instruction, and repetition can be useful in skill building. Some students with learning disabilities who have difficulty processing written information can also benefit from completing writing assignments, tutorial lessons, and drill-and-practice work with the aid of computers. For example, a standard word processor can be a valuable tool for individuals with dysgraphia, an inability to produce handwriting reliably.

Input

Quiet work areas and ear protectors may make computer input easier for individuals with learning disabilities who are hyper-sensitive to background noise.

Software that aids in efficient and accurate input can also assist. Some people can compensate for high rates of input errors by using spell checkers, thesauruses, and grammar checkers. In addition, word prediction programmes (software that predicts whole words from fragments) have been used successfully by students with learning disabilities. Similarly, macro software which expands abbreviations can reduce the necessity to memorize keyboard commands and can ease the entry of commonly used text.

Output

Some individuals with learning disabilities find adaptive devices designed for those with visual impairments useful. In particular, large-print displays, alternative colours on the computer screen, and voice output can compensate for some reading problems. People who have difficulty interpreting visual material can improve comprehension and the ability to identify and correct errors when words are spoken or printed in large fonts.

Documentation

Some individuals with learning disabilities find it difficult to read. Computer documentation provided in electronic forms can be enlarged on the screen and/or read aloud with speech synthesis systems to manage.

Students Approach

The attitude and self-advocacy skills of students with disabilities may be two of the most important factors in determining their success or failure in postsecondary education. Students with disabilities need to be prepared to work collaboratively with the institution's disability coordinator to enable them to have an equal opportunity to participate in an institution's programmes and activities. To ensure that students with disabilities possess the desired levels of self-advocacy to succeed in postsecondary education, high school educators may want to encourage the students to take the following steps.

Understand Their Disabilities

Students with disabilities need to know the functional limitations that result from their disabilities and understand their strengths and weaknesses. They should be able to explain their disabilities to an institution's disability coordinators or other appropriate staff. As part of this process, students should be able to explain where they have had difficulty in the past, as well as what has helped them overcome such problems and what specific adjustments might work in specific situations. To assist students in this area, high school educators can encourage high school students to be active participants in their IEP or Section 504 meetings. High school personnel also can suggest that students practice explaining their disabilities, as well as why they need certain services, to appropriate secondary staff or through role-playing exercises to prepare them to engage in such conversations with confidence in a postsecondary setting.

Accept Responsibility for Their Own Success

All students, including those with disabilities, must take primary responsibility for their success or failure in postsecondary education. Students with disabilities, in particular, are moving from a system where parents and school staff usually advocated on their behalf to a system where they will be expected to advocate for themselves. An institution's staff will likely communicate directly with students when issues arise and are generally not required to interact with students' parents. In general, students with disabilities should expect to complete all course requirements, such as assignments and examinations. Students with disabilities need to identify the essential academic and technical standards that they will be required to meet for admission and continued participation in an institution's programme. Students also need to identify any academic adjustments they may need as a result of their disabilities to meet those standards and how to request those adjustments. Students with disabilities need to understand that, while federal disability laws guarantee them an equal opportunity to participate these laws do not guarantee that students will achieve a particular outcome, for example, good grades.

Take an Appropriate Preparatory Curriculum

Because all students will be expected to meet an institution's essential standards, students with disabilities need to take a high school curriculum that will prepare them to meet those standards. If students with disabilities plan to attend a rigorous postsecondary institution, they, like their peers without disabilities, need to make high school curriculum choices that support that goal. High school guidance counsellors and state VR agency counsellors, in particular, can play an important role in students' curriculum planning.

For all students, good study skills and the ability to write well are critical factors of success in postsecondary education. High school educators can help students in these areas by offering or identifying opportunities, such as workshops, courses or tutoring programmes, that emphasize the importance of reading, writing and good study skills. In addition, staff should encourage students to enroll in classes that will focus on writing and study skills in their freshman year of postsecondary education.

Learn Time Management Skills

Although a primary role of high school educators is to provide monitoring, direction and guidance to students as they approach the end of their high school career, staff also need to prepare students to act independently and to manage their own time with little to no supervision. High school educators can assist students by identifying resources that will help them learn time management and scheduling skills.

Acquire Computer Skills

Because postsecondary students use computers to complete a multitude of tasks, from registering for classes to accessing course material and obtaining grades, it is essential that students learn to use computers if they are to be prepared for postsecondary education. Ideally, students with disabilities need to start using computers as early as possible in school to increase their familiarity with, and their comfort level in using, computers. Students with visual impairments, hearing impairments, learning disabilities or mobility impairments may have problems with inputting data or reading a computer monitor. Assistive technology can help certain students with disabilities use computers and access information.

Consider Supplemental Postsecondary Education Preparatory Programmes

A variety of institutions of postsecondary education have summer programmes in which students can participate while they are still in high school, or after graduation, to ease their transition to postsecondary education. These programmes often expose students to experiences that they are likely to encounter in postsecondary education, such as living in dorms, relating to other students and eating in dining halls. The programmes may also focus on instruction in certain subject areas, such as math or English, or in certain skills, such as computer, writing or study skills, that can prepare a student to be successful in postsecondary education. High school educators can assist students with disabilities by identifying such programme opportunities in their area of residence.

Research Postsecondary Education Programmes

Students with disabilities may select any programme for which they are qualified but should be advised to review carefully documentation standards and programme requirements for their programme or institution of interest. For example, students should pay close attention to an institution's programme requirements, such as language or math, to avoid making a large financial and time commitment only to realize several years into a programme that they cannot, even with academic adjustments, meet an essential requirement for programme completion. Campus visits, which include visits to the disability services office, can be helpful in locating an environment that best meets a student's interests and needs. In addition, while all institutions have a legal obligation to provide appropriate services, certain colleges may be able to provide better services than others due to their size or location.

4

Integrated Education in India: Challenges and Prospects

India has made impressive economic gains in the last few decades and currently has the 4 largest economy in terms of purchasing power parity. Despite this improvement, more than 260 million people in India live in poverty. The reciprocity of poverty producing disability, and disability resulting in poverty creates unique challenges for the integrated education movement in India. This paper begins with a brief history of special education in India, including changes to government legislation and policy in the move towards more integrated educational provision. A number of strategies are presented to address the current challenges that Indian administrators and educators face in the move towards more integrated education.

Inclusive and Integrated Education

With the release of the Salamanca Statement in 1994 (UNESCO), a large number of developing countries started reformulating their policies to promote the inclusion of students with disabilities into mainstream schools. While a large number of developed countries (e.g. USA, Canada, Australia) now have policies or laws promoting "inclusive education," a number of developing countries continue to provide educational services to students with disabilities in "segregated" schools. Typically, inclusive education means "that students with disabilities are served primarily in the general education settings, under the responsibility of [a] regular classroom teacher. When necessary and justifiable, students with disabilities may also receive some of their instruction in another setting, such as [a] resource room". Historically, many educational systems have adopted an integrated education model as an interim approach in the move towards inclusive education. In the "integrated education" model "whenever possible, students with disabilities attend a regular school". The emphasis, however, is upon the student to fit the system rather than the system to adapt to meet the educational needs of a student. In India, "integrated education" has been provided mainly to students with mild disabilities who are considered "easy" to include into regular school programmes. Students with severe disabilities, in a majority of cases, do not attend a school, or in rare cases, attend a special school.

From Segregated to Integrated Education

Caring for "the old, the sick and the disabled" is a part of the cultural heritage of India. Exploring the roots of welfare services for persons with disabilities, Karna states:

From time immemorial, it has been the part and parcel of the cultural heritage of India to provide help and sustenance to the poor and destitute. . . . The Hindu religion emphasised the value of compassion, charity, philanthropy and mutual aid. The guild system, as existed in ancient India, also contributed to the promotion of such practices for the disadvantaged strata of society.

The custom of joint family and kinship provided an in-built mechanism to support such practices. According to Miles (2000), rudimentary attempts to educate students with disabilities were made in India long before such attempts were made in Europe. He cites, for example, that specially adapted curricula was used 2000 years earlier as evidenced by children's toys that were excavated in diggings in Taxila. Also, the ancient "gurukul" system of education that existed in India for centuries was sensitive to the unique cultural, social, and economic needs of the students and their families and imparted life skills education recognizing the potential within each student (Singh, 2001). However, these educational and rehabilitation practices were lost during the colonial period.

The formal education of children with disabilities began in India in 1869 when Jane Leupot, with the support of the Church Missionary Society, started a school for "blind students" in Benares (Miles, 1997). Miles also reported that the first formal school for children with intellectual and physical disabilities was established in the eastern part of India in Kurseong in 1918.

The education of children with disabilities in segregated settings continued well after India gained independence from Great Britain in 1947, with various non-government organizations assuming increasing responsibility for their education. By 1966 there were 115 schools for students with a visual impairment, 70 schools for students with a hearing impairment, 25 schools for students with an orthopedic disability and 27 schools for students with an intellectual disability. According to Pandey & Advani (1997), by 1991 there were about 1,200 special schools for students with various types of disabilities in India.

One of the major initiatives from the Government of India to promote "integrated education" is the programme of Integrated Education of Disabled Children (IEDC). In 1974, the Ministry of Welfare, Central Government of India, initiated the IEDC programme to promote the integration of students with mild to moderate disabilities into regular schools. The programme was also designed to promote the retention of children with disabilities in the regular school system. Children were to be provided with financial support for books, stationery, school uniforms, transportation, special equipment and aids. The state governments were provided with 50 percent of the financial assistance to implement this programme in regular schools. However, the programme met with little success. Rane (1983), in his evaluation of this programme in the State of Maharashtra, reported that (a) the non-availability of trained and experienced teachers, (b) lack of orientation among regular school staff about the problems of disabled children and their educational needs, and (c) the non-availability of equipment and educational materials were major factors in the failure of the programme. Also, a lack of coordination among the various departments to implement the scheme was another major factor in the failure of the IEDC plan (Azad, 1996; Pandey & Advani, 1997). Mani (1988) reported that by 1979-80, only 1,881 children from 81 schools all over the country had benefited from this programme.

Due to its shortcomings, the IEDC programme was revised in 1992. Under the revised scheme, 100 percent assistance became available to schools involved in the "integration" of students with disabilities. Various non-government organizations are now fully funded to implement the programme. According to the most recent estimates, the IEDC is being implemented in 26 States and Union Territories, serving more than 53,000 students enrolled in 14,905 schools (Ministry of Information and Broadcasting, 2000). In this regard, Kerala has shown remarkable success. The IEDC programme is implemented in 4,487 schools in this state with 12,961 children being served (Ministry of Information and Broadcasting, 2000).

In 1987, the Ministry of Human Resource Development (MHRD), in association with UNICEF and the National Council of Educational Research and Training (NCERT) developed the Project for Integrated Education for the Disabled (PIED). The aim of the project was to strengthen the IEDC plan (NCERT, 1987). Instead of confining the programme to a particular institution or school, PIED adopted a "Composite Area Approach" that converted all regular schools within a specified area, referred to as a block, into integrated schools. These schools had to share resources such as specialized equipment, instructional materials and special education teachers. One key aspect of the project was the teacher training component. The teacher training programme, available to teachers in each selected block, followed a three-level training approach:

1. a five day orientation course for all the teachers in the regular schools,
2. a six-week intensive training course for 10 percent of the teachers, and
3. a one-year multi-category training programme for eight to ten regular school teachers.

The teachers who completed the one-year multi-category training programme were required to act as resource teachers.

This project produced several positive results. Jangira and Ahuja (1993) reported that as a result of improved programme planning and better management skills now made available to the teachers, the capacity of various states to implement integration programmes was enhanced. Both regular school teachers and students became more receptive towards students with disabilities (Azad, 1996). About 13,000 children with disabilities received educational services in regular schools (Azad, 1996). More than 9,000 teachers received training to work with disabled students in integrated settings (Azad, 1996). The success of the PIED project led to an increased commitment by the Department of Education to integrate students with disabilities (Jangira & Ahuja, 1993).

In 1996, the Government of India enacted the Persons with Disabilities (Equal Opportunities, Protection of Rights and Full Participation) Act (PWD Act) of 1995 (Ministry of Law Justice and Company Affairs, 1996). The Act provided for both preventive and promotional aspects of rehabilitation. It covered such aspects as education, employment, non-discrimination, prevention and early detection, social security, research and manpower development, and affirmative action. Seven categories of disability were covered in the legislation, namely "blindness," "low vision," "leprosy cured," "hearing impairment," "locomotor disability," "mental retardation" and "mental illness."

The PWD Act required the Central, State, and Union Territory Governments to ensure that all children with disabilities had access to a "free and appropriate" education until the age of 18 years. It also called upon these three tiers of Government to promote "integrated education." The Act outlined a comprehensive education scheme to provide transportation facilities, remove architectural barriers, supply free books and other study materials, grant scholarships, restructure curriculum, and modify the examinations system for the benefit of children with special needs. In order to expand educational opportunities for children with disabilities, the Central Government, in its last Five-Year Plan (1997-2002), set aside 1,000 million rupees specifically for the provision of integrated education.

Baquer & Sharma (1997) considered the passage of the PWD Act as a landmark step in the history of rehabilitation services in India. They stated:

In a country like India the numbers of disabled are so large, their problems so complex, available resources so scarce and social attitudes so damaging, it is only legislation which can eventually bring about a substantial change in a uniform manner. Although legislation cannot alone radically change the fabric of a society in a short span of time, it can nevertheless, increase accessibility of the disabled to education and employment, to public buildings and shopping centres, to means of transport and communication. (p. 274)

If fully implemented, this Act has the potential to change the educational status of more than 30 million children with disabilities who currently do not have access to any form of education. However, providing education to such a vast number of children with disabilities in the world's second most populated country will require a number of challenges and issues to be addressed at both the macro and micro levels of Indian society.

Challenges to Implement Integrated Education

The challenge of poverty associated with disability: With an estimated 1,027 million people, India is the world's second most populated country. It has 17 percent of the global population and 20 percent of the world's out-of-school children. Despite impressive gains in the last few decades (11th largest industrial power, 4th largest economy in terms of purchasing power parity) India still has more than 260 million people living in poverty. A large number of children with disabilities live in families with income significantly below the poverty level. According to Rao (1990), while disability causes poverty, it is also possible that in a country like India, poverty causes disability. The combination of poverty and disability results in a condition of "simultaneous deprivation." According to Harriss-White (1996), this is a syndrome that sets up barriers to the participation of persons with disabilities in the normal routines and activities of the community, including regular schooling. Recently, the Ministry of Rural Development, Government of India, has allocated 3 percent funds in poverty alleviation programmes targeting families of children with disabilities (B.L. Sharma, 2001). However, motivating poor families, with all the associated costs to send their child to school, is proving to be a big challenge.

The challenge of modifying deeply held attitudes: Attitudes of the non-disabled are proving to be a major barrier in the social integration of persons with disabilities. "The more severe and visible the deformity is, the greater is the fear of contagion, hence the attitudes of aversion and segregation towards the crippled". Such attitudes reinforced by religious institutions may militate against any attempts to include students with disabilities into regular schools. For example, Hindus (who constitute 85 percent of the total population in India) believe that disability is a consequence of misdeeds performed in the previous life (often referred to as the doctrine of Karma). Many Hindu religious institutions and temple trusts, therefore, do not think a part of their duty is to help persons with disabilities, because they consider the disability to be the result of a person's misdeeds in his previous life (Rao, 1990). Any attempts to improve the life of a person with a disability may be considered a "defiance of the wills of Allah or as interference with a person's karma". Alur (2001), in her study found that disability in India is not seen as something "normal" or "natural," rather it is seen as an "evil eye." Guilt, stigma and different kinds of fears tend to be paramount in such families. She further concludes that "the contradiction here was that Indian society, although integrated in accepting and valuing diversity in so many ways, has a social role construct of disability which is negative, discriminatory and exclusionary"(n.p.). Kannan, (2000), states that in order to harness the great potential of more than 30 million people with disabilities, it is essential that "prejudice, mental and irrational myths concerning disability, is eradicated."

Dissemination and public education: People, including parents and school personnel, are largely unaware of the full intent of the recent legislation passed by Indian Parliament. A large number of school personnel are also not aware of funding available to include students with disabilities in regular schools. There is some evidence that those educators who are knowledgeable about government policies and laws concerning integrated education tend to have positive attitudes towards implementing such programmes (U. Sharma, 2001). There is also evidence when parents are knowledgeable and supportive of integrated education, they tend to have a positive effect on school personnel (U. Sharma, 2001). Thus, unless people, especially parents of children with disabilities and school personnel, are made knowledgeable about the various provisions enshrined in the Act, the Central and State governments' commitment to providing integrated education will be in vain. Although some attempts are being made to disseminate information about the Persons with Disabilities Act to parents, to government officials and non government organizations.

There is also a greater need to have a National Resource Centre for Disabilities. Such a centre would work to collect, and disseminate information on various aspects of disability (B.L. Sharma, 2001). The centre would provide information through various TV and radio programmes as well as through internet (B.L. Sharma, 2001). The centre would also fulfil the role of scrutinizing all mass communication programmes (TV, radio and even entertainment programmes) to ensure that disability is not portrayed in a negative manner.

The centre could also start documentary projects (e.g. video programmes) that feature inclusion being implemented in different parts of India. Such programmes are likely to make a positive impact on school educators who often believe that inclusion can work only in Western or developed countries.

The challenge of providing adequate levels of training to key stakeholders: The majority of school personnel in India are not trained to design and implement educational programmes for students with disabilities in regular schools. Most teacher training programmes in India do not have a unit on Disability Studies. The universities, which do cover some aspects of special education in their teacher training programmes, fail to train teachers adequately to work in integrated settings. For example, there is limited coverage of information about practical strategies. Also, placement of pre-service teachers in special or integrated schools is rarely given consideration.

Great variations are noted in the content, process, and examination of existing special education programmes as well in the country (Myreddi & Narayan, 2000). However, the situation may improve in the coming years as the Rehabilitation Council of India (RCI) will periodically evaluate special education programmes to ensure that each programme meets minimum standards (Rehabilitation Council of India, 1996). The number of trained special educators is also limited. The most recent report of the Rehabilitation Council of India (1996) states that the number of trained special education teachers is extremely small considering the number of children with disabilities that require their services. At the time of the publication of this report there were only 9,492 specially trained teachers. Of these, 4,295 were trained to teach students with mental retardation, 1,079 were trained to teach students with visual disabilities, 4,011 were trained to teach students with hearing impairments, and 107 were trained to teach students with locomotor disabilities in India. To address this severe shortage of trained teachers, the Rehabilitation Council of India recommended that an additional 44,000 teachers needed to be trained by the end of the Ninth Five-Year Plan (1997-2002). However, it should be noted that even if these targets were to be achieved, *only* 10 percent of the population of children with disabilities would be served (Rehabilitation Council of India, 1996). RCI must consider reformulating existing teacher training programmes for special educators, with a greater emphasis on integrated education. Special educators could be a key resource as they can be used to train regular school educators in implementing integrated education. They can also act as an itinerant teachers working in partnership with a number of regular school educators to advise them on practical issues related to education of students with disabilities.

Inadequate resources: The majority of schools in India are poorly designed and few are equipped to meet the unique needs of students with disabilities. The lack of disability friendly transportation services and accessible buildings are considered by some to be far greater problems than social prejudice and negative attitudes (for example, Chatterjee, 2003). Both the Central and State governments will have to provide increased resources to this aspect of education to ensure successful implementation of integrated practices in schools.

Over and above some of these challenges that India shares with other developing countries are some distinctive features that will make the implementation of educational reform particularly difficult. India is a multilingual, multicultural, multireligious country, and its people are stratified along sharp socio-economic and caste lines. Therefore, unless the challenges are carefully identified and systematically addressed, inclusion will remain a policy on paper. The forthcoming section presents some strategies that policy makers in India may find useful to implement integrated education successfully.

Possible Strategies to Address Some of the Challenges

Training of teachers: If integrated education is to become a reality in India, then the training of teachers has to become a top priority. The educational authorities in India may adopt a policy of training one teacher from each school or a cluster of schools. The teacher would need to be provided with intensive training to work with various disabilities and could then act as an integration specialist or an inclusion facilitator for one or a number of schools located in close proximity. A similar strategy has already worked well in certain parts of India when several school teachers were specifically trained to work in integrated settings under the PIED programme and is recommended by several researchers in India (Jangira, 1995; Jha, 2002; Myreddi & Narayan, 2000). Also in-service teachers would need continued training to update their skills and knowledge of integrated education strategies.

It is clear that regular school educators need training in issues related to the implementation of integrated education. A question that arises with regard to such training is the identification of the specific content that should be included in these training programmes. Given the enormous diversity in India (cultural, linguistic, socio-economic, etc.), further research is clearly warranted. Sharma (1992) suggest that the curriculum for pre-service training programmes should be carefully developed, incorporating feedback from special and regular educators. Some research has been conducted in India that points out that educators need basic skills, professional knowledge, communication and interaction skills (K. Sharma, 1992; U. Sharma & Pillay, 1997), knowledge about assessment techniques, and resource management (Das & Pillay, 1999), knowledge of multigrade teaching, instructional techniques, and peer-tutoring and cooperative learning techniques to include students with disabilities into regular classes.

Need to design innovative system of training: Several authors have cautioned that India will not be able to successfully implement integrated educational services unless regular school educators are trained at mass scale. Comments on this situation as follows: "the number of persons who need training is very large and the conventional training methods cannot simply meet the requirements." Therefore, there is a need to design some innovative models to train educators at mass level. One possibility to educate such a large number of teachers is by using Distance Open Learning or DOL (Ramanujam, 2001). Indira Gandhi National Open University (IGNOU) has a history of successfully running courses for a larger number of students using DOL mode. IGNOU, in association with Rehabilitation Council of India, is considering offering various courses to the trainers of children with disabilities, including teachers. It is expected that such training, accompanied with ongoing in-service training, would prove very useful for school educators. It would, however, be important that practical aspects of implementing integrated education form a key part of any such course.

Need for collaboration between different ministries: Different ministries in India administer various services for persons with disabilities (Alur, 2001). For example, while "integrated education" is the responsibility of Ministry of Human Resource Development, education in special schools is the responsibility of Ministry of Social Justice and Empowerment. This is just one example of the waste of already limited resources. India cannot afford to have such administrative arrangements. There is a need for streamlining administrative arrangements so that funds provided to different ministries for persons with disabilities can be used effectively.

Involve NGO's in implementing integrated education programmes: There are more than one million NGO's working in India. Although not all of them are working in the education sector, a large number still provide educational services to children with disabilities. These organizations can play a significant role in implementing integrated education because they are widely located in India and can serve both urban and rural school communities. Unfortunately, a large majority of NGOs still believe that segregated education is the best way to educate students with disabilities. It would, therefore, be necessary to train the key stakeholders in these NGO's about the benefits of integrated education as well as practical aspects of implementing integrated education in regular schools.

Establish an alternate system of examination: Most school educators in India are concerned that integration of students with disabilities would result in lowering school standards because these students won't be able to pass exams. This seems to be a genuine concern of teachers because it can influence their promotion. Thus, it is necessary to establish an alternative system of examination for students with disabilities. Such an examination system is already in practice in the USA. Students in this system are asked to do activities that demonstrate their abilities rather than disabilities. It is expected that teachers in India would feel more comfortable including students with disabilities in their classrooms if such a system existed.

School-university partnership: The multilingual, multi-cultural and multi-religious nature of India is often cited as a challenge in implementing any educational reforms. Local universities in each of the States and Union Territories may play a significant role in overcoming this challenge. Pilot projects involving local schools could be initiated by universities to explore strategies that may be appropriate for each region. Also, texts on practical strategies can be produced in the common language spoken by educators in each of the States.

Cross Border Higher Education Through ODL System Prospects and Challenges.

Open learning and distance education refers to approaches to learning that focus on freeing learners from constraints of time and place while offering flexible learning opportunities. For many students, open and distance learning (ODL) is a way of combining work and family responsibilities with educational opportunities.

Distance education (sometimes referred to as 'distributed learning' or 'distance learning') is any educational process in which all or most of the teaching is conducted by someone geographically removed from the learner, with all or most of the communication between teachers and learners being conducted through electronic or print mediums.

The 'open' nature of distance learning might be formally institutionalized in such policies as open admissions, and freedom of selection of what, when and where to learn. The openness of distance learning is also seen in relatively flexible organizational structures, delivery and communication patterns as well as the use of various technologies to support learning.

Who offers ODL ?

ODL at the tertiary level is offered by single-mode institutions, an increasing number of traditional universities, 'dual-mode' institutions, consortia of universities and virtual universities. In addition, recent years have seen the increasing emergence of new non-traditional providers of higher education such as private companies.

Single-mode institutions are those in which distance education is the sole mission to which teachers and administrative staff are exclusively dedicated. Course development, instruction, evaluation and other educational processes are tailored to the distance learner.

In dual-mode institutions there may be an administrative staff whose sole responsibilities are distance education, but usually it is the teachers of the parent body who provide the teaching. There is some allowance for distance teaching methods in course design, instruction and evaluation and teachers may have some special training.

Distance learning consortia consist of two or more distance learning institutions who share either in the design or delivery of programmes, or both. A virtual university has no campus and no faculty of its own; instead a virtual university makes available programmes and courses offered by other universities and colleges using technologies.

Increasingly, non-traditional providers including private, profit-oriented new companies are entering the global market, selling educational services online, especially to adult learners in the labour force. Some traditional education institutions are responding to such competition by establishing their own for-profit affiliates.

How is ODL Delivered?

ODL is delivered using a variety of print and electronic systems either through synchronous communication (learning in which all parties participate at the same time) or through asynchronous communication (learning in which parties participate at different times). The main systems are mediated by correspondence, audiovisual means (television and radio), multimedia (audio and text files), and the Internet.

- Correspondence delivery centres around a printed study guide, often accompanied by audio and video components such as records and slides. Interaction is by letters and other written or printed documents sent through postal systems.
- Educational television and radio delivery uses various delivery technologies – terrestrial, satellite and cable television and radio – to deliver live or recorded lectures to both individual home-based learners and groups of learners in remote classrooms where face-to-face support might be provided. Some systems offer limited audio or video conferencing links back to the lecturer or a moderator at a central point.
- Multimedia delivery includes text, audio, video and computer-based materials and usually has face-to-face learner support

delivered to both individuals and groups. This approach, instruction is no longer an individual's work, but the work of teams of specialists, media specialists, information specialists, instructional design specialists and learning specialists. Programmes are prepared for distribution to large numbers of learners usually located across a large geographical area.

- Internet-based systems refer to those in which multimedia (text, audio, video and computer-based) materials in electronic format are delivered to individuals through computers along with access to databases and electronic libraries. These systems enable teacher-student and student-student one-to-one, one-to-many and many-to-many interactions synchronously or asynchronously through email, computer conferences, bulletin boards, etc.

What is the Value of a Qualification Earned by ODL?

ODL poses new challenges to learners in assessing the value of their qualifications to either continue their studies or to find employment. Before registering in an ODL course, it is important to ask key questions concerning the learning experience, and the status of the institution. The Council for Higher Education Accreditation (CHEA) and the Western Cooperative for Educational Telecommunications (WCET) have each developed resources aimed at assisting learners to evaluate the learning experience offered by higher education providers. These resources are developed for students intending to continue their studies in United States higher education institutions, but are of interest to all students as they address key issues.

Prospects and Challenges

THOUGH the terms open learning and distance education (OL and DE) have been around for quite a long time, scholars continue to differ in their definitions. The idea of open learning was founded on the work of two scholars Célestin Freinet and Maria Montessori (1870 – 1952) who proposed the need for self-determined, independent and interest-guided learning in education.

Widdowson defines open learning as a flexible approach to education and training designed to make it more accessible, effective and responsive to individual needs. This definition places considerable responsibility on the learner and relies, in the main, on well produced course materials. To Greenberg, the concept of distance education encompasses "any planned teaching/learning experience that uses a wide spectrum of technologies to reach learners at a distance and encourages learner interaction and certification of learning." Open learning and distance education vary distinctively in their approaches of study. Whereas open learning allows learners flexibility and choice over what, when, at what pace, where, and how they learn, distance education is principally characterised by separation of geographic distance and time.

Thus, open learning could be offered on campus or at a distance, and distance education could be open or closed.

In spite of the differences in definition, the concepts of open learning and distance education share a common aspect in that they both provide alternative paths to the traditional mode of learning. In OL and DE, educationists use novel methods of imparting knowledge such as the internet and e-mail, message-board forums, telephone, CD-Roms, print materials, video cassettes and video-conferencing in addition to 'popular' classroom-based instruction. Among other major attributes, OL and DE provides the learners a greater sense of autonomy and responsibility for learning since it espouses the twin values of flexibility and accessibility, has multiple modes of knowledge dissemination, employs a multi-modal assessment system and usually involves mediated or technology-based education.

Some modern schools of thought fuse the concepts of OL and DE to coin the idea of open and distance learning (ODL). The Commonwealth of Learning (COL), for one, observes that most definitions of open and distance learning differ due to their varying focus on factors such as separation of teacher and student, institutional accreditation, mixed-media courseware, possibility of face-to-face meeting for tutorials, two-way communication, and use of industrialized processes.

The International Council for Open and Distance Education defines open educational practices as practices which support the production, use and reuse of high quality open educational resources through institutional policies, which promote innovative pedagogical models, and respect and empower learners as co-producers on their lifelong learning path.

Nowadays, ODL is seen as a viable means of widening and broadening access to education. Most nations in the developing world, Africa in particular, are aligning themselves towards its adoption across all levels of the education spectrum. Apart from increasing the opportunities on education access, other benefits of ODL include emerging market opportunities and opportunity to adapt to technology and environments. Distance education fuels the public's need for lifelong learning in education by providing access to learners not in the primary school age group, and at the same time allows educational institutions to adopt distance education as a means to adapt to the rapid changes in technology being used in education today.

Assisting Persons with Disabilities in the Age of Technology and Cybernetics

A lack of employment opportunities limits the ability of many people with disabilities to fully participate in society, as employment plays a number of important roles and functions for individuals:

- Economic: Employment provides income that is key to individual and family economic well-being, and builds skills for future well-being. The low employment and earnings levels of people with disabilities help account for their lower average household incomes and higher poverty rates.
- Social : Employment often provides greater social interaction and connections that reduce isolation and build social capital. This benefit is especially valuable for people with dis-abilities, who generally are less likely to participate in many social activities.
- Psychological: Employment provides a valued social role in our society and helps create a sense of personal efficacy and social integration that contributes to life satisfaction. People who regain employment following onset of a disability report higher life satisfaction and better adjustment than do people who are not employed.

Ensuring employment opportunities for people with disabilities is important not just for those individuals but also for employers, government, and society:

- Employers are projected to face labour shortages as the baby-boom generation retires, and nonemployed people with disabilities represent a valuable pool of human resources to help fill those needs.
- Corporations are increasingly recognizing the benefits of workplace diversity. Providing greater opportunities to people with disabilities enhances diversity in ways that improve employee performance and expand the customer base.
- Government receives the above benefits as an employer, and also benefits generally from increased employment of people

with disabilities as tax receipts increase and social expenditures decline.

Growing importance of computers and new information technologies: These technologies can have special benefits for workers with disabilities, helping compensate for physical or sensory impairments (e.g., using screen-readers and voice-recognition systems) and substantially increasing the productivity of many workers with disabilities. A study by Krueger and Kruse (1995) found that a) people with preexisting computer skills at the time of a spinal cord injury had a faster return to work and b) computer use especially enhanced earnings among people with spinal cord injuries; in fact, they earned the same as other computer users, whereas a substantial pay gap was associated with spinal cord injury among people who did not use computers at work.

Though computers may have special benefits for people with disabilities, there are disturbing gaps in computer training and Internet access. People with disabilities are less likely than those without disabilities to receive computer training or use computers at work or elsewhere, probably in large part because of resource constraints. In addition, people with disabilities are only one-fourth as likely as those without disabilities to connect to the Internet (Kaye 2000).

Increased use of telecommuting and flexible work arrangements: New information technologies have made home-based work more productive, which can have special benefits for people with disabilities—particularly those with transportation problems or medical concerns that require them to be close to home. In addition, the past 15 years have seen growth in other types of flexible work arrangements that can help accommodate the needs of people with disabilities, such as job-sharing and temporary agency employment. As described in this report's issue brief on "Work-Life Balance and Alternative Work Arrangements," workers with disabilities are more likely than those without disabilities to be doing home-based work for pay, and to be in several types of part-time and flexible job arrangements. Though such jobs often have disadvantages and it is clear that workers with disabilities should have full access to standard full-time jobs, the growth of several types of flexible and contingent jobs is promising for enhancing the employment of many people with disabilities who benefit from these arrangements.

Growing attention to workplace diversity: Most large corporations today have diversity programmes, and a growing number are including disability as one of the criteria for a diverse workforce. This topic is reviewed in more depth in the issue brief on "Corporate Culture."

Overall, the good and bad news presents a mixed picture for the employment of people with -disabilities. The occupational trends are worrisome, but with appropriate employer and government policies people with disabilities should be able to move into the fastest-growing occupations. This report is designed to contribute to this process, assessing the evidence and highlighting the policies that will maximize employment opportunities for people with disabilities in the 21st century.

Matching Person & Technology Model

The Matching Person & Technology Model organizes influences on the successful use of a variety of technologies: assistive technology, educational technology, and those used in the workplace, school, home; for healthcare, for mobility and performing daily activities. Specialized devices for hearing loss, speech, eyesight and cognition as well as general or everyday technologies are also included. Research shows that although a technology may appear perfect for a given need, it may be used inappropriately or even go unused when critical personality preferences, psychosocial characteristics or needed environmental support are not considered. The use and non-use of technology as conceptualized in the Matching Person & Technology Model has been validated by many researchers and authors representing the fields of occupational therapy, physical therapy, speech language pathology, psychology, and others. The Matching Person and Technology Model is operationalized by a series of reliable and valid measures that provide a person-centred and individualized approach to matching individuals with the most appropriate technologies for their use. The Matching Person & Technology Model and measures were developed by Marcia J. Scherer, Ph.D. beginning in 1986.

MPT Process with Accompanying Assessment Measures

- Initial Worksheet for the Matching Person and Technology (MPT) Model—to determine initial goals, potential interventions, and technologies needed to support attainment of the goals.
- History of Support Use—identifies supports used in the past and satisfaction with those supports.
- Specific technology matching:
  - o General—survey of technology use

  - o Assistive—assistive technology device predisposition assessment, cognitive support technology predisposition assessment and hearing technology predisposition assessment
  - o Educational—educational technology device predisposition assessment
  - o Workplace—workplace technology device predisposition assessment
  - o Healthcare—healthcare technology device predisposition assessment
- Follow-up versions of the measures to determine degree of use, comparison of expected benefit and realization of benefit and change in functioning and subjective well-being.

Evolution of Cybernetics

Cybernetics is a transdisciplinary approach for exploring regulatory systems, their structures, constraints, and possibilities. Cybernetics is relevant to the study of systems, such as mechanical, physical, biological, cognitive, and social systems. Cybernetics is applicable when a system being analyzed is involved in a closed signalling loop; that is, where action by the system generates some change in its environment and that change is reflected in that system in some manner (feedback) that triggers a system change, originally referred to as a "circular causal" relationship. Some say this is necessary to a cybernetic perspective. System dynamics, a related field, originated with applications of electrical engineering control theory to other kinds of simulation models (especially business systems) by Jay Forrester at MIT in the 1950s.

Concepts studied by cyberneticists (or, as some prefer, cyberneticians) include, but are not limited to: learning, cognition, adaptation, social control, emergence, communication, efficiency, efficacy, and connectivity. These concepts are studied by other subjects such as engineering and biology, but in cybernetics these are abstracted from the context of the individual organism or device.

Cybernetics was defined in the mid 20th century, by Norbert Wiener as "the scientific study of control and communication in the animal and the machine." The word "cybernetics" comes from the Greek latter meaning to "steer", "navigate and govern, hence is the government while is the governor or the captain." Contemporary cybernetics began as an interdisciplinary study connecting the fields of control systems, electrical network theory, mechanical engineering, logic modelling, evolutionary biology, neuroscience, anthropology, and psychology in the 1940s, often attributed to the Macy Conferences. During the second half of the 20th century cybernetics evolved in ways that distinguish first-order cybernetics (about observed systems) from second-order cybernetics (about observing systems). More recently there is talk about a third-order cybernetics (doing in ways that embraces first and second-order).

Fields of study which have influenced or been influenced by cybernetics include game theory, system theory (a mathematical counterpart to cybernetics), perceptual control theory, sociology, psychology (especially neuropsychology, behavioural psychology, cognitive psychology), philosophy, architecture, and organizational theory.

As with all forms of technology, advancements in cybernetics can be tracked by Progress Level.

Progress Level 5: Cybernetics is still in its formative stage. Most prosthetic units are of the nonpowered variety, but medical associations have approved certain electronic regulators for life-threatening conditions. The artificial heart is the most recognized example. Other common examples include pacemakers, artificial kidneys, and pancreas monitors (for high-risk diabetics). Nearly all PL 5 cybernetic attachments are simply designed to keep their recipients alive and reasonably healthy.

Elective cybernetics begins at this stage with the work of university professor Kevin Warwick, who develops methods of linking computer microchips to the human nervous system. His "cyborg chip" becomes the foundation for all future cybernetic components.

Progress Level 6: This era sees the first use of independently powered cybernetics, including servolimbs and subcutaneous cellular telephones. These begin mostly in military applications but soon become available to the public. Household pets all over the world are implanted with subcutaneous identity chips—as are important government figures and their families—after the technology proves safe and effective on prison inmates.

As cybernetics is still new and can have negative side effects, its adoption is not universal. Most people still prefer mundane equipment, which is generally cheaper, safer, and less troublesome to repair, replace, or upgrade. Cybernetics becomes the preferred choice only when mundane equipment is impractical or unavailable— or when the recipient is fixated on self-improvement.

Medical plans eventually come to offer at least baseline prosthetics to compensate for disabling injuries, such as the loss or partial loss of a limb, though such plans do not cover elective cybernetic surgery. Their concern is overall health—not "cosmetic" enhancement. For those who want more than just replacements, a new kind of clinic appears, offering cybernetic enhancements.

At this Progress Level, the first cybernetic regulation laws are passed—largely instigated by a few harshly publicized accidents involving cyborgs. These laws give rise to numerous black-market cybernetic clinics that install cybernetics without performing the required background checks.

Progress Level 7: By this era, cybernetics has become a mostly safe science. Flaws in earlier designs have been corrected. Cybernetics becomes more of a status symbol, and luminous skin grafts become the fashion accessory of choice. In some societies, newborn children are implanted with identity chips as an anti-kidnapping measure. Military applications include replacement eyes with heads-up targeting and GPS displays.

Insurance regulations relax considerably towards cybernetic replacements at Progress Level 7; enhancements are perfectly acceptable, though only as part of a prosthetic, rather than as elective cyber-surgery. Still, most cyborgs are members of military or law-enforcement organizations—or mercenaries.

Progress Level 8: Cyborgs are a common sight. In some societies, medical insurance frowns on noncybernetic replacements, as mechanical body parts are less expensive than flesh. Cybernetic technology has improved so much, in fact, that some cyborgs are virtually indistinguishable from living beings—except that they never appear to age.

Cybernetic Attachments

Two kinds of cybernetic attachments exist: replacements and enhancements. Replacements: Replacements are prosthetic or artificial units intended to replace lost limbs and damaged organs. Common replacements provide no benefits other than duplicating the essential functions of their biological counterparts, and they present little strain on the beneficiary's overall well-being. In appearance, a cybernetic replacement can be recognizably artificial or virtually indistinguishable from the real thing.

Enhancements: Enhancements bestow new abilities or improve the recipient in some fashion. Enhancements include skeletal reinforcement, subcutaneous communications hardware, and weapon mounts. Some enhancements have visible external components, while others are hidden beneath the skin. Enhancements put more of a drain on the body's resources, and recipients frequently suffer debilitating physical or mental side effects.

Construction and Repair

Cybernetic attachments are complex instruments with both electrical and mechanical components. Consequently, a character must have the Craft Cybernetics feat to build a cybernetic attachment.

Repairing a damaged or nonfunctional cybernetic attachment requires 10 hours of work and a successful Repair check (DC 25). A character needs both an electrical tool kit and a mechanical tool kit to facilitate repairs. Without one or the another, a character takes a –4 penalty on the check; without both kits, the penalty increases to –8.

Installation and Removal

Installing or removing a cybernetic attachment, regardless of whether it's a replacement or enhancement, requires a successful Treat Injury check. A character with the Cybernetic Surgery feat suffers no penalty on the check.

Removing a cybernetic attachment without proper surgery causes lasting physical trauma to the patient's body, dealing 1d4 points of permanent Constitution drain.

Number of Attachments

Only living creatures can have cybernetic attachments. In addition, a living creature can have a maximum number of cybernetic attachments equal to 1 + the creature's Constitution modifier (minimum 0).

A creature may have more cybernetic attachments installed on its body can it can bear. However, the creature gains 1 negative level per cybernetic attachment that exceeds its maximum allowed. For each negative level, the creature takes a –1 penalty on all skill checks and ability checks, attack rolls, and saving throws, and loses one effective level or Hit Die whenever level is used in a die roll or calculation. Further, a character with psionic powers loses the ability to manifest one power of the highest level she can manifest (player's choice), while a character with spellcasting ability loses the ability to cast one spell of the highest level he can cast. This loss persists until the negative level is removed.

Negative levels caused by having too many cybernetic attachments remain until the offending attachments are removed.

Benefits and Drawbacks

Cybernetic attachments provide countless benefits to their recipients. For example, cybernetic eyes can bestow darkvision, improve the accuracy of the recipient's ranged attacks, or emit pencil-thin laser beams. A cybernetic brain implant can improve the recipient's response time in a crisis, protect against mind-influencing attacks, or increase the flow of adrenaline throughout the body. The possibilities of cybernetic technology are endless. Although the benefits make cybernetics very alluring, the drawbacks are equally discouraging:

Electricity Vulnerability

A creature with one or more cybernetic attachments takes 50% more damage from any attack that deals electricity damage. This vulnerability to electricity can be offset by an anti-shock implant.

Negative Levels

Whenever a creature exceeds its maximum number of cybernetic attachments, it gains negative levels until the excess attachments are removed.

Susceptibility to Attack

External cybernetic attachments are subject to attacks as if they were objects worn by their recipients.

Massive Damage Effects

Massive damage wreaks havoc with cybernetic attachments. Whenever a creature with cybernetic attachments fails a Fortitude save against massive damage, the GM should roll percentile dice and consult Table: Massive Damage Effects to determine what happens.

Table: *Massive Damage Effects*

d% Roll	*Effect of Failed Fortitude Save*
01–30	Normal Effect
31–60	Attachment Disabled
61–80	Normal Effect and Attachment Disabled
81–100	Attachment Damaged and Side Effect

Normal Effect: The character immediately drops to –1 hit points and is dying.

Attachment Disabled: One cybernetic attachment (determined randomly or chosen by the GM) ceases to function until repaired. The character suffers the effects of the disability—as noted in the description of the cybernetic attachment— for as long as the attachment remains disabled.

Attachment Damaged: One cybernetic attachment (determined randomly or chosen by the GM) continues to function but develops an unpleasant side effect that persists until the attachment is repaired.

Side Effect: The character suffers a debilitating side effect as the result of a damaged attachment. Various side effects are presented on Table: Side Effects.

Table: *Side Effects*

d% Roll	*Side Effect*
01–08	*Blurred Vision:* Character suffers a 20% miss chance on all attacks.
09–17	*Constant Trembling:* Character takes a –2 penalty on Dexterity-based skill checks.
18–25	*Cybernetic Rejection:* Character suffers 1d4 points of Constitution damage per day.
26–34	*Dizziness:* Character takes a –1 penalty on attack rolls, saving throws, ability checks, and skill checks.
35–42	*Impaired Hearing:* Static distortion imposes a –2 penalty on all Listen checks.
43–50	*Impaired Vision:* Distorted images impose a –2 penalty on Spot checks.
51–59	*Insomnia:* Character can only sleep for minutes at a time and gains insufficient rest to heal naturally.
60–67	*Muscle Cramps:* Character moves at half speed.
68–76	*Muscle Fatigue:* Character takes a –2 penalty on Strength-based skill checks.
77–84	*Power Surge:* Character is shaken for 1 round if wounded; a successful Fortitude save (DC 12) negates.
85–93	*Psychosis:* Character suffers 1d4 points of Charisma damage per day, lapsing into a coma if the score drops to 0.
94–100	*Sensory Overload:* Character is stunned for 1 round if wounded; a successful Fortitude save (DC 15) negates.

Replacements

The most basic replacement limbs and organs don't bestow any special benefits, but they suffer the usual drawbacks. Some replacements of higher PL are built to counter certain drawbacks, as noted. They don't add measurably to the recipient's weight.

Each replacement description includes the following information:

Benefit: What the cybernetic replacement allows its recipient to do.

Type: Replacements can be external or internal. External replacements are subject to sunder attacks; internal replacements are not.

Hardness/Hit Points: The hardness and hit points of the replacement. Internal replacements don't have hardness.

Base Purchase DC: The purchase DC of the replacement (or the components to build it), at its specified Progress Level. Cybernetic attachments are cheaper to buy at higher Progress Levels; for each raised step in Progress Level, reduce the purchase DC by 2.

Restriction: The level of license required to purchase the replacement legally, and an appropriate black market purchase DC modifier.

Artificial Organ (PL 5)

An artificial organ fully replaces a defective or destroyed biological organ, such as a heart, lung, eye, or ear.

Benefit: The artificial organ duplicates the function of its biological counterpart. It provides no special game benefits.

Type: Internal.

Hardness/Hit Points: –/2.

Base Purchase DC: 19.

Restriction: None.

Prosthetic Arm (PL 5)

A prosthetic arm fully replaces a lost or destroyed biological arm. The prosthetic arm may begin at the shoulder, elbow, or wrist.

Benefit: The prosthetic arm duplicates the function of its biological counterpart. It provides no special game benefits.

Type: External.

Hardness/Hit Points: 3/5.

Base Purchase DC: 17.

Restriction: None.

Prosthetic Leg (PL 5)

A prosthetic leg fully replaces a lost or destroyed biological leg. The prosthetic leg may begin at the thigh, knee, or ankle.

Benefit: The prosthetic leg duplicates the function of its biological counterpart. It provides no special game benefits.

Type: External.

Hardness/Hit Points: 3/7.

Base Purchase DC: 17.

Restriction: None.

Artificial Organ Upgrade (PL 6)

This upgraded version of the PL 5 artificial organ not only replaces a defective or destroyed biological organ but is also more resilient than its technological predecessor.

Benefit: The artificial organ upgrade duplicates the function of its biological counterpart and cannot be disabled if the recipient takes massive damage.

Type: Internal.

Hardness/Hit Points: –/4.

Base Purchase DC: 21.

Restriction: None.

Prosthetic Arm Upgrade (PL 6)

This upgraded version of the PL 5 prosthetic arm not only replaces a lost or destroyed arm but is also more resilient than its technological predecessor.

Benefit: The prosthetic arm upgrade duplicates the function of its biological counterpart but has a greater hardness and more hit points than the basic PL 5 prosthesis.

Type: External.

Hardness/Hit Points: 5/10.

Base Purchase DC: 19.

Restriction: None.

Prosthetic Leg Upgrade (PL 6)

This upgraded version of the PL 5 prosthetic leg not only replaces a lost or destroyed leg but is also more resilient than its technological predecessor.

Benefit: The prosthetic leg upgrade duplicates the function of its biological counterpart but has a greater hardness and more hit points than the basic PL 5 prosthesis.

Type: External.

Hardness/Hit Points: 5/15.

Base Purchase DC: 19.

Restriction: None.

Advanced Artificial Organ (PL 7)

This advanced version of the PL 5 artificial organ and PL 6 upgrade not only replaces a defective or destroyed biological organ but is also more resilient and less impairing than its technological predecessors.

Benefit: The advanced artificial organ duplicates the function of its biological counterpart and cannot be disabled if the recipient takes massive damage. In addition, the advanced organ does not count towards the total number of cybernetic attachments the recipient can have before taking negative levels.

Type: Internal.

Hardness/Hit Points: –/4.

Base Purchase DC: 24.

Restriction: None.

Advanced Prosthetic Arm (PL 7)

This upgraded version of the PL 5 prosthetic arm and PL 6 upgrade not only replaces a lost or destroyed arm but is also more resilient and less impairing than its technological predecessors.

Benefit: The advanced prosthesis duplicates the function of its biological counterpart. In addition, this advanced prosthesis does not count towards the total number of cybernetic attachments the recipient can have before taking negative levels.

Type: External.

Hardness/Hit Points: 5/10.

Base Purchase DC: 22.

Restriction: None.

Advanced Prosthetic Leg (PL 7)

This upgraded version of the PL 5 prosthetic leg and PL 6 upgrade not only replaces a lost or destroyed leg but is also more resilient and less impairing than its technological predecessors.

Benefit: The advanced prosthesis duplicates the function of its biological counterpart. In addition, this advanced prosthesis does not count towards the total number of cybernetic attachments the recipient can have before taking negative levels.

Type: External.

Hardness/Hit Points: 5/15.

Base Purchase DC: 22.

Restriction: None.

Enhancements

Cybernetic enhancements are available starting at Progress Level 6. Unlike standard replacements, they bestow new abilities upon their recipients. Unless otherwise noted, enhancements don't add measurably to a recipient's weight.

Each enhancement description includes the following information:

Benefit: What the cybernetic enhancement allows its recipient to do.

Type: Enhancements can be external or internal. External enhancements are subject to sunder attacks; internal enhancements are not.

Hardness/Hit Points: The hardness and hit points of the enhancement. Internal enhancements don't have hardness.

Base Purchase DC: The purchase DC of the enhancement (or the components to build it), at its specified Progress Level. Cybernetic attachments are cheaper to buy at higher Progress Levels; for each raised step in Progress Level, reduce the purchase DC by 2.

Restriction: The level of license required to purchase the enhancement legally, and an appropriate black market purchase DC modifier.

Anti-Shock Implant (PL 6)

This tiny implant, embedded near the recipient's brain stem, protects itself and other cybernetic hardware against electricity damage.

Benefit: The implant negates the recipient's special vulnerability to electricity.

Type: Internal.

Hardness/Hit Points: –/1.

Base Purchase DC: 15.

Restriction: None.

External Weapon Mount (PL 6)

The recipient's prosthetic arm ends in a weapon instead of a hand.

Benefit: The recipient has a melee or ranged weapon attached to a prosthetic arm. Attempts to disarm the recipient of the attached weapon automatically fail, though the weapon can still be attacked (like any other weapon) in an attempt to destroy it.

Type: External.

Hardness/Hit Points: 10/5 (mount only).

Base Purchase DC: Melee weapon mount 15, ranged weapon mount 17 (the purchase DC does not include the prosthetic arm or weapon).

Restriction: Military (+3).

Identity Chip (PL 6)

Identity chips provide identification without requiring visual recognition— high-tech ID cards that function even when the wearer is unrecognizable.

Benefit: An identity chip functions as both legal ID and a credit card. The recipient can make Wealth checks even when separated from his funds.

Type: Internal.

Hardness/Hit Points: –/1.

Base Purchase DC: 5.

Restriction: None.

Injector Unit (PL 6)

This unit, attached the recipient's forearm or thigh, incorporates three medical hypo-syringes. Upon command, the unit can inject any or all of the medicinal substances into the recipient's bloodstream.

Benefit: The injector unit has three built-in hypos, and each hypo holds a single dose of one of the following medicinal chemicals: antitox (PL 6), boost (PL 6), neutrad (PL 6), sporekill (PL 6), or biocort (PL 7). As a free action during his turn, the recipient can contract his muscles to inject himself with any or all of these hypos, gaining the benefits immediately. A drained hypo can be removed and replaced as a full-round action.

Type: External.

Hardness/Hit Points: 2/5.

Base Purchase DC: 15 (medical hypos must be purchased separately).

Restriction: Licensed (+1).

Nightvision Optics (PL 6)

The recipient's eyes are replaced with ocular implants that enable the character to see better in the dark. All of the recipient's eyes must be replaced to gain any benefit.

Benefit: The recipient gains darkvision out to a range of 60 feet.

Type: Internal.

Hardness/Hit Points: –/2 (per eye).

Base Purchase DC: 19.

Restriction: None.

Skill Implant (PL 6)

This small brain implant enables its recipient to perform a specific skill more adroitly.

Benefit: The recipient gains a +2 competence bonus on checks made with one class skill of his choice. Different skills require different implants, and a skill implant cannot be modified to grant a bonus to another skill.

A recipient may have multiple skill implants, but each is considered a separate cybernetic attachment.

Type: Internal.

Hardness/Hit Points: –/1.

Base Purchase DC: 20.

Restriction: None.

Stabilizer (PL 6)

A stabilizer releases chemical coagulants into a dying recipient's bloodstream to prevent excess blood loss, effectively stabilizing him. A stabilizer is usually installed near the recipient's heart.

Benefit: If reduced to negative hit points, the recipient automatically stabilizes.

Type: Internal.

Hardness/Hit Points: –/3.

Base Purchase DC: 22.

Restriction: None.

Subcutaneous Body Armor (PL 6)

Subcutaneous body armor consists of small plates of flexible armor implanted under the recipient's skin.

Benefit: The character gains a natural armor bonus to Defense. The bonus depends on the density of the armor: Light +2, Medium +5, Heavy +8.

Type: Internal.

Hardness/Hit Points: –/varies. The armor has one-quarter the maximum hit points of the recipient.

Base Purchase DC: Light 15, Medium 20, or Heavy 25.

Restriction: Military (+3).

Subcutaneous Cell Phone (PL 6)

The recipient has a small transceiver installed underneath the skin of her throat. The transceiver is connected to a tiny speaker located in the recipient's ear.

Benefit: The recipient may carry on conversations using the subcutaneous cell phone without raising her voice above a whisper; Listen checks made to hear the recipient suffer a –4 penalty. The tiny speaker implanted in the recipient's ear enables her to hear the other side of the conversation, but others cannot.

Type: Internal.

Hardness/Hit Points: –/2.

Base Purchase DC: 16.

Restriction: None.

Telescopic Optics (PL 6)

The recipient's eyes are replaced with ocular implants that simulate the effects of binoculars, enabling the recipient to perceive distant objects more easily. All of the recipient's eyes must be replaced to gain any benefit.

Benefit: Telescopic optics reduce the range penalty for Spot checks to –1 for every 30 feet of distance (instead of –1 for every 10 feet).

Type: Internal.

Hardness/Hit Points: –/2 (per eye).

Base Purchase DC: 15.

Restriction: None.

Voice Stress Analyzer (PL 6)

Sensors attached to the recipient's optic nerves and inner ear analyze minute physical indicators from living beings (including increased pulse galvanic skin response) and enable the recipient to better determine the emotional states of others.

Benefit: The recipient gains a +4 equipment bonus on all Sense Motive checks.

Type: Internal.

Hardness/Hit Points: –/4.

Base Purchase DC: 17.

Restriction: None.

Anti-Flare Implants (PL 7)

The recipient's corneas are replaced with artificial ones equipped with flare suppressors that react instantly to bright flashes of light.

Benefit: Blinding effects produced by bright lights have no harmful or debilitating effect on the recipient.

Type: Internal.

Hardness/Hit Points: –/1 (per eye).

Base Purchase DC: 14.

Restriction: None.

Anti-Stun Implant (PL 7)

This implant, embedded near the spine, shields the recipient's nervous system against stunning attacks.

Benefit: The recipient cannot be stunned.

Type: Internal.

Hardness/Hit Points: –/4.

Base Purchase DC: 24.

Restriction: Military (+3).

Body Repair Weave (PL 7)

A delicate weave of subdermal biowires stimulates and repairs the body's damaged tissue.

Benefit: The recipient heals naturally at twice the normal rate.

Type: Internal.

Hardness/Hit Points: –/4.

Base Purchase DC: 21.

Restriction: Licensed (+1).

Data Archive (PL 7)

A data archive is a microcomputer implanted in the recipient's skull. It contains skill-related information stored on a series of biological data chips, or biochips.

Benefit: The recipient treats all skills as class skills. Furthermore, the recipient gains access to an information database that grants a +4 equipment bonus on all Knowledge checks.

Type: Internal.

Hardness/Hit Points: –/2.

Base Purchase DC: 27.

Restriction: None.

Feat Implant (PL 7)

Thanks to a chip implanted in the recipient's brain or a series of implants wired to the recipient's nervous system, the recipient gains special knowledge or some extraordinary ability.

Benefit: The feat implant gives the recipient a feat. The recipient must meet all of the feat's prerequisites to gain its benefits. If the feat implant is destroyed, the granted feat is lost as well. A feat implant cannot duplicate a metamagic or psionic feat.

Type: Internal.

Hardness/Hit Points: –/5.

Base Purchase DC: 25.

Restriction: Military (+3).

Fortified Skeleton (PL 7)

The recipient's skeleton is fortified with high-impact polymers, increasing his ability to shrug off physical damage.

Benefit: The recipient gains damage reduction 4/–.

Type: Internal.

Hardness/Hit Points: –/varies. The skeletal reinforcement has one-quarter the maximum hit points of the recipient.

Base Purchase DC: 32.

Restriction: Military (+3).

Initiative Implant (PL 7)

The initiative implant consists of a series of wires threaded around the recipient's spinal cord and attached to the recipient's nervous system. The implant stimulates faster response times.

Benefit: The recipient gains a +2 equipment bonus on initiative checks.

Type: Internal.

Hardness/Hit Points: –/10.

Base Purchase DC: 20.

Restriction: Military (+3).

Internal Weapon Mount (PL 7)

The recipient has a subcutaneous weapon embedded in her body, usually in a prosthetic forearm or hand. The weapon extends from the prosthesis and is visible when in use.

Benefit: The recipient has a melee or ranged weapon hidden under her skin. Attempts to disarm the recipient of the attached weapon automatically fail, and the weapon itself cannot be attacked unless it is extended. Extending or retracting the weapon is a free action.

Spotting a subcutaneous weapon requires a successful Spot check opposed by the recipient's Sleight of Hand check. The weapon's size applies a modifier to the Sleight of Hand check.

Type: Internal.

Hardness/Hit Points: 10/5 (mount only).

Base Purchase DC: Melee weapon mount 17, ranged weapon mount 19 (the purchase DC does not include the prosthesis or weapon).

Restriction: Military (+3).

Laser Optics (PL 7)

The recipient's eyes are replaced with ocular implants capable of firing thin laser beams. Benefit: Using laser optics is an attack action that does not provoke attacks of opportunity. A "laser eye" deals 2d6 points of fire damage, threatens a critical hit on a natural 20, and has a range increment of 20 feet. Each additional eye adds +2 to the damage roll (thus, a pair of laser eyes would deal 2d6+2 points of fire damage).

A creature equipped with multiple laser eyes must fire them simultaneously at the same target.

Type: Internal.

Hardness/Hit Points: –/2 (per eye).

Base Purchase DC: Single 25, pair 28.

Restriction: Military (+3).

Luminous Skin (PL 7)

Special skin grafts create luminous displays on the recipient's flesh. Most recipients use it purely for decoration, but the same technology can provide a built-in chronometre.

Benefit: The recipient can control the brightness of the luminescence as a free action, negating it entirely if desired. As its most intense, luminous skin can illuminate squares occupied by or adjacent to the recipient. The chronometre serves the same function as a wristwatch, including date, time, and alarm functions.

Type: Internal.

Hardness/Hit Points: –/– (luminous skin ceases to function when the recipient is killed).

Base Purchase DC: 4 (6 for chronometre version).

Restriction: None.

Microcomputer (PL 7)

The recipient has a miniature computer attached to his nervous system, usually at the base of the skull. Benefit: The recipient may attempt Computer Use checks as a move action, rather than a full-round action. The microcomputer reduces by half the time required to operate remotes. A data port in the back of the unit allows for the insertion of a standard interface cable (purchase DC 5), allowing the recipient to transfer data without the benefit of a modem.

Type: Internal.

Hardness/Hit Points: –/4.

Base Purchase DC: 35 (36 with integrated cellular modem).

Restriction: Restricted (+2).

Mindscreen Implant (PL 7)

A small implant in the recipient's brain protects him against mental attacks.

Benefit: The recipient gains a +2 equipment bonus on saving throws against mind-affecting attacks.

Type: Internal.

Hardness/Hit Points: –/2.

Base Purchase DC: 28.

Restriction: Military (+3).

Prosthetic Enhancer (PL 7)

This implant attaches to a prosthetic arm or leg, making it stronger.

Benefit: If attached to a prosthetic leg, the prosthetic enhancer increases the recipient's base speed by +5 feet. In addition, any unarmed attack made with an enhanced prosthetic leg deals an additional 1 point of damage.

If attached to a prosthetic arm, the prosthetic enhancer grants a +2 bonus on Strength- and Dexterity-based ability checks and skill checks. In addition, any unarmed attack made with an enhanced prosthetic arm deals an additional 1 point of damage.

A prosthetic enhancer does not count towards the total number of cybernetic attachments the recipient can have before taking negative levels.

Type: Internal.

Hardness/Hit Points: –/2.

Base Purchase DC: 22.

Restriction: None.

Rage Implant (PL 7)

This brain implant dramatically increases the amount of adrenaline and testosterone the recipient's body produces, temporarily boosting his strength and durability.

Benefit: The recipient can activate the implant as a free action once per day. Upon doing so, he temporarily gains a +4 bonus to Strength, a +4 bonus to Constitution, and a +2 morale bonus on Will saves, but he takes a –2 penalty to Defense.

The increase in Constitution increases the recipient's hit points by 2 per level, but these hit points go away at the end of the rage when his Constitution score drops back to normal. While raging, the recipient cannot use any Charisma-, Dexterity-, or Intelligence-based skills (except for Balance, Drive, Escape Artist, Intimidate, Pilot, or Ride), the Concentration skill, any abilities that require patience and concentration (including spellcasting and manifesting psionic powers), or any items that must be activated to function.

The rage lasts for a number of rounds equal to 3 + the recipient's (newly acquired) Constitution modifier. The recipient may prematurely end his rage.

At the end of the rage, the recipient loses the rage modifiers and restrictions and becomes fatigued for the remaining duration of the current encounter.

The increased Constitution triggered by the rage implant in now way obviates the negative levels bestowed for having too many cybernetic attachments.

Type: Internal.

Hardness/Hit Points: –/3.

Base Purchase DC: 24.

Restriction: Restricted (+2).

Skill Plexus (PL 7)

This unit, implanted in the recipient's brain, allows multiple skill implants to function as a single cybernetic attachment.

Benefit: The recipient may have up to four skill implants attached to the skill plexus, and together they are treated as a single cybernetic attachment. However, if the skill plexus is destroyed, all of the attached skill implants are destroyed as well.

Type: Internal.

Hardness/Hit Points: –/4.

Base Purchase DC: 25 (does not include skill implants).

Restriction: None.

Targeting Optics (PL 7)

The recipient's eyes are replaced with ocular implants that use a projected targeting reticle to improve the recipient's aim. All of the recipient's eyes must be replaced to gain any benefit.

Benefit: Targeting optics grant a +1 bonus on all attack rolls made with ranged weapons.

Type: Internal.

Hardness/Hit Points: –/2 (per eye).

Base Purchase DC: 17.

Restriction: Military (+3).

Feat Plexus (PL 8)

This unit, implanted in the recipient's brain, allows multiple feat implants to function as a single cybernetic attachment.

Benefit: The recipient may have up to four feat implants attached to the feat plexus, and together they are treated as a single cybernetic attachment. However, if the feat plexus is destroyed, all of the attached feat implants are destroyed as well.

Type: Internal.

Hardness/Hit Points: –/4.

Base Purchase DC: 25 (does not include feat implants).

Restriction: Military (+3).

Invisiware (PL 8)

This technology enables its recipient to turn invisible for a short time. Invisiware uses crystalline refractors grafted to the skin and powered by rechargeable solar battery units protruding from various points on the recipient's body (usually the spine).

Benefit: By using invisiware to bend light around its body, a creature can turn invisible. An invisible creature gains a +40 bonus on Hide checks if immobile, or a +20 bonus if moving. Pinpointing the location of an invisible creature that isn't attempting to hide requires a Spot check (DC 40 if the creature is immobile or DC 20 if it is moving).

While invisible, the creature gains 50% concealment against attacks from other creatures that correctly pinpoint its fighting space.

Activating or deactivating invisiware is a free action. However, the technology consumes a great deal of the battery power; after 10 rounds (1 minute) of use, the solar batteries must be recharged for 1 hour, during which time the invisiware cannot be activated.

Type: External.

Hardness/Hit Points: 4/20.

Base Purchase DC: 35.

Restriction: Military (+3).

Psi Implant (PL 8)

This brain implant stimulates neuron activity in underdeveloped regions of the recipient's brain, unlocking latent psionic abilities.

Benefit: The recipient gains the Wild Talent feat.

Type: Internal.

Hardness/Hit Points: –/2.

Base Purchase DC: 31.

Restriction: Military (+3).

Inclusion and Adaptations in Curriculum for Improving Performance of Children with Special Needs

A curriculum guide may be general or specific and can be a way of determining what to teach, how to teach it, and in what ways to teach material to diverse groups of students. Sometimes these guides are used by students especially at the college level to determine what material they ought to master in their fields. Alternately, teachers, who are trying to build lesson plans with a variety of objectives, could utilize different forms of a curriculum guide, and these might be used by anyone from an early childhood educator to a college professor.

Since the term curriculum guide means different things, getting a handle on a definition that will always apply is challenging. Often, a guide is specific to a subject or to one aspect of a subject. For instance there exists guides to different important moments in history. They can list ideas of how to teach that moment to appeal to different types of learners, in addition to listing the main ideas that need be gleaned from study of that moment or epoch. Some guides would include suggested activities, worksheets, additional readings and other things that could be adapted to a broad range of grades or that are specific to a certain grade.

When construed broadly, intended outcomes of the general curriculum for students with low-incidence disabilities do not differ essentially from those expected for all students. Community inclusion, with the opportunity to achieve a high quality of life, is the ultimate goal for all citizens. State curriculum frameworks in core content areas, local content options, and district-level vision and mission statements about stakeholders' aspirations for students all drive the general curriculum. Right down to the level of the community school, the question is, *How might that curriculum be accessed by students with disabilities? How can participation be accomplished and effective progress be ensured?* While specialized curricula and instructional practices must continue to be employed to address disability-specific needs, today the unique needs of students with disabilities must be understood in a broader context of the general curriculum.

Curriculum and Instructional Practices

Curriculum and instructional practices are not easily separated conceptually one from the other. In the present context, *curriculum* is treated as content and *instruction* is meant as those teaching practices that engage students in curriculum. However, in reviewing the literature, disentangling the meaning of *curriculum* from *instruction* often proves unwieldy. Thus, for purposes of presentation, we combine both curriculum and instructional practices for each of the low-incidence disabilities discussed. While IDEA continues to classify students with disabilities according to category, in many instances curriculum and instructional practices can be applied more generically. Students with complex healthcare issues, significant developmental delays, and severe multiple disabilities require approaches that offer intensive levels of support. Students who are blind, deaf, deaf-blind, and autistic may in some cases require the same degree of support, but they also require more specialized curriculum and teaching approaches (in, for example, technology and literacy). Additionally, such students may require specialized resources from related service providers (such as orientation and mobility instructors or audiologists).

Facing the Challenge of Curriculum Access

Physical facilities, technology, media and materials, and human resources all contribute to the quality of what transpires in schools. Yet there remains great disparity in quality from community to community. And these disparities, in turn, yield uneven results for students from community to community. Such unevenness is particularly troubling when observed in communities with high concentrations of students from poor families, English language learners, or members of racial minorities. Also troubling is the achievement gap observed between disabled and non-disabled student populations. Standards-based reform and its reliance upon broad-scale assessment represents an attempt to improve overall performance of American students and to narrow the achievement gap observed in diverse student populations, including students with disabilities.

Pugach calls for a "curriculum-centred dialogue" that will enable general and special educators to confront several crucial and fundamental issues embedded in curriculum. These include the following:

1. The appropriateness and quality of the general education curriculum for all students

2. The degree to which the general education curriculum meets the needs of students from various cultural, linguistic, and socioeconomic backgrounds
3. The relationship of the curriculum to the disproportionate numbers of students of colour in special education

All teachers inevitably ask *what do my students need to know and be able to do?* In order to answer these questions, teachers must identify, locate, or develop curriculum—that which is generally believed to constitute the "what" or substance of education. This substance of education can be taken apart and understood in many different ways. For example, curriculum can be divided into domains or subject areas. Some domains may be considered "core" or vital, while others may be considered "extra" or supplementary (e.g., extra-curricular activities). Curriculum can also be examined in terms of its scope, depth, or sequence.

Today, the aims or purposes of curriculum are stated in the form of "standards." For each domain, that which students need to know is often referred to as *content standards*, and that which students need to be able to do in order to demonstrate what they know is frequently called *performance standards*. Standards are generally sequenced so that entry-level or prerequisite knowledge, skills, and dispositions can be specified along paths or strands for each domain. Standards may be broadly stated or narrowly defined. (When broadly stated, standards permit flexibility in the multiple ways in which a standard can be achieved. When narrowly defined, standards may permit more precise benchmarking for indicating within a particular standard the level a student has achieved.)

Blending General and Specialized Curriculum

Hitchcock, Meyer, Rose, and Jackson (2002) define the general education curriculum as the overall plan for instruction adopted by a school or school system. Nolet and McLaughlin (2000) acknowledge the uniqueness of the general education curriculum for each school system—and each student—when they recommend procedures for "finding" the general education curriculum. Wehmeyer (et al., 2002) acknowledges that the general curriculum is defined broadly because Congress intends for it to be determined locally. How students with disabilities ultimately access the general curriculum depends on the assessment, planning, and evaluation skills of their local IEP team members (consisting of both general and special educators). They need to examine the content of what is taught to non-disabled agemates, select entry points to the curriculum, determine appropriate accommodations for instruction and assessment, and determine curriculum modifications and alternates for assessment. They also need to determine what, if any, specially-designed instruction in expanded areas or domains of the curriculum is necessary to address needs arising from disability that also limit access to the general curriculum. Individual protections that reside at the heart of IDEA remain in place, so while curriculum is of primary importance, individual students will continue to be the focus of a free, appropriate, and public education.

What curriculum would support, complement, or augment student access to the general curriculum? For students with significant developmental or multiple disabilities, compilations of specialized curriculum have been published by Browder (2001) and by Ryndak and Alper (1996; 2003). These and other sources have been reviewed for inclusion in the low-incidence categories below. In the end, what students with low-incidence disabilities need to know and be able to do will depend on the expectations and standards embraced by their IEP team. A quality education for students with low-incidence disabilities will be a blending of curriculum designed to address disability-specific or unique needs and curriculum designed for optimal functioning in a democratic society.

Blind/Low Vision

Curriculum for blind students was developed largely by residential schools during the 19th and early 20th centuries (Frampton, 1940). Content mirrored the curriculum of the day with significant alteration in teaching practices and communication systems for conveying that curriculum. Most notable is the use of Braille. Today, IDEA presumes that all students with IEPs who have vision impairments shall use Braille as their primary literacy medium unless the team determines that print is more efficient. Braille, however, was not always held in such high esteem. It took over 100 years—a period known as "the war of the dots"—for Braille to become established as the reading medium of preference for the blind.

Curriculum for students with low vision began to appear in the early part of the 20th century when so-called "partially sighted" children were separated from schools for the blind for educational purposes (Jackson, 1983). Due to concern that students with very high myopia (nearsightedness) would lose more vision through eyestrain, curriculum materials were enlarged and supplemented by aural reading (listening).

This "sight saving philosophy," (Hathaway, 1959) as it was known, persisted well into the 1960s until Barraga's 1964 discovery that efficiency of vision improved through use. The new resulting "sight utilization philosophy" persisted into the 1980s, when declining Braille literacy rates among blind students were observed to correlate with unemployment. Hand in hand with the sight utilization philosophy was an increase in public day school attendance by blind students. Children who may have learned Braille at residential schools were now using enlarged print or print with optical magnification. In the minds of many advocates, this over-emphasis on the importance of sight utilization deprived many severely visually impaired students of the opportunity to learn Braille. Hence, the 1990s ushered in a new era of curriculum emphasizing Braille literacy.

Just as literacy is the focus of most of the current reform initiatives because of its connection with employment, so Braille literacy has taken centre stage with the observation that nearly three-fourth's of blind people today are unemployed. In fact, fluent Braille users are among the most successfully employed blind sub-group. Reasons for the decline in Braille literacy among blind and visually impaired individuals are complex, but IDEA now requires that IEP teams undertake a learning media assessment (LMA) (Koenig & Holbrook, 1995) to determine the most efficacious approach to learning and literacy.

During the 1950s and 1960s, public day school programmes for blind and visually impaired students expanded rapidly. Resource models, itinerant teaching services, and teacher-consultation models emerged and soon overtook residential school placement as the preferred approach for meeting blind students' educational needs. Prior to IDEA, advocates for public school programming downplayed or, at least, de-emphasized the unique and challenging needs of these students when entering the general educational environment. They argued that blind students needed the same curriculum as every other student and that teachers could supply just a few additional skills and resources (Abel, 1959). These additional skills and knowledge areas became known as the "plus curriculum." Today, the plus curriculum is known as the "expanded core" curriculum, to emphasize that it must go hand-in-hand with the "common core" curriculum.

The expanded core curriculum is derived from the unique or disability-specific needs of blind and visually impaired students identified and elaborated by Hatlen and Curry (1987). The table below is adapted from Hatlen (1996b).

Table: *Core Curriculum for Blind and Visually Impaired Children and Youths*

Existing Core Curriculum	
English Language Arts	Other languages, to the extent possible
Mathematics	Science
Health	Physical Education
Social Studies	Fine Arts
Business Education	Economics
History	Vocational Education
Expanded Core Curriculum	
Compensatory or functional academic skills, including communication modes*	Orientation and mobility
Social interaction skills	Independent living skills
Recreation and leisure skills	Career education
Use of assistive technology (AT)	Visual efficiency skills

****Note:*** *For this area of the expanded core curriculum for blind and visually impaired students, a distinction must be made between compensatory skills and functional skills. Compensatory skills are those needed by blind and visually impaired students in order to access all areas of core curriculum. Mastery of compensatory skills will usually mean that a visually impaired student has access to learning in a manner equal to that of sighted peers. Functional skills refers to skills that students with multiple disabilities learn that provide them with the opportunity to work, play, socialize, and take care of personal needs to the highest level possible.*

Components of the expanded core curriculum present educators with a means of addressing the needs of visually impaired students who also have additional disabilities. The educational requirements of this population are often not met since their lack of vision is often considered "minor," especially when a child is severely impacted by cognitive and physical disabilities. Each area in an expanded core curriculum can be further defined to address educational issues confronting these children and to assist parents and educators to fulfill their needs.

Hatlen's (1996) expanded core curriculum was first brought to national attention by Corn, Hatlen, Ryan, and Siller (1995) in response to the Improving America's Schools Act of 1994. Corn (et al., 1995) has argued that states and school districts ought to be held accountable for ensuring that blind and visually impaired students receive adequate and appropriate instruction in these expanded core areas as well as in common core areas. Out of that work, a national agenda for educating blind and visually impaired children has identified a number of goals around which national consensus in the field has emerged. Insistence on the primacy of Hatlen's expanded core curriculum is a critical component of that agenda.

As early as 1879, Congress recognized the importance of meeting the curricular needs of blind students when it passed the Act to Promote the Education of the Blind (Koestler, 1976). Today, this Act provides a line item for each state for the purchase of educational technology, media, and materials through the American Printing House for the Blind (APH). Depending on the number of blind students residing in any particular state, a quota account is established on an annual basis for supplementing the curricular needs of blind students. Under IDEA, the responsibility for meeting educational needs of blind students remains with states and school districts, so APH resources are not intended as comprehensive but rather as a supplement to the material needs of blind students. (Visiting APH's web site reveals directions for accessing an online database of products and links to resources keyed to Hatlen's (1996b) common core and expanded core curriculum areas.)

Over the past thirty years, comprehensive treatment of the challenge of educating students who are blind or visually impaired can be found in the comprehensive works edited by Lowenfeld (1973), Scholl (1986), and, most recently, Koenig and Holbrook (2000). More narrowly focused resources can be found in Chen (1999) for the essential elements of early intervention programming; in Ferrell (1985) for early childhood education; in Wormsley and D'Andrea (1997) for Braille literacy; in Wolffe and Sacks (2000) for social skills curriculum; in Levack (1994) for use of low vision; in Blasch, Wiener, and Welsh (1997) for orientation and mobility; in Corn (2000) for assistive technology; and in Wolffe (1999) for career education.

As a field, education of the blind and visually impaired recognizes the disproportionate numbers of students within its service population who are identified as multiply-disabled and deaf-blind. This is why Corn's (et al., 1995) description of the national agenda for educating visually impaired students includes those with multiple disabilities. While there are curriculum resources specifically identified for blind students with multiple disabilities (Sacks & Silberman, 1998), more generally applicable approaches for this population are described below.

Deaf/Hard-of-Hearing

Curriculum for the deaf has also developed within residential schools of the 19th and 20th centuries. Throughout this time period, controversy surrounded the development of a curriculum for the deaf. Debate centred around whether to maintain an emphasis on teaching sign language in the curriculum for deaf students or to follow an oral approach focused on lip-reading and listening skills as well as on how to speak. Today, this controversy continues at the language level the core of human communication. On one side is the position that deafness is a difference and not a disability; Deafness is a culture with its own native language—American Sign Language (ASL). On the other side is the position that deafness is a disability, creating in an individual significant limitations in communicative competence; measures must be taken in order to compensate for these limitations. (For example, cochlear implants provide access to the stimulus for hearing speech sounds and establish conditions for learning to speak and to use amplification [hearing aids].)

Crucial curricular content for deaf students include language, reading, and writing; Deaf culture, speech development, and aural habilitation. A curriculum in language often consists of teaching students English sentence patterns, starting with basic patterns and moving to increasingly complex structures. A curriculum in reading regularly involves using books with relatively simple grammatical structures or basal reading material that is designed so that sentence patterns increase in difficulty from book to book. A typical writing curriculum requires students to learn the rules of different types of discourse and the rules of grammar. Curriculum in language, reading, and writing today can be best described as a balance of analytical and holistic methods (Turnbull, et al., 2002).

Learning about Deaf culture is an important curricular goal for all students who are deaf or hard-of-hearing, regardless of educational setting. One goal of instruction about Deaf culture is to help students develop understanding of the culture of the Deaf community so that they can participate to whatever extent they wish. A second goal is to help transmit Deaf culture to the next generation of individuals who are deaf or hard-of-hearing.

Curriculum regarding speech development is aimed at helping children develop breath control, vocalization, voice patterns, and sound production. This curriculum focuses both on producing spoken language and on improving speech. Aural habilitation curriculum involves helping students use their remaining hearing effectively. Depending on a student's capability, learning goals might include awareness of sound, localization of sound, discrimination of sound differences, or recognition of sound. For some it may be recognition of speech used by others.

Literature concerning academic/vocational content of curriculum for the deaf contains disappointingly few articles, reflecting an historical lack in the field. Pagliaro (1998a; 1998b) wrote about the impact of mathematics reform on the education of deaf students and documented the poor preparation of math teachers for instructing the deaf. LaSasso (1999) has reviewed the literature on problems with test-taking skills among deaf students and has stated that the teaching of test-taking skills should be part of students' programmes. Furlonger (1998) has looked at career awareness of deaf and hearing adolescents in New Zealand and found significant differences in career measures and vocational maturity, in favour of hearing respondents. He proposed more attention to career awareness and vocational preparation.

In order to be effective, curriculum must be instituted early. Magnuson (2000) investigated the cognitive development of two deaf boys in Sweden enrolled in a sign-based preschool. One had been identified, and habilitation started, by four months of age, and the other had not been diagnosed until two years of age. Magnuson reported differences in social and linguistic development of the two boys in favour of the one who had been diagnosed at four months. She concluded that the boy who started at age two lacked early stimulation, resulting in poor language development.

Teaching Approaches

In deaf education, three distinct communication approaches are identified for teaching the deaf and hard-of-hearing. These approaches are the bilingual-bicultural approach, the auditory-oral approach, and the total communication approach.

Bilingual-Bicultural Approach

The position of the bilingual-bicultural approach is that ASL is the natural language of Deaf culture and that ASL should be the primary language choice for deaf students, with English considered a second language. When using this approach, the objective is to provide a foundation in the use of ASL, with its unique vocabulary and syntax rules, and, at the same time, to provide ESL instruction for English vocabulary and syntax rules. With this approach, ASL is the method of communication in the classroom. Kemp (1998) has discussed the difficulty of learning ASL and the misperception that it may be learned easily. He argued that, like all complex and subtle languages, mastery beyond a basic level requires extensive exposure and practice, and he concluded that ASL should be approached with respect and with the understanding that mastery will occur only over time. On a similar note, Galvan (1999) has reported that there were differences in sign complexity by three to nine years of age between native signing deaf children of deaf parents and early signing (before five years of age) deaf children of hearing parents.

Mason and Ewoldt (1996) have presented the position that a whole-language approach to literacy and bilingual-bicultural (bi-bi) education complement each other. Additionally, Andrews, Ferguson, Roberts, and Hodges (1997) have reported on a bi-bi programme with seven deaf children of diverse racial and ethnic backgrounds in east-central Texas from 1993 to 1996. They found grade-level achievement at first grade, showing that language development was not delayed. Knoors and Renting (2000) have reported on the involvement in different tasks of six deaf children in the Netherlands using spoken Dutch and the Sign Language of the Netherlands (SLN). They found there was greater involvement during activities led by a deaf teacher using SLN.

Auditory-Oral Approach

The position of the auditory-oral approach is that students with hearing impairments can develop listening/receptive language and oral language expression skills. It emphasizes the use of residual hearing, amplification, and speech/language training. When using this approach, the objective is to facilitate the development of oral (spoken) English. The method of communication used by a student would be oral (spoken) English (Gargiulo, 2003).

Research on teaching practices related to this method has thus far been inconclusive. It does appear, however, that hearing-impaired infants born to Deaf parents using ASL may exhibit significantly improved language development (Hunt & Marshall, 1999). Research conducted by Moores (1996) suggests that parents who use a total communication approach, including manual signs, fingerspelling, and spoken language with their child and with each other enhance their child's acquisition of language. It has also been shown to be important to switch from a child-centred to a family-centred approach. There is a great need for families to have access to comprehensive information about educational options for their children (Gargiulo, 2003). The debate between manualism or oralism continues to be a heavily charged issue.

Total Communication Approach

The position of the total communication approach is that simultaneous use of multiple communication techniques enhances an individual's ability to communicate, comprehend, and learn (Gargiulo, 2003). When using this approach, the basic objective is to provide a multifaceted approach to communication in order to facilitate whichever method works best for each individual. The method of communication used by a student should be a combination of sign language, fingerspelling, and speech-reading. Grushkin (1998) has argued that fingerspelling has been under-utilized and that educators should take advantage of its high potential for equivalence to English orthography.

Inclusion of Deaf and Hard-of-Hearing Children

There are many strategies for teaching students with hearing impairments. It is important to promote acceptance of these students, and to provide an environment where students feel accepted and where modifications can be made without causing undue attention to be focused on individual students. This can be aided by efforts to welcome a student to their new classroom, by discussing the student's hearing loss with him/her and letting him/her know his/her teacher is willing to help, by having the student or another person—with the student's approval—explain about the student's hearing loss to the entire class if appropriate, by making modifications seem as natural as possible so that the student is not singled out, by accepting the student as an individual and being aware of his/her assets and limitations, and by encouraging the student's special abilities or interests. Adapted from Turnbull, several factors that appear to contribute to effective placement in general education settings are listed below:

- Classroom teachers need time to learn about their student and deafness. A student's team, usually including their general education teacher, consultant, interpreter, and speech language pathologist need time to share information and plan instruction.
- Professional staff and a student's parents must be committed to making placement successful and feel confident about a student's ability to be successful.
- School and district leadership must provide the kinds of support that promote positive outcomes, such as providing adequate

professional staff, paraprofessional staff, computers, and an adequate budget for the purchasing of materials and equipment.

- Professional staff must provide information about the needs of students who are deaf/hard-of-hearing and must be engaged in activities that enable them to understand programme design, clarify their roles and activities, and identify appropriate instructional strategies.
- Parents need to be involved on a daily basis and not relegated merely to IEP planning.
- Teachers of the deaf must have occasional opportunities to teach a whole class or to team teach with a general education teacher.
- A school must offer structured and supportive extracurricular activities.

Environmental Concerns

Another important suggestion for teachers of hearing impaired students is to provide them with preferential seating in their classroom. A hearing-impaired student should have a seat near where the teacher usually teaches. The student should be able to see the face of the teacher without straining. The student should be seated away from noise sources, including hallways, radiators, and pencil sharpeners. The student should sit where light is on the teacher's face and not in their eyes. If the student has a better ear, that ear should be turned towards the teacher. The student should also be allowed to move when necessary for demonstrations or other classroom activities.

Teachers should also increase visual information made available, since the student will use lip-reading and other visual information to supplement what he or she hears. The student will need to see the teacher's face in order to lip-read. The teacher should use visual aids whenever possible and should demonstrate what the student is supposed to understand whenever possible. A chalkboard should be used for assignments, new vocabulary words, and key phrases.

Other suggestions for classroom teachers are to minimize classroom noise, modify teaching procedures, and have realistic expectations of students. Teaching modifications allow a student to benefit from instruction and decreases the need for repetition. Teachers can aid these efforts by being sure a student is watching and listening when others are talking to him/her, by being sure a student understands what is being said and having him/her repeat information or answer questions, by rephrasing (rather than repeating) questions, by repeating or rephrasing things said by other students when appropriate, and by introducing new vocabulary to a student in advance prior to a lesson.

Adapted Educational Methods

Instructional interventions for students with hearing impairments include adapted methods of communication as well as the use of audiologists and interpreters. Different instructional interventions may be required depending on the severity of hearing loss. These include hearing aids, personal FM systems, favourable seating, medical management, auditory skill-building, help with self-esteem, sound-field FM systems in the classroom, and/or special educational support.

There are four basic types of hearing aids available: 1) in-the-ear aids, 2) behind-the-ear aids, 3) body aids, and 4) bone-conduction aids. Assistive listening devices (ALDs) can also be used to enhance participation and responsiveness of people with hearing loss. In addition, students sometimes use auditory trainers—specifically, FM systems—in their educational settings. These amplification systems are easy to use, enhance signal-to-noise ratio, and are often more effective than hearing aids in managing acoustical problems inherent in many classrooms. (With sound-field systems, the teacher wears a small microphone, and his or her voice is transmitted to various speakers placed around the room or on a desktop).

It is also important that teachers ensure that hearing aids and other amplification devices are used when recommended. Teachers should understand that most hearing aids make sounds louder but not necessarily clearer. Students' hearing devices should be checked daily to ensure that they are always in proper working order. Students should be encouraged to and trained to care for their own hearing device.

Everyday alerting devices can be adapted to meet the needs of hard-of-hearing students. These include wristwatches, doorbells, flashing-light clocks, flashing lamps, pillow vibrators, and specially-designed smoke detectors. Captioning is available on many television programmes to make entertainment more accessible to people with hearing impairments. In addition, a telecommunication device for the deaf (TDD) can be used by individuals with severe hearing impairments to help them communicate by telephone. (A TDD is a small keyboard with an electronic display screen and a modem attached.) Amplified telephones are also available in a wide range of models and capabilities.

Easterbrooks and Mordica have examined teachers' ratings of functional communication skills of deaf children with cochlear implants and concluded that a teacher's role in implant use warrants more attention and that all factors should be considered before advocating or choosing this "financially, emotionally, and therapeutically challenging option".

Using Technology

Computers have many possible applications for students with hearing impairments. Special programmes offer the opportunity for students to learn at their own comfort level and pace, and special programmes are available for speech drill, auditory training, speech-reading, sign language instruction, and supplemental reading and language instruction.

There is a need to encourage reflection upon teacher practice and to promote increased application of computer technology in educational curricula. To achieve this goal, a greater understanding of the relationship between teacher variables and teacher adoption of computer use is needed. This information may be used to help teachers become familiar with how computers work in the classroom and how they can be used for instruction.

For technology to work in schools, it is critical that teachers support the concept of instruction with computers and use them constructively with students. Stubbs (1990) found that in enhancing teacher technology training programmes, the three primary means of support are equipment budget, access to equipment, and support personnel. Congress has suggested that teachers need more than just access to resources of hardware and software. They also need "opportunities to discover what the technologies can do, [to] learn how to operate them, and [to] experiment with ways to best apply them in the classrooms".

Deaf-Blind

Students who are deaf-blind present a unique challenge to families, schools, and communities. Despite their designation, they represent an extremely heterogeneous population. Given their relatively small size in number, as well as their diversity, curriculum and instructional arrangements must remain flexible. Varying amounts of remaining vision, residual hearing, cognitive capacity, psychosocial status, and motor integrity all contribute to a complex set of needs.

In an overview of deaf-blindness, Miles (2000) makes several important recommendations, which we discuss below.

Communication

The most important challenge for parents, caregivers, and teachers of students who are deaf-blind is meaningful communication, which can be thought of as a conversation; it uses body language, gestures, and both signed and spoken words. The conversation begins with taking notice of what the deaf-blind child is paying attention to and communicating a shared interest. Unlike sighted or hearing children, who might respond to gestures, facial expressions, or sounds, children who are deaf-blind will often need touch to communicate shared interest. Pausing after each interaction allows time for the deaf-blind student to respond. Successful interaction depends on respecting the child's timing, which may be slow. These back and forth interactions with their pauses are the conversations which become the basis for language learning. Symbolic communication is the next step. Simple gestures or objects can accompany the introduction of words. These gestures or objects serve as symbols or representations for activities, teaching the child that one thing can stand for another, and also helping the child to learn to anticipate events.

An additional challenge is providing an environment rich in language that is meaningful and accessible. Such an environment can be created through the use of whichever symbol system is most accessible to the child.

Principal communication systems for persons who are deaf-blind are these: ASL, Braille writing and reading, fingerspelling, gestures, large-print writing and reading, lip-reading of speech, object symbols, picture symbols, Pidgin signed English, sign language, signed English, Tadoma method of speech-reading, touch cues. A reliable and meaningful routine that can be communicated to a deaf-blind student is also important. Touch cues, gestures, and use of object symbols are some typical ways in which to let a child who is deaf-blind know what is about to happen to him or her. An anticipated routine can help to decrease the anxiety associated with a deficit of sensory information.

Orientation and Mobility

A deaf-blind child will need help learning to move about in his or her environment. Attention must be paid to the immediate physical space surrounding a child so that the physical space rewards movement with stimulation to encourage further movement. Orientation and mobility specialists, as well as physical and occupational therapists, teachers of the visually impaired, and health professionals, can be helpful.

Individualized Education

Education for a deaf-blind student must be highly individualized. Assessment is critical both for estimating underlying intellectual capacity and for creating appropriate educational programmes. To discourage isolation, it is important to involve people who are familiar with both blindness and deafness. These services should be obtained as early as possible to ensure maximum opportunities for learning and meaningful contact.

Transition

Near the end of a school-based education of a deaf-blind student, transition and rehabilitation services will be necessary to find appropriate work and living arrangements. Teamwork will be required "among specialists and agencies concerned with such things as housing, vocational and rehabilitation needs, deafness, blindness, orientation and mobility, medical needs, and mental health" (Miles, 2000). Central to such a transition process, of course, is the deaf-blind person and his or her interests and needs.

Inclusion in Family

A major challenge is the inclusion of a deaf-blind child in the flow of family and community life. Parents must learn to identify subtle rewards, such as hand or body movements, instead of typical responses to care such as smiles. Parental perceptions and expectations of developmental milestones and successes may also need to be altered.

Teaching Strategies and Content Modifications

People who are deaf-blind who have high-quality lives have several things in common: they accept themselves as individuals with unique experiences and gifts, their educational experiences have maximized their ability to communicate and function in a typical environment, and they live and work in accepting families and communities.

Recommended teaching strategies and content modifications for a student with deaf-blindness are offered by Moss and Hagood (1995). The authors begin by asserting that students with deaf-blindness have unique educational needs. Without sight or hearing, he or she relies on doing in order to learn. Small-group or individual instruction becomes critical, as large-group instruction might only be useful during activities in which a student is consistently active (such as playground activities). New experiences may be difficult for a deaf-blind student. As trust is essential, bonding between student and instructor is critical.

It is important to create balanced interaction by taking turns, to encourage a student to be responsive; directive instruction is therefore less valuable. Safety is also of high importance, both in the environment and in creating a feeling of safety in which to move around independently. An orientation and mobility specialist can help develop safe routes for travel and to identify obstacles in an environment.

A student with deaf-blindness should have a curriculum focused on bonding and developing interactions and routines for expanding the frequency and functions of communication. This student needs instruction to piece together inputs, and he or she must be taught both to accept and use such instruction. An additional priority should be to develop a communication foundation for learning. A student might first have to be taken step-by-step through new activities to learn what will be expected of him or her. After he or she understands what is expected, this support should be removed to allow the development of independence. Learning should be functional, and clear goals and objectives must be developed for a deaf-blind student. Objectives should be limited in number, as it will take much practice before a student can generalize what he or she has learned to other situations. Vocabulary concepts should be broad, and consideration of the extent to which they can be generalized is important. A deaf-blind student needs a great deal of support. This support can at first be provided by teaching staff, but can later be modeled for other students in class for use during play or other learning situations. Specialized training and support may be needed for teachers without knowledge or experience in the specific area of deaf-blindness.

Significant Developmental Delay

Students with significant developmental delay represent a special population for whom expectations are generally low. However, like all people, these students have many unique strengths and specific talents in certain areas. It is important to see beyond disability and come to know and appreciate each individual. It is a daunting challenge for educators to ensure these students have access to the general curriculum.

The field of educating students with severe disabilities has undergone change in some key curricular trends. In the 1970s, as programmes were first created for individuals with severe disabilities, educators sometimes borrowed ideas from early childhood curriculum. By the late 1970s, Brown (et al., 1976) had challenged the field to focus instead on functional, age-appropriate skills. In the 1980s, many educators began to rely on emerging behavioural methods to teach students the skills believed to be prerequisites to community placements. Skills including food preparation, housekeeping and laundry, home safety and first aid, telephone use, dining out and buying snacks, shopping, community mobility, and community leisure were all taught by a variety of systematic instructional procedures. As more opportunities for school inclusion emerged in the late 1980s and 1990s, professionals often focused on *social* inclusion. Inclusive education provided a means for students to cultivate a circle of friends. Today, focus has shifted to instructional inclusion. As Ford, Davern, and Schnorr (2001) note, the current mandate for assessment and accountability for students with significant cognitive disabilities will influence curriculum decisions for years to come. Most states' standards focus on what Vanderwood, Ysseldyke, and Thurlow (1993) have described as academic and functional literacy outcomes. In contrast, many IEPs for students with severe disabilities focus on functional and social skills reflective of the more recent curriculum trends for this population. When states first began working on alternate assessments, many focused on functional outcomes with no link to actual state standards. Almost every state alternate assessments examine the same standards as general assessments either by expanding state standards, linking standards to a set of functional skills, or assessing standards plus an additional set of functional skills (Thompson & Thurlow, 2001). Thative language—American Sign Language (ASL). On the other side is the position that deafness is a disability, creating in an individual significant limitations in communicative competence; measures must be taken in order to compensate for these limitations. (For example, cochlear implants provide access

Curriculum

Planning curriculum starts with the individual needs of a student rather than a disability label or the availability of a separate programme that typically serves a particular type of student. After a student has been identified as having a disability, it is then possible to link student-specific goals and outcomes to general education curriculum standards. Planning should focus on an individual's capacities and assets. Family members and friends should be involved in planning. A collaborative team should analyze the general education curriculum and routines to identify when and how the learning needs of a student, expressed in terms of foundational skills, can be addressed within the context of the general education classroom.

The following assumptions, based on *Choosing Options and Accommodations for Children* (COACH), are inspiring in developing curriculum for students who are significantly developmentally delayed:

- Design of curriculum should be related to life outcomes that are valued
- Families should be considered consumers and partners in the design of curriculum
- Collaboration is essential in the design and delivery of quality education
- Curriculum objectives should be developed based on priorities and outcomes valued by a student and his or her family rather than professionals representing different disciplines
- Problem-solving strategies are instrumental in the design of effective curriculum and should be appropriately included

At each grade level, all students are expected to demonstrate proficiency in core curriculum areas as measured by each state's assessment system. It may be appropriate and feasible for a student with severe cognitive disabilities to demonstrate competence on all, part, or none of the core curriculum content for a given grade level (or unit addressed for a given grade level). When the needs of students are expressed in terms of critical or foundational skills, well-established strategies are available to identify opportunities for these skills to be addressed within the context of the general education curriculum. The five areas described below represent domains of a functional curriculum from which instructional targets can be selected and blended with the general curriculum. Browder (2001) and Ryndak and Alper (2003) provide extensive treatments of these curriculum areas.

Functional Reading: Functional reading involves being able to recognize specific sight words and to use them in the performance of daily routines. Most reading instruction targets the outcome of literacy; that is, students are expected to be able to read whatever printed material they may encounter.

Functional Math: Functional math refers to basic math skills needed to perform skills of daily living. It includes money management, time management, measurement, counting, and simple computation. In a typical general education curriculum, students learn number and computation skills needed to perform these tasks by the end of second grade. Individuals with significant cognitive disabilities often have not mastered basic math skills needed in daily living activities by this age, and will need to learn these concurrently with their applications to time and money management.

Community and Leisure Skills: With the appropriate support, all students can participate actively in their communities. The purpose of teaching community and leisure skills is not to "ready" students to be part of their communities but to help them benefit from these experiences more fully. Community and leisure skills are included in nearly all life-skills curricula. An important way that schools can prepare students for both current and future community and leisure opportunities is to directly involve them in these activities through community-based instruction.

Home and Personal Living Skills: Nearly all published curricula for students with severe disabilities include home and personal living skills. A large body of research now exists regarding how to teach skills such as eating, dressing, using the toilet, brushing the teeth, housekeeping, food preparation, and laundry skills (Konarski & Diorio, 1985; Westling & Fox, 1995).

Communication and Social Skills: Communication skills are often among the top priorities for students with significant cognitive disabilities. To be able to communicate with peers facilitates social interactions in inclusive settings. Many instructional interactions rely on communicative responses. Self-determination is also promoted through self-expression.

Three major components of communication are form, content, and function. When the form of communication is speech, teachers focus on syntax, including such skills as sentence structure, grammar, and inflection. When the form is an augmentative or alternative communication system (a non-speech system), teachers focus on teaching students to use that system effectively. Content of communication includes vocabulary and topics discussed. Function of communication relates to the purpose of communication.

Instructional Adaptations

Special educators must be focused on developing programmes of high-quality instruction for students with significant cognitive disabilities that are anchored to the general education curriculum. These students continue to exceed our expectations if they have access to appropriate curricula and are taught using effective instructional practices.

Curriculum and instructional practices include basic skills and functional life-skills content designed to help students learn the work, domestic, or leisure skills needed for independent living: self-care skills, social interaction, recreation and leisure skills, job training, and community-based instruction (Drew, Logan, & Hardman, 1992; Morgan, Moore, McSweyn, & Salzberg, 1992; Patton, Beirne-Smith, & Payne, 1990). School adjustment skills such as interaction with peers, working in groups, participating, communicating, complying with schedules and requests, improving general work habits (following directions, working with others, accepting supervision, meeting demands for quality work, demonstrating occupational safety skills, recognizing the importance of attendance and punctuality, working at a satisfactory rate) are also critical. Additionally, attention skills, memory skills, functional academics (using money, carrying on conversations, learning survival words), choice making, learning strategies, time management, organizational skills, generalization skills, self advocacy, community-based instruction, self-direction, health and safety, functional academics, should also be included in the curriculum.

Fisher and Frey (2001) have described ways in which students with significant cognitive disabilities have accessed the core curriculum in the past and have identified the services and supports necessary for participation in general education classrooms. In their work they describe the experiences of three students with significant disabilities (one elementary student, one middle school student, and one high school student) who had been members of general education classrooms in urban schools for at least three years. In their observations of these students, four themes emerged: (a) individualized, content-specific accommodations and modifications; (b) collaboration among members of a student's teaching team; (c) involvement of peers; and (d) disconnection between the students' IEPs and curriculum and instruction. Practical implications of Fisher and Frey's research are that students with significant cognitive disabilities should receive their special education services within general education classrooms. Thus, one implication of Fisher and Frey's work is that students must be included in general education classrooms in order to access these types of curricula and curriculum supports.

To succeed in general education classrooms, students with significant cognitive disabilities must also have access to personal supports and technology supports (Fisher, Frey, & Sax, 1999). Schools that want to implement inclusive schooling practices would be well advised to ensure that general and special education teachers have access to planning time if they expect innovations in curriculum to take hold.

Researchers investigating instructional adaptation have identified a variety of strategies for facilitating the inclusive education of students with severe disabilities. For example, incorporating choice, by allowing students to choose a Language Arts assignment, revealed dramatically decreased levels in undesirable behaviour (disruptive and off-task) (Powell & Nelson, 1997). Furthermore, allowing students to choose the order in which they complete academic tasks has been shown to result in increased levels of desirable classroom behaviour (Dunlap, et al., 1994). Priming, or pre-practice, has also been documented as an effective classroom intervention for students with significant cognitive disabilities. Priming consists of previewing information or activities that a student is likely to have difficulties with before they actually engage in that activity (Wilde, Koegel, & Koegel, 1992). Priming has been shown to be effective in reducing disruptive behaviour in students with autism and in increasing on-task behaviour during class storybook reading activities and in increasing initiations of social interaction with typical peers. Partial participation is another strategy for adjusting curriculum to facilitate the educational inclusion of students with severe disabilities . Partial participation, also known as multi-level instruction, consists of allowing a student with a disability to participate in the same projects and instructional activities as the rest of their class, with specific modifications to the activity so that it suits a student's specific abilities and needs.

Teachers have been taught to successfully implement instructional adaptations found to be effective for students with disabilities, including giving clear directions; appropriate, immediate feedback; and mnemonic recall strategies. General educators have been taught to effectively implement instructional adaptations in mathematics and reading and writing.

Self-management

Teaching a student self-management in the classroom allows that student to function independently without relying on a teacher or a one-on-one aid. Self-management allows individuals with disabilities to become actively involved in the intervention process as well as more involved in their classroom environments. This increased involvement has the potential to improve autonomy by reducing dependence on adult intervention, which in turn provides a student with more opportunities to interact with classmates without the stigma of a one-on-one aid. Self-management has been suggested as an ideal intervention for students with significant cognitive disabilities to enable them to participate in full inclusion classroom settings (Reid, 1996).

Cooperative learning

A number of studies have demonstrated that teaching social skills to students with severe disabilities and their non-disabled peers in cooperative groups in integrated settings results in increased frequency, duration, and quality of social interactions.

Peer tutoring

Peer tutoring consists of any instructional strategy where two students work together on an academic activity, with one student providing assistance, instruction, and feedback to the other (DuPaul & Eckert, 1998). Peer tutoring strategies and their variants have been demonstrated to be effective in producing improvements in on-task behaviour and math performance (DuPaul & Henningson, 1993) and in on-task behaviour and social interactions (Locke & Fuchs, 1995).

Friendships

Inclusive classrooms are an excellent setting in which to evaluate and design interventions to promote friendships for students with disabilities; at the least, they provide these students with the opportunity to interact socially.

Educational Strategies

Horner, Flannery, and Snell's work (1996) on intellectual disabilities addresses the broad structure for educational strategies that meets the needs of students with severe intellectual disabilities. They recognize that special education is in a critical period for assessing educational strategies used with students with severe disabilities. For several years, these students have been at the door of the regular school and regular classroom. They are now part of the school reform movement. Horner and his colleagues have foreshadowed the real challenge of educational reform as defining systems that produce valued instructional gains while supporting the social inclusion that had become a key value in the education of these students. How to educate students with severe disabilities in the general education classroom without overburdening the general educator, or disrupting the education of students without disabilities, remains the question of the day. To achieve that goal (a) new strategies are needed for general educators, and (b) the strategies for educating students with severe disabilities must be expanded and integrated with those available to regular educators. Teachers of students with severe disabilities come to this task with a strong foundation in instructional systems and curriculum options grounded in direct instruction, systematic instructional delivery and data-based outcome measures. Good strategies exist for designing functional curricula that are sequenced to promote rapid, generalized acquisition. What continues to be less available are clear strategies and strategies for organizing broader variables related to quality education. The strategies we need today are strategies for how students should be grouped, how school-wide systems should be set up, and how funding should be used to achieve broader educational goals of all students (including those with the most severe disabilities).

Significant Physical and Multiple Disabilities

Curricula most important to students with significant physical disabilities include skills that increase their personal independence, mobility within classroom, school, home, workplace, and community environments, and self-care skills. Self-advocacy varies according to a student's individual strengths and needs. "Goals ultimately include enhancing functional mobility, increasing communication, and enhancing capabilities in attending to daily living skills" (Geyer, et al., 1998), and enhancing self-determination in achieving quality of life. Essentially, special instruction in mobility skills, daily living skills, occupational skills, and, in severe cases, functionality in the everyday environment, are the critical needs of this population.

With high absence rates, modifications need to be made so that students can keep up with their peers (i.e., with the use of videotapes, telephone communications, schoolmates as tutors) (Culatta & Tompkins, 1999). Service from an interdisciplinary team of professionals that collaborate is ideal (Heward, 1996) although Hunt and Goetz (1997) argue for a transdisciplinary model—the same one or two professionals delivering all services to ensure continuity. Collaboration efforts of professionals, families, and students working together as a community to deliver services, the use of assistive technology (AT) to enhance a student's capabilities, and adapting the general curriculum are all highly recommended.

Other considerations for students with physical disabilities include applying principles of proper and customized positioning and seating; making classroom materials and work areas accessible, modifying the height, slant, or angle of work areas to meet individual students' needs; stabilizing work materials as needed, and using technology and adaptive equipment (mobility aids, hand controls, arm/wrist supports, page-turning devices, modified keyboards, scanners, voice-recognition programmes, mouth-operated devices, etc.) (Sands, et al., 2000).

Education of classmates to help them understand their peers' disabilities and encouraging students with health impairments to discuss their needs and the characteristics of their condition with peers to lessen anxiety for all are also important practices (Wood & Lazzari, 1997).

Autistic Spectrum

The Diagnostic and Statistical Manual of Mental Disorders (fourth edition) (DSM-IV) (American Psychiatric Association, 1994) defines autism as a disability "characterized by severe and pervasive impairment in several areas of development: reciprocal social interaction skills, communication skills, or the presence of stereotyped behaviour, interests, and activities." Individuals with this disability have considerable difficulty in interacting with others socially and in communicating verbally. They also often engage in self-stimulating behaviour and can have a very limited number of routines and interests.

"Effective intervention in autism appears to require early and intensive educational support that addresses the behavioural, social, and communication deficits associated with that disorder" (Rapin, 1997). Curriculum created for the autistic population includes a behavioural component, which focuses on decreasing self-injurious and or/self-stimulatory behaviour as well as a functional element with language skills (Biklen, 1990). Other tasks recommended to be introduced include attention skills, memory skills, functional academics (using money, carrying on conversations, learning survival words), communication skills, social interaction skills, learning strategies, time management, organizational skills, generalization skills, and self advocacy. Some programmes also have curricula that include teaching an autistic person skills to help them cope with and appropriately control external environmental stimuli.

Some common practices of teachers of autistic children include having clearly defined behavioural expectations, frequently acknowledging appropriate behaviours, evaluating programmes and making adaptations on an ongoing basis through a team approach, and targeting support to address students who need intense skill development and practice. These teaching practices can be applied to all areas of an autistic person's skill development: behavioural, communicational, and functional. However, there are certain teaching practices that specifically relate to each type of skill listed above.

A teacher may help improve an autistic individual's behaviour by formally assessing conditions that bring about inappropriate behaviours. Understanding the origin of problematic behaviours enables a teacher to then help an autistic individual learn new skills that will help him/her to achieve a desired result (e.g., receiving attention or obtaining a break). Teachers should also give positive consequences for using a new skill and occasionally use negative consequences for inappropriate behaviour. Teachers can provide a variety of structured opportunities in which their students may practice skills so they can transfer their knowledge to different settings. Some popular teaching practices for conveying functional skills include the following: "embedding opportunities to practice functional life skills in daily activities in the natural setting where they would occur; using concrete, age-appropriate, real-life teaching materials; demonstrating new routines in a sequential manner, checking for understanding at each step; and using a variety of modes for expressive and receptive communication skills".

Sands, Kolzeski, and French (2000) have identified various curricula and teaching practices that are currently in use for children with autism. Their educational interventions include sensory-motor therapy, communication therapy, social skills training, applied behaviour analysis, and multi-treatment programmes.

Sensory-Motor Therapy

Sensory-motor therapy curriculum is based on the idea that an autistic person has difficulty discerning and reacting to environmental stimuli because damaged sensory and motor pathways causes him/her to be either over-aroused or under-aroused. This over- or under-stimulation can cause an autistic individual to feel pain or discomfort. The need to engage in repetitive/ritualistic behaviour is believed to be caused by an autistic person's need to control the amount of stimulation entering his or her nervous system. The purpose of sensory-motor therapy curriculum is to teach autistic students how to perceive environmental stimuli through alternative pathways in order to help them become desensitized to environmental stimulation. Ultimately, this should foster the maturation of his/her nervous system and result in an increased ability to learn social and communication skills. According to Dempsey and Foreman (2001), sensory-motor therapy includes the following components:

- *Sensory Integration Training* In this type of therapy, an occupational therapist performs activities to stimulate a child's skin to reduce sensitivity to outside stimulation. These activities can include massage, brushing or stroking the body of an autistic person in specific areas such as the joints, and having the autistic person walk on a balance beam or jump on a trampoline. Sensory integration training is believed to help "improve the sensory processing capabilities of the brain" resulting in increased vocalization, "eye contact, learning, and motor skills."
- *Auditory Integration Training* This type of therapy is based on the belief that autistic people have hypersensitive hearing, and that this is what causes a great deal of their learning and behavioural problems (Berard, 1993). In auditory integration training, an "audiogram is completed to determine the frequencies at which the individual's hearing appears to be too sensitive. Training then occurs for approximately 10 hours over a two-week period, in which a person listens, through headphones, to music in which the identified frequencies are altered out."
- *Music Therapy* Music therapy uses music to help an autistic individual either through listening or playing an instrument him- or herself to work through his/her linguistic, emotional, learning, and motor skills difficulties.

Communication Therapy

According to language therapists, an autistic child may share the same interest and capability as non-autistic children to learn how to communicate with others and express him- or herself. Therefore, the curriculum of communication therapies focuses on learning language skills. Using a systematized approach emphasizing positive reinforcement, teachers using applied behaviour analysis have succeeded in teaching autistic individuals how to speak or to use sign language or pictures to communicate.

Social Skills Training

Sometimes the world can appear to be a cruel place to a person who has autism. Because of their lack of social skills, an autistic individual may frequently take offense at innocent remarks and often appears awkward in social gatherings. Thus, the curriculum of social skills training focuses on teaching students how to act appropriately and how to function in society. Skills included in this curriculum are understanding social cues, reading body language, participating in conversations, looking at situations from other people's points of view, and communicating emotions. Social skills training may include role playing activities and the use of social stories:

- *Role Playing* In role playing, an autistic student is presented with a social situation that he/she might encounter in daily life. (For example, greeting another person.) The student then acts out what he or she should do in the scenario. Sometimes a student might be videotaped during role play. After acting out the scene and possibly viewing it on video, the student's teacher provides feedback about the student's performance and may engage the student in conversation about what was done correctly or what could be done better next time.
- *Social Stories* The social stories methodology was created to teach people how to read social cues. In order to do this, a teacher will show an autistic individual a picture of a social situation that might take place in daily life. Easy-to-read captions accompany each of the pictures. These captions explain how each of the illustrated individuals might be feeling according to their body language, and how to act appropriately when they see the same body language in others.

Applied Behaviour Analysis

Applied behaviour analysis is based on the notion that the neurological system of people with autism has not formed connections that allow learning and socialization to take place as it does for most people. It can be considered more of a teaching technique than a curriculum. It focuses on teaching cognitive, communication, and social skills in a highly structured fashion. Skills are broken down into small steps and taught using "a specific cue or instruction, and by using prompts" (Dempsey & Foreman, 2001). Appropriate responses are rewarded, and inappropriate actions are ignored (not reinforced). This specific teaching practice is based on applied behaviour analysis. Learning goals for a student are determined by an individual analysis of the student's needs in terms of academic skills, life skills, and social skills. These are taught within a highly structured environment that is made consistent and predictable for a student.

Multi-Treatment Programmes

Multi-treatment programmes utilize an assortment of curriculums and teaching techniques to serve the needs of autistic students. For example, Project TEACCH (Treatment and Education of Autistic and related Communication handicapped Children) uses a variety of behavioural teaching practices to help students learn how to care for themselves and conduct themselves suitably. Much of their curriculum is taught in a highly structured learning environment. Another programme, called Giant Steps, integrates techniques used in sensory-motor training and applied behaviour analysis. In addition to providing an education in a self-contained classroom, Giant Steps allows opportunities for autistic students to be mainstreamed in public schools. Treatment of an autistic individual is a daunting task. His/her neurological condition does not allow him/her to process information in ways that most people do. In addition, each child with autism does not respond the same way to any given treatment. What might be successful for some might not produce the same results for others. Thus, although the skills spelled out in the curricula explained above should be acquired by those with autism, teaching practices used will have to cater to individuals.

Classroom Management for the Children with Special Needs

There are times when the real issue may not be the child but rather in the teaching style of the classroom teacher, that is, having unrealistic expectations, being critical, or being overlay demanding. In such instances, help for the teacher can come in the form of classroom management techniques. Classroom management techniques are strategies developed to help handle various problems and conflicts within a classroom. An administrator, psychologist, or any realistic and diplomatic team member who feels comfortable with this type of situation may offer these practical suggestions to the teacher. There are many classroom techniques and modifications that should be tried before taking more serious steps. These include the following:

- Display daily class schedule with times so that the student has a structured idea of the day ahead
- Change seating
- Seat the student with good role models
- Use peer tutors when appropriate
- Limit number of directions
- Simplify complex directions
- Give verbal as well as written directions
- Provide extra work time

- Shorten assignments
- Modify curriculum but change content only as a last resort
- Identify and address preferred learning styles
- Provide manipulative materials
- Provide examples of what is expected
- Use colour coding of materials to foster organizational skills
- Develop a homework plan with parental support
- Develop a behaviour modification plan, if necessary
- Uses lots of positive reinforcement
- Use technology as an aid

Help Classes

Certain children may require only a temporary support system to get them through a difficult academic period. Some schools provide additional non special education services, such as help classes, that may be held during lunch or before or after school. These classes can clarify academic confusion that could lead to more serious problems if not addressed.

Remedial Reading or Math Services

Remedial reading or math services are academic programmes within a school designed to help the student with reading or math by going slower in the curriculum or placing him or her with a smaller number of students in the classroom for extra attention. These services can be recommended when reading or math is the specific area of concern. Remedial reading and math classes are not special education services and can be instituted as a means of alleviating a child's academic blems.

In-School Counselling

In-school counselling is normally done by the school psychologist, social worker, or guidance counselor, and is designed to help the child deal with the issues that are currently problematic for him or her. Sometimes, a child may experience a situational or adjustment disorder (a temporary emotional pattern that may occur at any time in a person's life without a prior history of problems) resulting from separation, divorce, health issues, newness to school district, and so on. When this pattern occurs, it may temporarily interfere with the child's ability to concentrate, remember, or attend to tasks. Consequently, a drop in academic performance can occur. If such patterns occur, the school psychologist may want to institute in-school counselling, with the parent's involvement and permission. This recommendation should be instituted only to address issues that can be resolved in a relatively short period of time. More serious issues may have to be referred to outside agencies or professionals for longer treatment.

Progress Reports

A progress report is a synopsis of the child's work and behaviour in the classroom sent home to the parents in order to keep them updated on the child's strengths and weaknesses over a period of time (e.g., every day, each week, biweekly, or once a month). Sometimes, a child who has fallen behind academically will "hide" from the real issues by avoiding reality. Daily progress reports for a week or two at first and then weekly reports may provide the child with the kinds of immediate gratification and positive feedback necessary to get back on track. They offer the child a greater sense of hope and control in getting back to a more normal academic pattern.

Disciplinary Action

This recommendation is usually made when the child in question needs a structured boundary set involving inappropriate behaviour. If a child demonstrates a pattern of inappropriate behaviour, disciplinary action is usually used in conjunction with other recommendations because such patterned behaviour may be symptomatic of a more serious problem. The appropriate disciplinary actions necessary should be discussed with the school psychologist, and how it should be implemented must be carefully considered before it begins.

Change of Programme

A change of programme involves examining the child's programme and making adjustments to his or her schedule based on the presenting problem. This recommendation usually occurs when a student has been placed in a course that is not suited to his or her ability or needs. If a student is failing in an advanced class, then the student's programme should be changed to include more modified classes.

Consolidation of Programme

There are times when reducing a student's course load is necessary. Consolidation of a programme involves taking the student's programme and modifying it so that the workload is decreased. If a child is "drowning in school," then that child's available energy level may be extremely limited. In such cases, you may find that he or she is failing many courses. Temporarily consolidating or condensing the programme allows for the possibility of salvaging some courses, because the student's available energy will not have to be spread so thin.

Referral to Child Protective Services

Child Protective Services is a state agency designed to investigate cases of possible neglect and abuse of children. A referral to Child Protective Services (CPS; name can vary by state) is mandated for all educators if there is a suspicion of abuse or neglect. The school official or staff does not have a choice as to referral if such a suspicion is present. Referrals to this service may result from physical, sexual, or emotional abuse and/or educational, environmental, or medical neglect.

Screening

If the CST feels the prereferral strategies are not working after a realistic period of time, team members may recommend a screening for a suspected disability. The source of this suspicion may emanate from the team, a staff member, or the parent. Keep in mind that the team does not have to diagnose a specific disability, but only suspect one in order to begin the referral for a more comprehensive assessment to a multidisciplinary team. This team will administer a comprehensive evaluation conducted by a multitude of professionals to decrease the possibility of subjective and discriminatory assessment.

Screening measures may include a variety of tests and procedures that can be sensitive enough to allow team members the opportunity to determine the presence of a suspected disability. Other than the very obvious cases involving attempted suicide, neglect, abuse and so on, which must be dealt with immediately, a child with a suspected disability is defined as a child who exhibits one or more of the following symptoms for more than six months:

- Serious inconsistencies in intellectual, emotional, academic, or social performance
- Inconsistency between ability and achievement and/or ability and classroom performance
- Impairment in one or more life functions, that is, socialization, academic performance, or adaptive behaviour

In order to accomplish this screening, team members utilize

- Abbreviated intelligence tests

- Selected subtests or screening versions of individual achievement tests
- Informal reading inventories
- Checklists
- Observation scales
- Rating scales
- Prereferral data already discussed

If the screening determines the possibility of a suspected disability, then the CST must make a more formal referral to the district's multidisciplinary team for a comprehensive assessment.

Person Centred Approach an Approach to Encounter Psychological Thrust of Children with Special Needs

Person Centred Approaches began with a search for better ways to include people with disabilities in the society. Person Centred Approaches are:

- focused on the individual and the people who love them
- person led, not service led
- rooted in respect for the individual and a belief that they belong in a community of their chosing
- a way of encouraging people around the individual to learn together
- a way of developing a shared vision of the future with the individual

Person-centred planning is changing how people view the futures of individuals with severe disabilities. This approach, also known as personal futures planning, is a radical change from how services have been planned and delivered to persons with disabilities in the past. In fact, it is being referred to by some as a "paradigm shift"—a completely different way of looking at services for persons with disabilities. So before you say "we are already doing that," you may need to learn more about how this approach is empowering people to move beyond the traditional service system to follow a more personal and more powerful path.

Person-centred planning goes well beyond the traditional individualized planning processes that occur in the development of individualized educational programmes (IEP), transition plans for youth who are leaving school, and rehabilitation plans for adults.

These approaches have focused on the services that "the system" can offer an individual and the family. The systems approach has unsuccessfully tried to create "slots" or placements in schools, social services, and rehabilitation agencies to serve the needs of persons with disabilities. However, the system has always been hampered by the absence of enough money to meet all of the diverse needs, and individuals have been forced to accept and be grateful for what was available, even if it did not fit their personal situation and aspirations. In addition, research on the traditional planning process casts doubt on the degree to which parents become full partners with professionals in making plans for their children's futures.

The person-centred approach relies much less on the service system by organizing truly individualized, natural, and creative supports to achieve meaningful goals based on the individual's strengths and preferences. No longer is planning based on "the services available at the present time" which has been the age-old excuse that has restricted our thinking, planning, and actions. The person-centred approach creates a team of people who know and care about the individual with a disability, who come together to develop and share a dream for the person's future, and who work together to organize and provide the supports necessary to make that dream a reality.

5

Inclusive Education in the Indian Perspective

The purpose of education is to ensure that all students gain access to knowledge, skills, and information that will prepare them to contribute to America's communities and workplaces. The central purpose becomes more challenging as schools accommodate students with increasingly diverse backgrounds and abilities. As we strive to meet these challenges, the involvement and cooperation of educators, parents, and community leaders is vital for the creation of better and more inclusive schools.

Inclusion is an educational approach and philosophy that provides all students with community membership and greater opportunities for academic and social achievement. Inclusion is about making sure that each and every student feels welcome and that their unique needs and learning styles are attended to and valued.

Inclusive schools put the values upon which America was founded (pluralism, tolerance, and equality) into action; they ask teachers to provide appropriate individualized supports and services to all students without the stigmatization that comes with separation. *Research shows that most students learn and perform better when exposed to the richness of the general education curriculum, as long as the appropriate strategies and accommodations are in place.*

At no time does inclusion require the classroom curriculum, or the academic expectations, to be watered down. On the contrary, inclusion enhances learning for students, both with and without special needs. Students learn, and use their learning differently; the goal is to provide *all* students with the instruction they need to succeed as learners and achieve high standards, alongside their friends and neighbours.

India is committed to fulfilling the goal of education for all and 'inclusive education' is now a feature of various government documents and plans. However, between 35 and 80 million of India's 200 million school age children do not attend school. In addition, fewer than five percent of children who have a disability are in school. Research based in the UK's University of Cambridge analyses how 'inclusive education' is understood in India and what influences decisions to include or exclude children.

Inclusive education in India is seen by many as a matter of providing education for children with disabilities. Many more children are excluded on grounds of gender, regional or caste differences but these are not considered. While it is recognised that these children need to be included efforts to do so are not well co-ordinated. Programmes for pre-school children, child workers, children from particular castes and tribes and those with special educational needs are all run by different government ministries.

The research was carried out in a sample of schools in Delhi recognised as having made progress towards becoming more inclusive. Although all but one of the schools in the sample are private and fee paying this does not mean that that private schools are for the elite: in Delhi and elsewhere in India there has been an enormous growth in private education due to the perceived failures of state education. Many of these private schools receive grants from the state.

Through interviews with teachers and head teachers and observation of lessons, the authors found that:

- Schools believe they deserve the label 'inclusive' as they include students who otherwise would be denied admission to the mainstream and are developing a range of responses to meet their special needs.
- Whilst head teachers are familiar with the term 'inclusive education' – and have picked up this term at conferences – most teachers are unfamiliar with the concept.
- Interviewees regard efforts towards inclusive education as being shaped by Western influences, rather than being based on Indian reality.
- Changes have been driven by government and parental pressure: teachers have hardly been involved and the voice of the child has been completely neglected.

- Decisions to include children were governed by issues such as the degree and nature of disability, perceived 'IQ', and behaviour of the child.
- Teachers received little or no formal training to help them meet the needs of children with different abilities and have made only small changes to their teaching methods: they primarily depend on informal and outside support from home tutors and parents.

Most practitioners seem resigned to the continuation of a system that excludes many and regards children's personal inabilities and characteristics of mainstream education as the reasons why they cannot be included.

Arguing that Education for All will only be achieved through inclusion, the authors call for:

- the development of a shared understanding in Indian schools of what inclusive education means that is communicated effectively amongst schools with a view to forming common goals
- more teachers to be involved in decision-making processes within schools
- teacher training courses to address increased diversity in the classroom.

Providing access to education is only the first stage in overcoming exclusion from education. There needs to be a shift in perspectives and values so that diversity is appreciated and teachers are given skills to overcome the cycle of failure and frustration which inevitably results from limited teaching practices.

Challenges for Vocational Education and Sustainable Rehabilitation of Persons with Disabilities

Disability has gained recognition as a development issue at international level. The United Nations Convention on the Rights of Persons with Disabilities (UNCRPD) (UN, 2006) provides vast opportunities to increase awareness of disability around the world. The convention was based on the social model of disability, which focuses uponequal access; social opportunities; health; education; employment; political, economic and social development; and elimination of legal and social barriers.

In spite of the emphasis on the right-based approach to disability, about 82% of disabled people worldwide live below the poverty line.

An estimated 65-80% of 60 million disabled people in rural areas of India do not have access to basic minimum facilities. 'Disability' still remains overwhelmingly marginalised at mainstream developmental research, institutional, policy and programme levels. Social and economic discrimination, architectural, transportation, institutional and policy barriers continue to prevent disabled people from accessing any opportunities.

In the contemporary world economic factors determine a person's quality of life, dignity and value. The World Health Organisation (WHO) suggests that secured access to livelihoods can reduce poverty among disabled people.

'Livelihoods' not only refers to the ability to earn but also the opportunity to develop one's full potential with control over factors that shapes his/her life and contribute to society's development.

Sustainable rural livelihoods approach emphasizes access to resources; market and economic services; removal of barrier to participation; reform in basic services and improvement in rural infrastructure to improve the livelihoods of all, including disabled people.

However, the situation regarding employment and livelihoods for disabled people depicts a poor picture. The statistics suggest that unemployment for working age disabled people in developing and industrialised countries is between 80-90% and 50-70% respectively. Further more, unemployment among disabled women is almost 100% in developing countries.

As per the Government of India's Planning Commission poverty estimate for 2009-2010, Odisha is one of the poorest states in the country. Therefore, the conditions of disabled people in Odisha may be worse.

The Census of India (2001) finds the highest disability rate (3.8%) in Puri district in Odisha and their employment rate is 26% in urban, and 25.1% in rural, areas. However, a recent study in Odisha suggests that 77.8% of disabled people survive as dependants and among the rest, 45% are self-employed and 29% are daily labourers. The experience in Puri suggests that most disabled people in rural areas lack access to livelihoods.

Training Persons With Disabilities

Before entering into a new venture, even if it is to be a small-scale enterprise, a person needs to have sufficient knowledge of the work involved in order to make the business successful. In several cases, training is needed in order to learn more about the technical aspects and procedures that will ensure success. This training is often not readily available to persons with disabilities. Several vocational training centres will not accept a person with a disability because they assume that such a person will "slow down" the learning process of other participants. Financing the necessary training is therefore another issue that cannot be ignored. How much does it cost? Who will finance it?

Governments and non-governmental organizations around the world are developing special programmes for persons with disabilities. Because such persons did not always have the opportunity to go to school, or could study for only a few years, many disabled persons can barely read or write, or are totally illiterate. Training programmes must be especially developed to take this into account and use hands-on training techniques to teach new skills to persons with disabilities.

Creating the Opportunity for Disabled Persons to Become Self-reliant

Trainers must realize their responsibility towards trainees with disabilities because they will play a major role in the future of the trainees; their work will offer disabled persons a chance for a better life with self-reliance, food security and an improved quality of life.

The main objective is to enable rural persons with disabilities to become economically self-reliant through income generation as small-scale entrepreneurs. The trainer must keep this in mind at all times during the training. All trainees participate in the training by choice and because they believe that the training course will give them the tools necessary for improving their livelihood. It is the responsibility of the trainer to convince trainees that they can do anything and everything they set their minds to.

Considerations for Training of Rural Disabled Persons

Training must take into consideration the activities of trainees within their community. In Asia, rice sowing and harvesting are the busiest times of the year for farmers and, therefore, it is very difficult to organize training during these periods.

Trainees may also have received different levels of education and, therefore, they must be encouraged to work as a team, helping one another. Both trainees and trainers must learn to work together towards a common goal, which is to succeed in starting a small-scale enterprise. If the trainees help each other, they can all learn from one another and will feel happier during the training.

Trainees must be well prepared for training in farming and rural activities. They must understand that it is not possible to close the enterprise during the weekend. Rural poor people often work seven days a week since some activities cannot be stopped. For example, animals need to be fed and crops need to be watered every day of the week. Trainers must arrange their schedule according to rural daily realities.

The use of a small-scale entrepreneur's experience can be very helpful and highly encouraging for trainees with disabilities. Trainers should include specialists in enterprise development, disability matters, and agriculture and rural affairs. The training can be provided either by one person with all these specializations or by a strategically selected training team.

Trainers may work on a rotating schedule. Communication between trainers, trainees, consultants and all parties involved is necessary for an effective outcome.

Motivation and Capacity-building

Trainers will have to prepare trainees for basic learning and for unexpected events that will certainly occur during and following the training.

Four Main Learning Steps

The objectives and priorities in training rural people with disabilities for enterprise development are:

1. To improve daily living skills
2. To impart technical capabilities and capacities
3. To develop entrepreneurial skills
4. To establish a network and strategic partnerships

***To Improve Daily Living Skills*:** Trainers should focus on the daily realities of the trainees' community life by direct discussion with the trainees and offering appropriate advice:

- Accept who you are and learn to love yourself as you are
- Think positively, and be convinced that you CAN DO
- Be an active member of your family and community
- Be responsible for your life by ensuring food security and quality, and practice good eating habits for yourself and your family

- Be aware of your needs
- Participate in your family and community activities as an equal member
- Confront and surmount problems through open-minded interactions among themselves and in addition, through personal prayers, meditation, reflection and physical exercises.

Trainees must be made aware of their personal limitations and potentials; they must never allow other people to determine what they can and cannot do. Training sessions should create the atmosphere of a large family reunion in order to encourage exchange, sharing, discussion, compassion and emotional strengthening. Trainees must learn to listen to the experiences of others in order to learn how to overcome some of the problems and be successful in improving their quality of life.

Finally, enterprise development will offer trainees the chance to become self-reliant once they are convinced that they are capable of doing, even if they do it differently. Surmounting new challenges is never easy but always brings a feeling of achievement and success.

***To Impart Technical Capabilities and Capacities*:** Trainers must concentrate on the skills required for the successful accomplishment of all tasks associated with the chosen small-scale enterprise that is to be established in a rural area. These skills and tasks will vary from one business to another.

For persons with physical disabilities, certain techniques may be needed to replace the "conventional way" of doing things. For example, using the feet or mouth instead of hands has proven very efficient. Certain tools and devices can also be adapted to a person's physical disability.

Because training has to be conducted over a limited period of time, the quality of trainers becomes extremely important. Several programmes developed by government and non-governmental organizations use specialized trainers. Nevertheless, trainees prefer trainers who are successful entrepreneurs themselves and can explain from experience the "do's" and "don'ts" of establishing and running a small-scale enterprise.

***To Develop Entrepreneurial Skills*:** All aspects of a sustainable rural enterprise must be reviewed and well understood. For details see Part III.

***To Establish a Network and Strategic Partnerships*:** Regular communication with trainers and all parties involved will provide trainees with timely information about existing training programmes. Trainees should fully exploit opportunities for collaboration with various agencies and organizations. This will also facilitate their acceptance as full members of their community.

The following are examples of organizations and institutions that can be contacted for future collaboration or partnership.

1. Agriculture extension offices
2. Local disability training centres
3. Technical colleges
4. Universities
5. Private companies
6. Local community small enterprises
7. Organizations for persons with disabilities (local, national and international levels)
8. Non-government organizations (local, national and international levels)
9. Central government agencies (e.g. Ministry of Invalids, Ministry of Social Welfare, Ministry of Labour, Ministry of Health)
10. Local government agencies
11. UN agencies such as FAO, ILO, UNDP, UNICEF, UNIDO, WHO.
12. Others

Finally, because of the importance of marketing in any business venture, strategic partners and associations may support trainees in advising on market opportunities and become potential partners and clients.

Selecting Trainees

The selection of trainees should be based on well-defined criteria. Although many persons with disabilities can perform all required tasks, their motivation is crucial for success. Careful selection of the trainees is, therefore, vital for the successful replication of the enterprise and its future sustainability.

Persons with disabilities are capable of accomplishing most of the tasks involved in enterprise development. Nevertheless, certain activities may need to be adapted and strategies developed to compensate for the disability. Moreover, two persons with the same disability do not necessarily have the same capabilities and, consequently, it becomes necessary to understand their abilities while developing the strategy. Every person is different and therefore should be allowed to test his or her capabilities and limitations. Trainees must be allowed to develop their own personal way of accomplishing the tasks required in the enterprise. Trainers must be able to give advice, support and direction.

Trainee Selection Procedure

1. Identification of the candidates: In most countries, the names and addresses of persons with disabilities are registered with a government office responsible for their welfare, such as the Ministry of Invalids, the Ministry of Social Welfare or the Ministry of Health. Provincial or municipal governments may also have information on persons with disabilities. Radio or television announcements can be used to invite candidates for training on enterprise development. Information on training should be provided to disabled persons located in the remotest rural areas.
2. Pre-selection: The disabled person's age and type of disability should be verified. Ideally, the age should be between 20 and 35 years. Nevertheless, it has been demonstrated in some cases that the selection of younger or older candidates was fully justified and highly rewarding for both trainees and trainers with the success of the trainee's new enterprise. Persons with multiple disabilities may have difficulties following a training course because of limited mobility and their capability for active participation must be verified. Candidates with basic literacy will also, generally speaking, find the training course more enjoyable and easier to understand; they are also more likely to succeed and, therefore, may be given priority.
3. Diversity of location: Care must be taken to avoid market saturation. A diversity of locations for training in the same type of enterprise is necessary. Moreover, if trainees are selected from different locations, they will have the opportunity to replicate their enterprise and become trainers in their community.
4. Each candidate visited at home: Trainers must meet each candidate at his or her home. This will allow trainers to verify if the candidate has family and community support, as well as the financial and other material resources for establishing the new enterprise.

5. Verification of commitment: Trainers must check the will and commitment of the trainees and their families to attend the training course. This is especially true when the trainee has to leave home to attend the training which may last for several months.
6. Verification of motivation: Trainers must make sure that the candidates are highly motivated to learn about enterprise development and new skills.
7. Verification of availability: Trainers must make sure that the candidate is capable, committed and ready to leave home to learn. In case of a person with multiple disabilities, a family member may have to accompany the trainee.
8. Final selection: Trainers must sit together and evaluate each candidate, decide whether or not a candidate should be selected, and justify their decision. This will ensure impartial and objective selection. Trainers must always keep in mind that the training is not only for enterprise development but should also serve as a re-education of the disabled towards their full integration as active and self-reliant participants in society.

Size of the Training Group

The number of trainees will depend on the number of trainers. A ratio of five to one or six to one has been shown to be successful. With only five or six interns, it is possible for a trainer to better understand the physical, psychological and emotional needs of the trainees. The trainer should always keep in mind that the training programme is not only for enterprise development but also for self-motivation and confidence-building to ensure that the disabled person-turned-entrepreneur can be an active and self-reliant participant in community development.

Gender Issues

Training in enterprise development offers a good opportunity for women with disabilities. Small-scale enterprise development allows both women and men with disabilities to earn a living close to home. A small-scale enterprise can be set up near the house allowing the woman to take care of home and children while generating supplementary income. It can also offer single women, single parents or widows an opportunity to establish a sustainable business that will enable them to become financially self-sufficient. Experience has shown that women can learn just as well as men, the skills needed for successful enterprise development. Attention must be given to the safety and security of women when training in mixed groups.

Issues and Considerations to be Addressed Prior to Training

1. To ensure that trainees do not abandon the course before its completion, it should be ascertained if they have left their home in the past, whether for re-education, training or work. This will show how they cope with living away from home.
2. Trainees who have never left their family should be allowed to train closer to home rather than be sent to a distant training centre.
3. Trainees who have never undergone re-education are often incapable of taking care of themselves. This must always be considered when planning a training programme especially during budget preparation because offering re-education with skills training will take more time. Ideally, the trainees should have undergone re-education. Trainees with multiple disabilities may need continuous assistance.
4. Some trainees may also have been over-protected by their families and not used to accomplishing certain tasks on their own. As a result, it may be quite difficult for them to overcome certain physical challenges and trying to do so may cause serious emotional confusion. Trainees must initially understand that enterprise development may require specific tasks that can be difficult. They must have decided to attend the training because they truly want to learn new skills and not because family members have decided that it would be a good idea for the disabled person to learn new skills.
5. Many persons above 60 years of age have never had the opportunity to learn new skills or to undergo professional re-education or formal education. Learning enterprise development skills may be difficult for them and this is why it is recommended that trainees be between 20 and 35 years of age. Homogeneity within the group is also important. When trainees are both men and women, care must be taken that all women are not very young and men older. Different types of disabilities can also create different problems. For example, the needs of the visually impaired are different from those of the hearing impaired and the physically disabled.
6. Some trainees with multiple disabilities or with specific physical or mental disabilities may be incapable of systematic learning.

For example, mentally-disabled persons may need additional attention. Although they may be capable of accomplishing specific tasks, especially repetitive actions, they may not necessarily be capable of analysis and decision-making. Other members of the group must understand the mental capabilities of their peers and can help during training by giving additional explanations and training.

7. Safety and security must be ensured for women attending mixed training courses. Appropriate facilities must be available for women trainees with disabilities to ensure their safety and privacy.
8. Following up on the trainee's progress after the establishment of his or her enterprise is crucial for its continuation. Like any other new entrepreneur, the disabled person will face problems, expected or not, usually shortly after set-up or during installation. A resource person, ideally the trainer, should be available for follow-up action and troubleshooting. This will protect trainees-turned- entrepreneurs from being overwhelmed with problems, which can often be solved easily. Failure must be avoided to ensure that the new entrepreneur becomes more self-confident and, therefore, self-reliant.

Developmental Disability

Developmental disability is a term used in the United States and Canada to describe lifelong disabilities attributable to mental or physical impairments, manifested prior to age 18. It is not synonymous with "developmental delay" which is often a consequence of a temporary illness or trauma during childhood.

Causes

There are many social, environmental and physical causes of developmental disabilities, although for some a definitive cause may never be determined. Common factors causing developmental disabilities include:

- Traumatic brain injury resulting from accidental causes or physical abuse (blunt force, shaken baby syndrome);
- Infection before, during or after birth;
- Growth or nutrition problems (prenatally, perinatally, or postnatally);
- Abnormalities of chromosomes and genes;

- Birth long before the expected birth date — also called extreme prematurity;
- Poor maternal diet and absent or minimal health care;
- Drug abuse during pregnancy, including alcohol intake and smoking;
- Drug-related prenatal developmental insult from prescription or over-the-counter drugs;
- Environmental toxins;
- Severe physical maltreatment (child abuse), which may have caused brain injury and which can adversely affect a child's learning abilities and socio-emotional development

Developmental disabilities affect between 1 and 2% of the population in most western countries, although many government sources acknowledge that statistics are flawed in this area. The worldwide proportion of people with developmental disabilities is believed to be approximately 1.4%. It is twice as common in males as in females, and some researchers have found that the prevalence of mild developmental disabilities is likely to be higher in areas of poverty and deprivation, and among people of certain ethnicities.

Associated Issues

Physical Health Issues: There are many physical health factors associated with developmental disabilities. For some specific syndromes and diagnoses, these are inherent (such as poor heart function in people with Down syndrome); however lack of access to health services and lack of understanding by medical professionals is also a major contributing factor. People with severe communication difficulties find it difficult to articulate their health needs, and without adequate support and education might not recognize ill health. Epilepsy, sensory problems (such as poor vision and hearing), obesity and poor dental health are over-represented in this population. Life expectancy among people with developmental disabilities as a group is estimated at 20 years below average, although this is improving with advancements in adaptive and medical technologies, and as people are leading healthier, more fulfilling lives, and some conditions (such as Freeman-Sheldon syndrome) do not impact life expectancy.

Mental Health Issues (Dual Diagnoses)

Mental health issues, and psychiatric illnesses, are more likely to occur in people with developmental disabilities than in the general population. A number of factors are attributed to the high incidence rate of dual diagnoses:

- The high likelihood of encountering traumatic events throughout their lifetime (such as abandonment by loved ones, abuse, bullying and harassment)
- The social and developmental restrictions placed upon people with developmental disabilities (such as lack of education, poverty, limited employment opportunities, limited opportunities for fulfilling relationships, boredom)
- Biological factors (such as brain injury, epilepsy, illicit and prescribed drug and alcohol misuse)
- Developmental factors (such as lack of understanding of social norms and appropriate behaviour, inability of those around to allow/understand expressions of grief and other human emotions)
- External monitoring factor: all people with developmental disabilities that are in a federal- or state-funded residence require the residence to have some form of behavioural monitoring for each person with developmental disability at the residence. With this information psychological diagnoses are more easily given than with the general population that has less consistent monitoring.
- Access to health care providers: in the United States, all people with developmental disabilities that are in a federal- or state-funded residence require the residence to have annual visits to various health care providers. With consistent visits to health care providers more people with developmental disabilities are likely to receive appropriate treatment than the general population that is not required to visit various health care providers.

These problems are exacerbated by difficulties in diagnosis of mental health issues, and in appropriate treatment and medication, as for physical health issues.

Abuse and Vulnerability

Abuse is a significant issue for people with developmental disabilities, and as a group they are regarded as vulnerable people in most jurisdictions. Common types of abuse include:

- Physical abuse (withholding food, hitting, punching, pushing, etc.)

- Neglect (withholding help when required, e.g., assistance with personal hygiene)
- Sexual abuse
- Psychological or emotional abuse (verbal abuse, shaming and belittling)
- Constraint and restrictive practices (turning off an electric wheelchair so a person cannot move)
- Financial abuse (charging unnecessary fees, holding onto pensions, wages, etc.)
- Legal or civil abuse (restricted access to services)
- Systemic abuse (denied access to an appropriate service due to perceived support needs)
- Passive neglect (a caregiver's failure to provide adequate food, shelter)

Lack of education, lack of self-esteem and self-advocacy skills, lack of understanding of social norms and appropriate behaviour and communication difficulties are strong contributing factors to the high incidence of abuse among this population.

In addition to abuse from people in positions of power, peer abuse is recognized as a significant, if misunderstood, problem. Rates of criminal offense among people with developmental disabilities are also disproportionately high, and it is widely acknowledged that criminal justice systems throughout the world are ill-equipped for the needs of people with developmental disabilities—as both perpetrators and victims of crime.

Challenging Behaviour

Some people with developmental disabilities exhibit challenging behaviour, defined as "culturally abnormal behaviour(s) of such intensity, frequency or duration that the physical safety of the person or others is placed in serious jeopardy, or behaviour which is likely to seriously limit or deny access to the use of ordinary community facilities". Common types of challenging behaviour include self-injurious behaviour (such as hitting, headbutting, biting), aggressive behaviour (such as hitting others, screaming, spitting, kicking, swearing, hairpulling), inappropriate sexualized behaviour (such as public masturbation or groping), behaviour directed at property (such as throwing objects and stealing) and stereotyped behaviours (such as repetitive rocking, echolalia or elective incontinence).

Challenging behaviour in people with developmental disabilities may be caused by a number of factors, including biological (pain, medication, the need for sensory stimulation), social (boredom, seeking social interaction, the need for an element of control, lack of knowledge of community norms, insensitivity of staff and services to the person's wishes and needs), environmental (physical aspects such as noise and lighting, or gaining access to preferred objects or activities), psychological (feeling excluded, lonely, devalued, labelled, disempowered, living up to people's negative expectations) or simply a means of communication. A lot of the time, challenging behaviour is learned and brings rewards and it is very often possible to teach people new behaviours to achieve the same aims. Challenging behaviour in people with developmental disabilities can often associated with specific mental health problems.

Experience and research suggests that what professionals call "challenging behaviour" is often a reaction to the challenging environments that those providing services create around people with developmental disabilities. "Challenging behaviour" in this context is a method of communicating dissatisfaction with the failure of those providing services to focus on what kind of life makes most sense to the person, and is often the only recourse a developmentally disabled person has against unsatisfactory services or treatment and the lack of opportunities made available to the person. This is especially the case where the services deliver lifestyles and ways of working that are centred on what suits the service provider and its staff, rather than what best suits the person.

In general, behavioural interventions or what has been termed applied behaviour analysis has been found to be effective in reducing specific challenging behaviour Recently, efforts have been placed on developing a developmental pathway model in the behaviour analysis literature to prevent challenging behaviour from occurring.

Societal Attitudes

Throughout history, people with developmental disabilities have been viewed as incapable and incompetent in their capacity for decision-making and development. Until the Enlightenment in Europe, care and asylum was provided by families and the church (in monasteries and other religious communities), focusing on the provision of basic physical needs such as food, shelter and clothing. Stereotypes such as the dimwitted yokel, and potentially harmful characterizations (such as demonic possession for people with epilepsy) were prominent in social attitudes of the time. Early in the twentieth century the eugenics movement became popular throughout the world. This led to the forced sterilization and prohibition of marriage in most of the developed world and was later used by Hitler as rationale for the mass murder of mentally challenged individuals during the Holocaust. The eugenics movement was later proven to be seriously flawed and in violation of human rights and the practice of forced sterilization and prohibition from marriage was discontinued by most of the developed world by the mid 20th century.

The movement towards individualism in the 18th and 19th centuries, and the opportunities afforded by the Industrial Revolution, led to housing and care using the asylum model. People were placed by, or removed from, their families (usually in infancy) and housed in large institutions (of up to 3,000 people, although some institutions were home to many more, such as the Philadelphia State Hospital in Pennsylvania which housed 7,000 people through the 1960s), many of which were self-sufficient through the labour of the residents. Some of these institutions provided a very basic level of education (such as differentiation between colours and basic word recognition and numeracy), but most continued to focus solely on the provision of basic needs. Conditions in such institutions varied widely, but the support provided was generally non-individualized, with aberrant behaviour and low levels of economic productivity regarded as a burden to society. Heavy tranquilization and assembly line methods of support (such as "birdfeeding" and cattle herding) were the norm, and the medical model of disability prevailed. Services were provided based on the relative ease to the provider, not based on the human needs of the individual.

Ignoring the prevailing attitude, Civitans adopted service to the developmentally disabled as a major organizational emphasis in 1952. Their earliest efforts included workshops for special education teachers and daycamps for disabled children, all at a time when such training and programmes were almost nonexistent. In the United States, the segregation of people with developmental disabilities wasn't widely questioned by academics or policy-makers until the 1969 publication of Wolf Wolfensberger's seminal work "The Origin and Nature of Our Institutional Models", drawing on some of the ideas proposed by SG Howe 100 years earlier. This book posited that society characterizes people with disabilities as deviant, sub-human and burdens of charity, resulting in the adoption of that "deviant" role. Wolfensberger argued that this dehumanization, and the segregated institutions that result from it, ignored the potential productive contributions that all people can make to society. He pushed for a shift in policy and practice that recognized the human needs of "retardates" and provided the same basic human rights as for the rest of the population.

The publication of this book may be regarded as the first move towards the widespread adoption of the social model of disability in regard to these types of disabilities, and was the impetus for the development of government strategies for desegregation. Successful lawsuits against governments and an increasing awareness of human rights and self-advocacy also contributed to this process, resulting in the passing in the U.S. of the Civil Rights of Institutionalized Persons Act in 1980.

From the 1960s to the present, most U.S. states have moved towards the elimination of segregated institutions. Along with the work of Wolfensberger and others including Gunnar and Rosemary Dybwad, a number of scandalous revelations around the horrific conditions within state institutions created public outrage that led to change to a more community-based method of providing services. By the mid-1970s, most governments had committed to de-institutionalization, and had started preparing for the wholesale movement of people into the general community, in line with the principles of normalization. In most countries, this was essentially complete by the late 1990s, although the debate over whether or not to close institutions persists in some states, including Massachusetts.

Individuals with developmental disabilities are not fully integrated into society. Person Centred Planning and Person Centred Approaches are seen as methods of addressing the continued labelling and exclusion of socially devalued people, such as people with a developmental disability label, encouraging a focus on the person as someone with capacities and gifts, as well as support needs.

Services and Support

Today, support services are provided by government agencies (such as MRDD), non-governmental organizations and by private sector providers. Support services address most aspects of life for people with developmental disabilities, and are usually theoretically based in community inclusion, using concepts such as social role valorization and increased self-determination (using models such as Person Centred Planning). Support services are funded through government block funding (paid directly to service providers by the government), through individualized funding packages (paid directly to the individual by the government, specifically for the purchase of services) or privately by the individual (although they may receive certain subsidies or discounts, paid by the government). There also are a number of non-profit agencies dedicated to enriching the lives of people living with developmental disabilities and erasing the barriers they have to being included in their community.

Education and Training

Education and training opportunities for people with developmental disabilities have expanded greatly in recent times, with many governments mandating universal access to educational facilities, and more students moving out of special schools and into mainstream classrooms with support.

Post-secondary education and vocational training is also increasing for people with these types of disabilities, although many programmes offer only segregated "access" courses in areas such as literacy, numeracy and other basic skills. Legislation (such as the UK's Disability Discrimination Act 1995) requires educational institutions and training providers to make "reasonable adjustments" to curriculum and teaching methods in order to accommodate the learning needs of students with disabilities, wherever possible. There are also some vocational training centres that cater specifically to people with disabilities, providing the skills necessary to work in integrated settings, one of the largest being Dale Rogers Training Centre in Oklahoma City.

At-home and Community Support

Many people with developmental disabilities live in the general community, either with family members, in supervised-group homes or in their own homes (that they rent or own, living alone or with flatmates). At-home and community supports range from one-to-one assistance from a support worker with identified aspects of daily living (such as budgeting, shopping or paying bills) to full 24-hour support (including assistance with household tasks, such as cooking and cleaning, and personal care such as showering, dressing and the administration of medication). The need for full 24-hour support is usually associated with difficulties recognizing safety issues (such as responding to a fire or using a telephone) or for people with potentially dangerous medical conditions (such as asthma or diabetes) who are unable to manage their conditions without assistance.

In the United States a support worker is known as a Direct Support Professional (DSP). The DSP works in assisting the individual with their ADLs and also acts as an advocate for the individual with a developmental disability, in communicating their needs, self-expression and goals.

Supports of this type also include assistance to identify and undertake new hobbies or to access community services (such as education), learning appropriate behaviour or recognition of community norms, or with relationships and expanding circles of friends. Most programmes offering at-home and community support are designed with the goal of increasing the individual's independence, although it is recognized that people with more severe disabilities may never be able to achieve full independence in some areas of daily life.

Residential Accommodation

Some people with developmental disabilities live in residential accommodation (also known as group homes) with other people with similar assessed needs. These homes are usually staffed around the clock, and usually house between 3 and 15 residents. The prevalence of this type of support is gradually decreasing, however, as residential accommodation is replaced by at-home and community support, which can offer increased choice and self-determination for individuals. Some U.S. states still provide institutional care, such as the Texas State Schools. The type of residential accommodation is usually determined by the level of developmental disability and mental health needs.

Employment Support

Employment support usually consists of two types of support:

- Support to access or participate in integrated employment, in a workplace in the general community. This may include specific programmes to increase the skills needed for successful employment (work preparation), one-to-one or small group support for on-the-job training, or one-to-one or small group support after a transition period (such as advocacy when dealing with an employer or a bullying colleague, or assistance to complete an application for a promotion).
- The provision of specific employment opportunities within segregated business services. Although these are designed as "transitional" services (teaching work skills needed to move into integrated employment), many people remain in such services for the duration of their working life. The types of work performed in business services include mailing and packaging services, cleaning, gardening and landscaping, timberwork, metal fabrication, farming and sewing.

Workers with developmental disabilities have historically been paid less for their labour than those in the general workforce, although this is gradually changing with government initiatives, the enforcement of anti-discrimination legislation and changes in perceptions of capability in the general community.

In the United States, a variety of initiatives have been launched in the past decade to reduce unemployment among workers with disabilities—estimated by researchers at over 60%. Most of these initiatives are directed at employment in mainstream businesses. They include heightened placement efforts by the community agencies serving people with developmental disabilities, as well as by government agencies.

Additionally, state-level initiatives are being put launched to increase employment among workers with disabilities. In California, the state senate in 2009 created the Senate Select Committee on Autism and Related Disorders. The Committee has been examining additions to existing community employment services, and also new employment approaches. Committee member Dr. Lou Vismara, chairman of the MIND Institute at University of California, Davis, is pursuing the development of a planned community for persons with autism and related disorders in the Sacramento region. Another committee member, Michael Bernick, the former director of the state labour department, has established a programme at the California state university system, starting at California State University East Bay, to support students with autism on the college level. Other Committee efforts include mutual support employment efforts, such as disability job networks, job boards, and identifying business lines that build on the strengths of persons with disabilities.

Day Services

Non-vocational day services are usually known as day centres, and are traditionally segregated services offering training in life skills (such as meal preparation and basic literacy), centre-based activities (such as crafts, games and music classes) and external activities (such as day trips). Some more progressive day centres also support people to access vocational training opportunities (such as college courses), and offer individualized outreach services (planning and undertaking activities with the individual, with support offered one-to-one or in small groups).

Traditional day centres were based on the principles of occupational therapy, and were created as respite for family members caring for their loved ones with disabilities. This is slowly changing, however, as programmes offered become more skills-based and focused on increasing independence.

Advocacy

Advocacy is a burgeoning support field for people with developmental disabilities. Advocacy groups now exist in most jurisdictions, working collaboratively with people with disabilities for systemic change (such as changes in policy and legislation) and for changes for individuals (such as claiming welfare benefits or when responding to abuse). Most advocacy groups also work to support people, throughout the world, to increase their capacity for self-advocacy, teaching the skills necessary for people to advocate for their own needs.

Other Types of Support

Other types of support for people with developmental disabilities may include:

- therapeutic services, such as speech therapy, occupational therapy, physical therapy, massage, aromatherapy, art, dance/ movement or music therapy
- supported holidays
- short-stay respite services (for people who live with family members or other unpaid carers)
- transport services, such as dial-a-ride or free bus passes
- specialist behaviour support services, such as high-security services for people with high-level, high-risk challenging behaviours
- specialist relationships and sex education

Rehabilitation Counselling

Rehabilitation Counselling is focused on helping people who have disabilities achieve their personal, career, and independent living goals through a counselling process. Rehabilitation Counsellors can be found in private practice, in rehabilitation facilities, hospitals, universities, schools, government agencies, insurance companies and other organizations where people are being treated for congenital or acquired disabilities. While most rehabilitation counsellors focus on vocational services, in some states they qualify as both a Certified Rehabilitation Counselor (CRC) and a Licensed Professional Counselor (LPC), enabling them to focus on psychotherapy.

Over time, with the changes in social work being more psychotherapy-oriented, rehabilitation counsellors take on more and more community engagement work, especially as it relates to special populations.

History

United States: Historically, rehabilitation counsellors primarily served working-age adults with disabilities. Today, the need for rehabilitation counselling services extends to persons of all age groups who have disabilities. Rehabilitation counsellors also may provide general and specialized counselling to people with disabilities in public human service programmes and private practice settings.

Initially, rehabilitation professionals were recruited from a variety of human service disciplines, including public health nursing, social work, and school counselling. Although educational programmes began to appear in the 1940s, it was not until the availability of federal funding for rehabilitation counselling programmes in 1954 that the profession began to grow and establish its own identity.

Education/Training

Though no specific undergraduate degree is required, the majority of rehabilitation counselling graduate students have undergraduate degrees in rehabilitation services, psychology, sociology, or other human services-related fields. As a Masters degree is required at a minimum, rehabilitation counsellors are trained at the graduate level, with most earning a Masters degree, and a few continuing on to the Doctoral level. The Council on Rehabilitation Education (CORE) accredits qualifying institutions, though not all programmes meet accreditation requirements, prohibiting some graduates from professional certification/ licensure. Rehabilitation counsellors are trained in the following areas:

- Individual and group counselling
- Medical and psychosocial information
- Problems and community engagement of special populations
- Evaluation and assessment
- Research utilization
- Employment and occupational choice
- Case and caseload management
- Job development and placement

Accredited rehabilitation counselor education programmes typically provide 60 credit hours of academic and field-based clinical training. Clinical training consists of at least a semester of practicum and a minimum of 600 hours of supervised internship experience. Clinical field experiences are available in a variety of community, state, federal, and private rehabilitation-related programmes.

Professional Certification/Licensure

The Commission on Rehabilitation Counselor Certification (CRCC) grants certification to counsellors who meet educational requirements and have passed an examination indicating that they possess the competency and skill to become a Certified Rehabilitation Counselor, (CRC in the United States; CCRC in Canada). A Masters degree is required to obtain certification. Certification as a rehabilitation counselor is not mandated by any state or federal laws, however eligibility to sit for the certification exam is mandated by federal law for those wishing to work for state/federal vocational rehabilitation systems. Some states have Licensed Rehabilitation Counsellors (LRC), which places LRCs at the same level as other licensed social service professionals. In other states the CRC qualifies the rehabilitation counselor to obtain the Licensure as a Professional Counselor (LPC). Certification is highly desirable to many employers.

Social Relevancy

Community service to a culturally and ethnically diverse population, professional functions, critical thinking, advocacy, applied research activities, and ethical standards are integrated throughout rehabilitation counselor preparation and development. Though rehabilitation counsellors are adept at understanding medical issues surrounding the disability (as proven by certification/licensure), they are trained in the social model of disability, which identifies systemic barriers, negative attitudes and exclusion by society (purposely or inadvertently) that mean society is the main contributory factor in disabling people. Rehabilitation Counsellors are often advocates in the community for people with disabilities outside of the workplace, with most doing some form of community engagement. As a good portion of counsellors have disabilities themselves, the counselling process often emphasizes self-advocacy skills. Rehabilitation counsellors can be found in the leadership of many prominent organizations that support human rights and civil rights for people with disabilities such as American Coalition of Citizens with Disabilities, National Black Deaf Advocates, etc.

Rehabilitation Counselling Careers

Careers in the Profession

In the United States, many rehabilitation counsellors work in a variety of arenas. The predominant placement of rehabilitation counsellors are state rehabilitation programmes as Vocational Counsellors, social service agencies as Administrators, and at the collegiate level as Disability Counsellors/Specialists:

State Rehabilitation Programmes

The predominant need for rehabilitation counsellors is within federal/state funded vocational rehabilitation programmes. While the Veterans Benefits Administration has its own vocational rehabilitation programme, the rest of Federal/State Vocational Rehabilitation Programmes are funded and regulated by the Rehabilitation Services Administration (RSA), a division of the U.S Department of Education. Although policies vary from state to state, rehabilitation counsellors who work in the federal/state systems typically must hold a masters degree in rehabilitation counselling, special education or a related field, and are required to be certified or be eligible to sit for the certification examination. People accepting employment in the federal/ state Vocational Rehabilitation programmes do so with the agreement they will meet these qualifications by a specified date to maintain employment.

Social Service Agencies/corporate Sector

Rehabilitation Counsellors can work in the non-profit/corporate sector in various ways. Though the majority start as counsellors, specializing in career counselling, most rehabilitation counsellors that work in the non-profit arena rise to the administration level, either in supervising staff or directing programmes for people with disabilities. Others supervise staff that work in case management programmes that serve people with disabilities. Some rehabilitation counsellors work with Independent Living Centres, doing community engagement, advocacy, outside referrals, and social service provision for people with disabilities. Entrepreneurial rehabilitation counsellors also work as consultants, establishing their own private service agencies. Counsellors in working with corporations focus on community relations or corporate service, serving as liaisons between companies and charities or service programmes.

College Disability Counsellors/specialists

By law all community colleges, colleges and universities are required to make reasonable accommodations for students with disabilities. To satisfy this requirement most collegial settings have a Disability Resources Centre, a Special Needs Coordinator or a similar office. Staff are responsible for coordinating services that *may* include but are not limited to: advocacy/liaison, computer access, counselling (academic, personal, vocational), equipment loan, information/referral services, in-service awareness programmes, notetakers, on campus orientation and mobility training for visually impaired students, priority registration assistance, readers, scribes, shuttle (on-campus), sign language interpreters, test proctoring/testing accommodations, and tutors.

Some adaptive technological accommodations *may* include but are not limited to: Adaptive computer technology (including voice activated and speech output), Assistive listening devices, Films/ videotapes about disabilities, Kurzweil personal reader, Large print software,Print enlargers (CCTV), Raised-line drawing kit, Tactile map of campus, Talking calculators, Tape recorders/APH Talking Book Machine, TDD for hearing impaired, Wheelchair, Wheelchair access maps.

Students who have documentation proving their disability status and the staff are trained to access or have knowledge of the necessary services according the students' unique need. As the college level is different from the primary school system, the same services that a student may have received within a special education programme in high school may not be required at the collegiate level. A wide variety of students with disabilities can be served, some examples are individuals with: learning disabilities, sensorial disabilities (hearing loss, vision loss, etc.), physical disabilities (cerebral palsy, etc.) and psychological disabilities.

The Growth of the Field

Job Outlook

As of 2010 there were 129,800 working in the field. Jobs for rehabilitation counsellors are expected to grow by 28 percent, which is much faster than the average for all occupations.

Professional Development

There are several professional organizations Rehabilitation Counsellors and other rehabilitation professionals belong to, including the American Rehabilitation Counselling Association, National Rehabilitation Counselling Association, and American Rehabilitation Action Network. Though there is no nationwide union or lobbying organization supporting rehabilitation counsellors (such as is the case with social workers, or psychologists), the Commission on Rehabilitation Counselor Certification (CRCC) does a lot of work in organizing rehabilitation counsellors that pursue the professional advancement of the young field.

Evolution of Vocational Education and Training with Special Reference to the Persons with Disabilities

Persons with physical and mental disabilities have been the target of discrimination across cultures for thousands of years. On virtually every continent there are records of isolation, exclusion, and even destruction of persons with disabilities.

Governmental treatment of persons with disabilities, beginning with their placement in institutions and moving slowly into the educational system and the workplace, is a relatively recent pattern.

India is one of the earliest known civilizations, covering an area of 3 287 263 sq km, extending from the snow-covered Himalayan heights to the tropical rainforests of the south. At 60 years of Independence, with the programmes based on the vision of the first Prime Minister to turn India into a technologically and industrially developed country, the country has now achieved multifaceted socio-economic progress. Today, having once been a food insecure country for very long, it has become self-sufficient in agricultural production and is presently the tenth industrialized country in the world and the sixth nation to have explored space.

Historical Perspective in India

Historically, in India, persons with disabilities (PWD) enjoyed co-existence with the general mass, though at different times, the treatment and attitudes were at variance. In other words, they were never excluded from society by confinement to institutions. Rather, they lived with their families. As far as education was concerned, even the Gurukula Ashram promoted the basic educational principles of special education like ascertaining the abilities and needs of each pupil, individualization of teaching targets and methods to match the skills and interests and preparing them to meet the social expectations of their prospective interests.

In intellectual disability, unlike other disabilities, the history of special education has not been very encouraging. The first school for intellectual disability was established in 1940 as per the report of the expert group of the National Planning for the Mentally Handicapped held in New Delhi on 12-17 November 1979. After independence, there has been some growth of special education in our country and it has been seen that during 1960 and 1975, 81 schools were established.

By 1979, the number of special education centres was 150. With the establishment of the National Institute for the Mentally Handicapped, availability of trained personnel and suitable models of service made the growth of special schools for children with intellectual disability very significant.

Intellectual Disabilities - Needs

Persons with disabilities have been there since the time when human beings evolved and started forming their assemblage. Out of all the types of disabilities, an intellectual disability poses greater challenges than the other types do. Persons with intellectual disabilities have a condition of arrested or incomplete development of mind, which is especially characterized by sub-normal intelligence, thus partially or totally restricting the person's ability to perform certain activities in their life. This is owing to impairment in cognitive, emotional or behavioural endowment. One of the key abilities for human beings to lead an independent life is to take decisions independently, which persons with mental retardation are, unfortunately, not endowed with. Therefore they have special needs, which basically include activities for daily living (ADL); instrumental activities of daily living (IADL); reading, writing and arithmetic skills; extra curricular activities, namely sports and games, art and cultural activities; social activities; vocational and employment activities; independent living skills; and community integration; etc. Every activity of persons with mental retardation has a meaning in their life, which they have to acquire through individualized education plan supported by related services. viz. audiology services, counselling services, early identification and assessment of disabilities in children, medical services, occupational therapy, orientation and mobility services, parent counselling and training, physical therapy, psychological services, recreation, rehabilitation, school health services, social work services in schools, speech-language pathology services, and transportation.

The families of persons with mental retardation, particularly the parents and siblings, do also have needs different from others, which cannot be segregated from the needs of children with mental retardation, if our intention is to extend proper rehabilitation services. Some of the important family needs are: information about the condition of the child, management of the child, services available, vocational rehabilitation, marriage of the child, emotional needs, societal acceptance of the child, government benefits and legislation, relief of burden (financial and respite), etc. The needs of the families having a child with mental retardation are very complex and call for developing support programmes for these families.

Indian Constitution and Legislation & Government Initiatives

India, being a signatory to the United Nations (UN) instruments, has undertaken the rehabilitation programmes on a massive scale. While recognizing the need to fulfil commitments as per the UN declarations and mandates, India being aware of its obligation under the Constitution of India, has introduced various programmes and schemes for the empowerment of persons with disabilities. Articles 15 and 41 afford protection to the rights of persons with disabilities. Disabled persons have been guaranteed the Fundamental Rights as available to other citizens of the country. These include equality of opportunity; non-discrimination; non-untouchability; no traffic in human beings; prohibition of employment of children; religious freedom; right to the language, script or culture; right to franchise; right to property; right to enforce fundamental rights; access to education in any educational institution, and the right to work.

The State has also the obligation to apply the Directive Principles of State Policy of securing a social order in promotion of the welfare of the people. The State Policy has to be directed towards minimizing inequalities, securing the right to an adequate means of livelihood and also ensure that the operation of the legal system promotes justice. Among many other provisions, the State also has the responsibility of promoting with special care the educational and economic interests of the weaker sections of the people including persons with disabilities.

The paradigm shift from the welfare and charity approach to rights based one towards the issues concerning persons with disabilities is encapsulated most effectively through the landmark enactment of the Persons with Disabilities (Equal Opportunities, Protection of Rights and Full Participation) Act, 1995. The Act establishes the responsibility on the appropriate Governments and society to ensure free education for persons with disabilities up to the age of 18 years, preference in employment in the public sector through the reservation of 3% of vacancies against identified posts and accessibility to buildings, roads, transport and other public services. The Act also prohibits discrimination in every sphere on the grounds of disability.

This was followed in 1999 by the enactment of the National Trust for the Welfare of Persons with Autism, Cerebral Palsy, Mental

Retardation and Multiple Disabilities Act. The objective of this enactment is to enable and empower persons with these disabilities to live as independently and as fully as possible within or close to the community to which they belong. It also addresses the needs of those persons who do not have family support and provides for their care and protection.

Education of Persons with Intellectual Disabilities –Some Experiences

It has been realized that education of persons with disabilities is very crucial for their development and living as independently as possible. Hence, it has also undergone great metamorphosis aiming at empowerment for independent living. Charity has given way to right as far as the education of persons with disabilities is concerned. Education has become a fundamental right of every child.

Equal opportunity is the bedrock of the growth of special education, which advocates not only access to education but also meaningful, appropriate and quality education adding value to the development of persons with disabilities. Special settings for the education of these children made them secluded from society and they were looked upon as a separate part of society. Concern regarding this arose in the pertinent welfare departments. Other government departments and the general population were not at all concerned about the education of these special children.

Evolving strategies to enlist the support of the Department of Human Resources Development and other developmental agencies has become a continual process for inclusion in India. Mainstreaming is one such concept for the practice of selectively placing students with disabilities in one or more 'regular' education classes. This approach presupposed that the student must fit in the school environment designed for regular children; thereby the equal opportunity principle has received a great blow of defeating the purpose. Then there came the concept of inclusion that expresses commitment to educate each child, to the maximum extent appropriate, in the school and classroom the student would otherwise attend. It involves bringing the support services to the child, rather than moving the child to the services, and requires only that the child benefit from being in the class, rather than having to keep up with the other students. This has further led to the concept of full inclusion in which all students, regardless of the handicapping condition or severity, will be in a regular class room full time. All services must be taken to the child in that setting.

These concepts have transformed from various philosophical frameworks, which cannot escape the practicality of limitations and constraints involved in implementation. Each of the systems of special education is interdependent, in which the severity of the disability plays a key role. For example, a special setting is surely needed if the condition of the child is severe or profound, which is most restrictive. As the disability condition moves towards mild in the continuum, the child's ability improves and he or she can come out of the restrictive environment and into open system. However, there are some factors that are irrespective of the condition of the disability, efforts of rehabilitation professionals, and Government support. One of these factors, which is very crucial for a successful inclusive education of children with disabilities, is a positive, favourable attitude of the community and teachers in the general stream, making available appropriate skills for a proper teaching process and making the school environment disabled friendly. Teacher readiness, school readiness, and community acceptance are the core aspects of educating children with disabilities. Continual consultations with and involvement of parents and family members is an integral part of the special education process.

Current Scenario

The Government of India, has implemented the rehabilitation programmes on a massive scale. In a systematic way, the work started in the early 1980's has been instrumental in building capacities in terms of trained teachers, development of teaching and learning materials, models of context specific educational and therapeutic services, promotion of Non-Government organizations (NGOs), extensive coverage of persons with disabilities under the scheme of providing aids and appliances, and use of technology for improvement in education. The programmes to sensitise the community, government machineries, and other developmental agencies are very significant in the acceptance of and providing support to persons with disabilities. Convergence of various governmental schemes for the empowerment of persons with disabilities is another bold step initiated by the Government. It has also made a purposeful endeavour to include disability rehabilitation as an area of critical social development responsibility and accountability of the national planning process from the 8th Five Year Plan onwards. During the 10th Five Year Plan, the outlay will be 14541 million Rupees, and the process of the 11th Five Year Plan to commence from 2007 will focus on the early intervention, education, employment, aiming at a barrier free and inclusive society.

Education of children with disabilities was not lost from the sight of various commissions of Government of India. The Kothari Commission (1964-1966) observes that the coveted goal of Universalisation of Elementary Education (UEE) depends upon the extent of success in bringing special groups of children within the educational network. However, not much was attempted to increase the coverage of children with disabilities in the educational network, who constituted just 0.07% of the total children at the elementary stage. This has increased to 1% with the review of National Policy on Education (1992). An integration approach was largely adopted. Children with locomotive disabilities, low vision and blindness are enrolled in regular schools in larger numbers when compared to those with intellectual disability and hearing impairment. This is owing to the fact that children with intellectual disability require significant adaptation in the curriculum and children with hearing impairment require teachers trained specifically in effective communication with these children. Teacher preparation in special education is very essential. Integration is to support the children in the content and process of teaching besides physical adjustments and rearrangements. Education through the integration mode has been imparted to a large number of children with disabilities by both governmental and non-governmental agencies in the country.

Integrated Education for Disabled Children (IEDC) was introduced in 1974 initially by the Ministry of Welfare and later on handed over to the Ministry of Human Resource Development, Department of Education, which is being implemented in over 20000 schools in India covering over 120000 children with disabilities. IEDC has contributed significantly in incorporating the special needs inputs in the teacher education curriculum for primary and secondary teachers prepared by District Institutes of Education and Training. It has also contributed in large scale production of print and non-print material. During the 1987-1994 period UNICEF assisted Project Integrated Education for the Disabled (PIED) under NCERT (National Council of Educational Research & Training) was taken up to provide education for all children with disabilities and to allow them and their families, neighbours and non-disabled children to interact in normal settings. It aimed to develop competencies in children with disabilities so as to provide a natural basis for adult life experiences in such a manner that they can perceive themselves as contributing members to socio-economic development of the society. Subsequently, the District Primary Education Programme was launched in 1994, in which 18000 regular teachers were trained to impart special education inputs to children with special needs. Janashala is another programme, which is a community school aiming to support ongoing efforts of the Government of India towards UEE with special focus on the problems of girls and underprivileged children.

In 1994, the Government of India launched the District Primary Education Programme (DPEP), a centrally sponsored scheme funded by the World Bank and other foreign agencies, which emphasized UEE through developmental management, a participatory process, and capacity building at all levels. DPEP covered IEDC as its component and adopted an area approach, in 18 states. Since UEE has not been achieved fully, the Government of India launched Sarva Shiksha Abhiyan (SSA - Education for All), which also made special provision for serving children with disabilities. It has set a target to provide useful and quality elementary education to all children in the 6-14 year age group by 2010, which promotes decentralized planning with full involvement of Panchayat Raj Institutions (PRIs). The programmes of SSA are as follows:

- Early detection and identification
- Functional and formal assessment
- Educational placement
- Provision of aids and appliances
- Support services
- Teacher training
- Resource support
- Individualised education plan
- Parental training and community mobilisation
- Planning and management
- Strengthening of special schools
- Removal of architectural barriers

According to the Census of India, out of 21.9 million persons with disabilities 10.8 million persons are literate, constituting 49 per cent. The rate of literacy by residence is 44.4% for rural and 63.9% for urban population with disabilities.

Employment of People with Disabilities

Throughout the world, paid work is a crucial aspect of culture and identity, with many individuals organizing their lives around employment. Employment helps define an individual's place in the community. The unemployed are often excluded from important activities and roles within the social group (Obermann 1980). Until recently, the expectation for people with disabilities was they usually would not work. For example, in the United States, prior to the passage of the Rehabilitation Act of 1973, employment policies rarely aimed to place people with disabilities in competitive employment positions (Blanck 2001). Benefits programmes for people with disabilities largely remain tied to income—only persons below a certain threshold income receive assistance (Blanck et al. 2009; Wehman et al.1997).

With the passage of the Individuals with Disabilities Education Act (1975) and the Americans with Disabilities Act (ADA) of 1990 (as amended in 2008), employment discrimination has been reduced and employment opportunities for people with disabilities have improved in the United States (Blanck 2008). This trend is not exclusive to the United States. However, employment outcomes for people with disabilities continue to lag substantially behind those of people without disabilities in the United States and worldwide (Blanck et al. 2007; International Disability Rights Monitor 2004). Since its adoption by the United Nations (UN) General Assembly in 2006, the UN Convention on the Rights of Persons with Disabilities has been signed by 114 nations with the promise, in part, of greater employment opportunities for all persons with disabilities. The Convention entered into force May 3, 2008 (Reina, Adya and Blanck 2007; United Nations 2006; United Nations).

Employment Rates

While reliable data on the employment of people with disabilities worldwide is difficult to come by, available data indicate people with disabilities have poorer employment outcomes than people without disabilities (International Disability Rights Monitor 2004). At least 650 million people have disabilities worldwide, with approximately 15-20% of each country's population affected by disability (Employers' Forum). In developing countries, 80-90% of people with disabilities of working age are unemployed (Zarocostas 2005). In industrialized countries, the situation is slightly better. However, individuals of working age with disabilities are still unemployed at a rate between 50% and 70%, at least twice the rate of those without disabilities (International Disability Rights Monitor 2004).

Regionally, the general trend is the same. In Asia, there are 370 million people with disabilities, 238 million of whom are of working age. Of those, the unemployment rate is typically twice that of the rest of the population and often as high as 80% (Perry 2002). In the European Union, 43% to 54% of individuals with disabilities are of working age and their unemployment rate is two to three times greater than for people without disabilities (International Disability Rights Monitor 2004). In Latin America and the Caribbean, approximately 80-90% of individuals with disabilities are unemployed, and those that are employed receive comparatively low wages.

Models of Disability

The employment outcomes mentioned above are greatly influenced by conceptual models of disability adopted by service providers. These models are tools for defining impairment and are important because they play a significant role in determining the strategies that government and society devise to help meet the needs of people with disabilities (Shapiro 1994). Numerous models of disability exist; however, the three most prominent are the medical model, the social model and the biopsychosocial model.

The medical model has been the dominant model in the formulation of disability policy for more than a century (Blanck 2001; Myhill and Blanck 2009). The primary tenet of the medical model is that disability results from the physical or mental limitations of the individual and is largely unrelated to the physical and social environment in which people live. As a result, the medical model focuses almost solely on the individual's impairment when forming disability policy and developing treatments and services for those living with a disability (Shapiro 1994). This model regards disability as a health or rehabilitation issue; therefore, the first step is to heal or find a cure for the disability. If this is unsuccessful, the model aims to provide the care and services to support the individual with a disability.

Because of the medical model's emphasis on care, people with disabilities may be excused from the normal obligations of society, such as work, and institutionalization and segregation are ultimately given justification. This has negative consequences for employment outcomes because it limits opportunities for people with disabilities to make choices, become economically self-sufficient, and reach their full vocational potential. Furthermore, this reinforces existing prejudices among employers about the inability of people with disabilities to do a job as well as individuals without disabilities (Shapiro 1994). In countries that employ primarily a medical model of disability, people with disabilities are rarely employed, and when they are employed, it is typically in segregated settings (Lunt and Thornton 1994).

The second major model of disability, and one that has become increasingly recognized and prominent in recent years, is the Social Model. The social model considers disability a consequence of environmental, social and attitudinal barriers that prevent people with disabilities from maximum participation in society. It implies that if attitudinal, physical, and institutional barriers are removed, many people with be viewed as having different abilities and greater opportunity to participate in society, rather than having disabilities and the inability to participate. The social model differs from the medical model because it places the focus on society, rather than on the individual. Furthermore, it focuses on the unique abilities and needs of each individual, while the medical model treats each individual that falls under the same disability classification in the same manner (Shapiro 1994).

The Social Model has had positive consequences for employment outcomes in the United States, Canada and Australia, among other countries, with many individuals with disabilities obtaining customized and competitive employment in the community. This focus helps change negative attitudes employers may have towards people with disabilities (Shapiro 1994). In contrast, the medical model of disability perpetuates sheltered or segregated employment opportunities, which are not part of the open labour market (Parent 2004; Shapiro 1994). This has important implications for people with disabilities and policy makers.

A third model, the biopsychosocial model adopted by the World Health Organization (WHO), is a framework that integrates the medical and social models of disability (Jette 2006; Wright 2004). The WHO (2001) determined that neither the medical model nor the social model of disability, by itself, was sufficient to fully understand or frame disability, although each had clear strengths. In the biopsychosocial model, disability is perceived to stem from the interactions between biological, psychological and social factors. Previously, the International Classification of Impairments, Disabilities, and Handicaps, formulated by the WHO, differentiated between impairments, disabilities, and handicaps (WHO 1980). Recently, it was revised and renamed the International Classification of Functioning, Disability and Health (or "ICF") (WHO 2001). The ICF uses a biopsychosocial approach to disability and acknowledges socio-environmental factors, sociodemographic factors, and behavioural factors that dictate the subjective experience of living with a disability.

The biopsychosocial model is evolving and will benefit from the continued development of both the medical and social models in their pure forms (Wright 2004). Because the biopsychosocial model is new, its impact on employment opportunities for people with disabilities is unclear. However, since it focuses on social and environmental factors, it is reasonable to assume that, like the social model, it would have a positive impact on employment opportunities for people with disabilities.

Employment Models for People with Disabilities

There are several primary models of promoting employment for people with disabilities implemented throughout the world. These include sheltered, supported, and customized employment. A useful distinction among employment models are those where people with disabilities work in a segregated environment of only workers with disabilities compared with an integrated environment of workers largely without disabilities (Kregel and Dean 2002). Notably, Article 27 of the UN Convention on the Rights of Persons with Disabilities emphasizes "the right ... to gain a living by work freely chosen or accepted in a labour market and work environment that is open, inclusive and accessible to persons with disabilities."

Another distinction is between models that pay and do not pay competitive wages (Kregel and Dean 2002). In sheltered employment, people with disabilities work together in a segregated setting and are trained and supervised by people without disabilities (Kregel and Dean 2002). The sheltered employment model assumes people with disabilities are less productive than workers without disabilities, and often pays a wage that is a fraction of wages given other workers (sometimes called a "subminimum wage"). In theory, people with disabilities are supposed to advance their productivity until they move out of segregated employment and into employment that pays a competitive wage.

There are challenges associated with the sheltered employment model. First, earnings received in sheltered settings are low or inconsequential, which often causes individuals to remain dependent on government cash benefit programmes. Second, sheltered employment isolates the person with a disability from the community. As a result, instead of reducing obstacles to employment, segregation lowers expectations and enhances negative public attitudes, making it more difficult for individuals with disabilities to obtain meaningful employment. Third, very few people in sheltered employment progress into competitive employment. Therefore, sheltered employment has been shown to have a limited long term impact on the productivity and community integration of people with disabilities.

In supported employment, an integrated model of employment, workers with disabilities are assisted throughout the employment process. A job coach may assist the individual to find a job, train for the job, and maintain employment through individual supports and accommodations (Parent 2004). Supported employment aims to place people in jobs that earn competitive wages, though in practice this is not always the case. Supported employment is grounded in the philosophical concept of self determination. It is based on core values, which emphasize the right to work, capacity to perform a job, individual strengths, personal goals and choices, and role of community in the person's growth and development (Wehman et al. 2003).

A new model of employment that aims to place individuals with disabilities in jobs earning competitive wages is customized employment. The term was first defined by the Office of Disability Employment Policy (U.S. Department of Labour):

Customized employment means individualizing the employment relationship between employees and employers. ... It is based on an individualized determination of the strengths, needs, and interests of the person with a disability .... It may include employment developed through job carving, self-employment, or entrepreneurial initiatives, or other job development or restructuring strategies ... to fit the needs of individuals with a disability. Customized employment assumes the provision of reasonable accommodations and supports necessary for the individual to perform the functions of a job ... (Office of Disability Employment Policy 2001, p. 38,004).

Customized employment embraces a "person-centred" approach. It begins with the person's needs, aspirations, talents and skills, which serve as a basis for contacting potential employers (Inge 2008b). Additionally, it emphasizes the person's choice and strengths and abilities. In customized employment, jobs are negotiated so that they best fit the individual, while individuals are placed in competitive settings and receive supports that match their individual needs. In the United States, this model is employed in One-Stop Service Delivery Systems, in which workforce investment, education, and other human service programmes collaborate to enhance access to services and long term employment outcomes.

Supported and customized employment models lead to desirable outcomes for persons with disabilities for a number of reasons. First, wages and hours worked are significantly higher, on average, than for individuals in sheltered employment (Conley 2003). According to a Maryland survey, individuals in customized and supported employment earn 3.5 times more than those in sheltered employment and work 30% more hours per week (Conley 2003). Second, individuals with disabilities gain social benefits from customized and supported employment (Ohtake and Chadsey 1999). Customized employment enables individuals with disabilities to make friends with individuals without disabilities, obtain cultural benefits from obtaining a job, since an individual's identity is often shaped by work, and become integrated in society outside of work (Ohtake and Chadsey 1999). Similarly, supported and customized employment models may diminish stigma associated with having a disability because they emphasize the person's abilities and productivity (Wehman et al. 2003).

Third, employing individuals with disabilities in competitive settings has benefits for corporations (Kregel 1999). Employers rate the performance of individuals with disabilities favourably in dependability, reliability, ability to get along with coworkers, loyalty to the company, and respect for authority (Kregel 1999). On-going case study research among partners with the Burton Blatt Institute (BBI) found:

- Employees with disabilities who report having supervisors who exhibit behaviours valuing diversity were less likely to report harassment as a result of their disability, and report higher levels of commitment and lower turnover intentions.
- Fairness of human resources practices significantly predicts employee organizational commitment, job satisfaction, citizenship behaviours, and turnover intentions.

Another study using nearly 30,000 employee surveys from 14 companies found disability is linked to lower average pay, job security, training, and participation in decisions, and to more negative attitudes towards the job and company (Schur et al. 2009). These "disability gaps" in attitudes vary across companies and worksites, with no attitude gaps in worksites rated highly by employees for fairness and responsiveness. The results indicate corporate cultures responsive to the needs of all employees are especially beneficial for employees with disabilities. Thus, hiring individuals with disabilities improves workforce diversity and overall company profitability and productivity (Kregel 1999).

Increasing numbers of people with disabilities are employed through models that focus on abilities and choice, such as customized employment. However, most individuals with disabilities worldwide still are employed in sheltered rather than competitive settings (Wehman et al. 2003). A useful distinction to understand the obstacles or barriers that prevent customized employment from becoming the dominant model is between those that affect labour supply and those that impact labour demand (National Council on Disability 2007; Wehman et al. 2003).

Supply and Demand

Supply and demand in the employment context refers to the supply (or availability) of trained, job-seeking workers in the labour market and the demand (or need) for these workers by industries. First, on the labour supply side, without effective accommodation it may be more expensive for an individual with a disability to work than it is for an individual without a disability, such as if personal assistance is needed getting ready for work, accessible transportation is not available, or medical costs are higher than for people without disabilities (National Council on Disability 2007). Second, on average, individuals with disabilities have lower levels of education and training. Third, people with disabilities often need jobs with greater flexibility, since certain disabilities require additional time for self-care, therapy, and medical appointments, and transportation issues may increase uncertainty in daily schedules. Fourth, people with disabilities often are hesitant to become employed because increased employment income may jeopardize eligibility for disability services and health benefits; these benefits may be tied to personal assets and income.

On the labour demand side, a common barrier to employment is discrimination, prejudice, stereotypes and misconceptions of ability, which often make employers reluctant to hire individuals with disabilities (National Council on Disability 2007). Second, corporate culture, in terms of organizational practices and the attitudes of managers, supervisors, and coworkers, can reduce employment opportunities for individuals with disabilities (Schur et al. 2009). Third, individuals with disabilities may require workplace accommodations; employers may be hesitant to hire individuals with disabilities due to mistaken fears of expensive accommodation and healthcare costs.

Empirical studies demonstrate, however, that most accommodations cost nothing or less than $500 and result in substantial benefits to employers. Thus, when existing employees require accommodations, such as for an acquired disability or health condition, the benefits and cost savings from not having to hire and train a replacement employee outweigh the accommodation costs by several thousand dollars. Fourth, there is often a lack of information on both sides of the labour market; some individuals with disabilities do not know what jobs they are capable of doing and how to obtain necessary training, while employers are unaware of resources available to help them hire individuals with disabilities.

Music Education and Therapy for the Children with Disabilities Need and Application

Music can be a motivating and fun way to teach all children and in particular children with special needs. It is unquestionable that through the medium of music many essential and enabling life skills can be learned and the benefits that playing and learning music can have on a child's growth and development are immeasurable. For some real life examples, please review our Piano Wizard success stories.

All children have the same need to express themselves and playing a musical instrument can provide an outlet for creative and emotional expression. When we think of music we don't often think of it as therapy. But it can be.

The playing of good quality percussion instruments during music therapy sessions can be of inestimable value for children who have difficulties in hearing, seeing, moving, thinking or responding; each can experience the music in their own unique way. The music is not the goal of music therapy. Cognitive stimulation, self-expression, self-awareness, or increased motor movements are some of the goals that music therapy can focus on and the music itself is simply a tool to achieve these goals.

Listening to music for enjoyment is very beneficial but active participation is even better. For children and adolescents with cerebral palsy, playing music may be an effective way to stimulate speech development and communication skills, express emotions, develop a sense of rhythm and provide opportunity for physical, cognitive and motor development whilst creating an environment for socialisation and fun.

Every child can be helped to learn to enjoy and to become involved in music to some degree and instruments tuned to a harmonic pentatonic scale which produce a soothing sound straightaway, makes playing them an instantly gratifying experience.

Playing music and music therapy has proven to be a very effective method in dealing with autism and aspergers syndrome. Most children diagnosed with Autism or Asperger's lack the social skills that enable them to participate fully in play and other social situations. Interestingly, many children with autism show a heightened interest in music. While they may be unable to easily communicate verbally with others, music is an avenue for many autistic people to express themselves and communicate in a non-verbal, non-threatening manner. Playing music puts the individual at ease, allowing for strides in social interactions to follow.

Easy access to musical instruments may provide an outlet that encourages children to use music to deal with emotional issues, especially when they are unable to express them through speech. Where words fail, music may be a medium through which to explore one's inner world and experiences. Often people with developmental delays and learning disabilities such as Down's syndrome will respond to music. The easy, non-challenging way in which pentatonic instruments can be played offers opportunities for response and expression to children and adults with such developmental delays.

Musical instruments in the classroom or playground offer blind or partially sighted children the opportunity to explore and musical sound and awareness. Instruments, which are simple to play and enable creative experimentation and tactile exploration, encourage the use of motor skills, thus developing coordination whilst stimulating the imagination.

Music is a tool that is used in pain management and healing for children undergoing medical procedures and as a comfort for those who have suffered a traumatic experience. Music can be a powerful distraction, turning the patient's attention away from pain and promoting relaxation as well as to help ward off depression, promote movement and ease muscle tension.

The use of music in group therapy has long been advocated and practiced in the music therapy profession, in addition to the purely musical benefits, playing in an ensemble is useful for working on concepts such as cooperation with others, coordination, and a sense of accomplishment. Making music and singing songs together in a group can build a harmonious cooperative spirit of support and encouragement for everyone. Children who experience severe obstacles in forming relationships with other children, adults and their environment can achieve security and joy in making music. Music making involves many of the fundamental elements of social interaction; turn taking, listening and responding to another person can all be augmented in music therapy.

To see, hear and play musical instruments at school or in community programmes is an important cultural experience for every child. While music therapy is an important discipline, you can also achieve benefits from making music on your own. Successful projects include sensory or music gardens where musical instruments have been installed outdoors, making them accessible at break times as well as for use with the curriculum. Playgrounds and outdoor spaces should be viewed as therapeutic settings and an outdoor music centre or garden could enhance learning and development for both children with and without special needs.

Music Therapy is a well-established, research-based profession in which music is used to accomplish therapeutic and educational goals. Music Therapy helps to improve cognitive, social, physical, psychological, and communication functioning. The Music Therapists at Alternatives For Children design and implement music sessions for individuals and groups based on the specific needs of the children. Music Therapy also provides an opportunity for the children to practice and generalize the skills they acquire throughout their school day.

Music therapy is considered a related service modality in special education (IDEA, 1997). Music therapy can play an important role in special education because many students with disabilities need special instructional treatment. Music is an ancient method for healing. It neutralizes negative feelings, increases stress tolerance level and harmonizes inner peace. The use of music therapy can help people who are crippled by varies cognitive and biopsychosocial problems. It can also help to improve the quality of life for people with disabilities of various kinds.

The IDEA (Individual with Disabilities Act) requires schools to provide related services and equipment for a student with a disability to ensure a "free and appropriate" public education. The reauthorization of IDEA (1997) mandates related services to be included into the Individual Education Programme (IEP). In 2001, with passage of the No Child Left Behind Act (NCLB), the U.S. Department of Education is embracing evidence based research in order to improve the effectiveness of educational intervention and in turn, academic achievement. Regular education and special education teachers are given increased responsibilities for students with disabilities in their classrooms. Recent research indicates that music therapy has a positive impact on students' cognitive development.

Students with disabilities arrive daily in music classes from kindergarten through high school. Effective integration of music in the content areas creates a learning environment that makes all children want to learn. Collett (1992) reported a successful music integrated curriculum which works well with bilingual and special education students. Music integration provide children with concrete, hands-on experiences that are essential to developing each child's ability to reason, think, solve problems, analyze, evaluate, and to enhancing creativity.

Several studies have investigated the effects of music therapy on children with cognitive disabilities. Straum (n.d.) suggested the use of music to assist students with autism disorder in the areas of social and language development. Autistic children have eliminated their monotonic speech by singing songs composed to match the rhythm, stress, flow and inflection of the sentence followed by a gradual fading of the musical cues. The author also argues that music can be used as a tool to encourage human development in cognitive, learning, perceptual, motor, social and emotional development. In a related study, Stambough (1996) conducted an action research at a music camp to 37 campers ages from 9-45, each suffers varies degree of a genetic condition called Williams Syndrome, which leads to cognitive impairment.

She found that several strategies and techniques, combined with a great deal of patience, helped to accommodate the special needs of the students.

Others researchers suggested steps for facilitating the integration of students with emotional or behavioural disorders into the regular music classroom. Results gathered from King & Schwabenlender (1994) reported various supportive strategies for promoting emotional well-being in children from a diverse background. Allow children to be expressive provides them with a sense of empowerment.

Implications

Special education teachers have used music to alter mood and assess emotional problems. Music allows the individual to invent emotions.

Music is viewed as an integral part of all children's lives. Children enjoy listening to music, singing, and humming. Music may effectively enhance the ability to cope with stress. The author suggested that music be found in both music classes and regular education classrooms.

She found that integrating literature with musical content helped to bring books alive and that musical classrooms encouraged children to relate and participate in the activities.

However, very few studies provided a comprehensive view of some disability categories such as autism, mental retardation (MR) or cognitive delays, attention deficit disorders (ADHD), learning disabilities (LD) and physical and other health impairments (POHI).

Below is a list of practical, relevant, and evidence based strategies teachers can use to help students with varies disabilities through music.

Speech and Language Impairments

Music is more than a leisure activity. It is more than verbal counselling. It is a sophisticated cognitive, linguistic, social and psychological treatment. Music provides a form of compensation

for those with language impairments as well as a means of facilitating language development.

1. Find a piece of music enjoyable to the student.
2. Encourage student to participate in the musical activities.
3. Have student verbally identify an instrument by name before he or she can play it.
4. Learn words and articulate particular phonemes through singing songs.
5. Create non-judgemental and nonverbal activities to help make student feels comfortable.
6. Create activities where any vocal sound is accepted as a creative part of the improvised music.
7. Incorporated vocal sounds that are spontaneously emitted and that are elicited from the music making.

Orthopedics and Health Impairments

Music affects heart beat, pulse rate, and skin responses.

1. Place an instrument at a strategically placed distance to increase hands or arms movement.
2. Swing a mallet to strike a drum to help increase the range of motion.

3. Have student hold a musical instrument may help the development of fine motor coordination.
4. Vary the intensity of clapping, jumping, stamping, pounding, swinging, and snapping, etc. according to the severity of the disability.
5. Use slow and gentle music to increase flexibility and to decrease hyper tense muscular contractions.

Cognitive Disabilities

Research in neurological functioning supports the association between music and cognitive development. Music organizes sounds and silences in a flow of time. It creates expectations and are then satisfied. It raises a question and solves it.

1. Use mnemonic devices for remembering sequences (the alphabet song).
2. Use categorical structures to differentiate (animal farm, colour, etc.).
3. Connect sound with a concept (a cow makes a "moo" sound").

Attention Deficit /Hyperactive Disorders and Learning Disabilities

Music focuses on accuracy and attention. Learning how to play an instrument can improve attention, concentration, impulse control, social functioning, self-esteem, self-expression, motivation and memory.

1. Connect a particular vocal sound with a particular body movement.
2. Provide more than one neural pathway by using multi-sensory channels.
3. Use visual, auditory and kinesthetic (striking a drum, clapping hands).
4. Use the inherent structure in songs to reinforce a sense of internal order.
5. Use rhythm, steady pulse, and basic beat of music as a model to help student to experience order, sequence, and a sense of consistency.

Gifted and Talented

Music focuses on deeper psychological process and allows creative expression. Challenge gifted students to adapt their existing abilities in ways that enable them to produce music.

Emotional and Behavioural Disorders

Music creates physiological responses, which are associated with emotional reactions. Music explains the tension release sequence associated with emotional arousal (Abeles, 1980). The speed and intensity of the musical beat creates the different feelings in each type of song. The opportunity to play an instrument can be used as a reinforcer for on task behaviour.

1. Use small group music therapy to facilitate socialization and interpersonal interactions.
2. Encourage student to play different instruments in the songs.
3. Allow student to express individually while participating as a group.
4. Use the common musical beat to unite group cohesion and concrete group dynamic.
5. Use music activities that require a member to imitate the body movement or rhythmic pattern of another member.
6. Teach student to take turn when there is only one instrument available to share within a group.
7. Use sharing space while playing musical instrument to control impulse.

The effects of music therapy on children with disabilities are numerous. This paper introduced the background of music and children with disabilities. It explained the rationale behind music integration in an inclusive classroom. Music therapy contributions to cognitive, psychosocial and academic development. It provided practical guidelines to use music to accommodate children with disabilities.

6

Training of Disabled on Rural Enterprise Development

Small-scale enterprise development is not for everyone, whether disabled or not, and needs a high level of discipline, dedication, persistence and creativity as well as a lot of work. The micro-entrepreneur must be capable of decision-making and have the ability to manage employees (if any) and accounts. Furthermore, small-scale enterprise development for persons with disabilities involves a multitude of additional challenges, which require specific attention and strategies. Before setting up a small-scale enterprise, it is necessary to:

Deal with Specific Challenges: In any business venture, specific challenges need to be addressed. These include:

- *seed money*
- *physical location of the business venture*
- *construction or other physically demanding work*
- *management skills*
- *accounting skills*
- *marketing skills*
- *maintenance of equipment, machinery and premises.*

In the case of persons with disabilities, their physical and mental capabilities have to be reviewed for suitability to the enterprise.

Ask these questions:

1. What are my strengths?
2. What are my weaknesses?

3. How can I compensate for my weaknesses?
4. What are my current personal needs?
5. Who will be working with me?
6. Choose the right business

The right business certainly varies from one person to another. Personal preferences, along with physical and mental capabilities are the main deciding factors. Nevertheless, the focus should be on market demand and its limitations to determine if the business can be successful.

A planned small-scale enterprise should be able to produce sufficient income to justify the time and energy invested in the venture. Family support also plays a major role in the selection of the business since a disabled person needs help in accomplishing certain tasks, especially during the start-up of the enterprise.

1. Make a list of what you would like to do.
2. *Also make a list of what you are good at doing.*

Go through the following steps to guide the choice of business:

· Start with what you like	® *Remain realistic*
· Investigate the market and its needs	® *Try to be objective*
· Review the competition	® *Competition means a market*
· Avoid saturated markets	® *Look for opportunity*
· Make sure you can do it yourself	® *Hiring means spending money*
· Consult with others	® *Discretely, not to divulge ideas*
· Discuss with your family	® *Check impact on family*

Keep in mind that if there is competition, it means there is a market. Discreet investigation is therefore advisable.

Write Down your Ideas so You Will Not Forget

***Review Market Demand and the Competition*:** Review of the competition is necessary. Competition means there is a market, but how big is the market?

It is important not to saturate the market and to supply the right type of product or service; something that is in demand.

Ask these questions:

1. Who are my competitors?
2. Who are my customers?

3. How much can the market absorb before saturation?
4. *Is there a shortage or surplus?*

Location of the market is also important for micro-entrepreneurs with physical disabilities. Agricultural produce, for example, has to be sold at the fresh market, which must be accessible to the disabled person micro-entrepreneur. If it is too far, proper transportation arrangements will be necessary or else the product will have to be sent by a hired delivery person or sold to a middle person. Hiring people increases production costs. Marketing is easier for a farm-based enterprise located within a small community where the production can be sold directly to the villagers.

Check Seasonability: Agriculture and farming produce are often seasonal. The following questions must be considered:

1. Is the crop or product available only during certain seasons?
2. Are raw materials available all year round?
3. Can the product be kept in storage?
4. Is the service or product only required during certain periods of the year?
5. Can there be off-season production?

Some products can be grown off-season generating substantial profits since there are few competitors during that period. Such products, although requiring more time and attention, can offer a niche market opportunity for micro-entrepreneurs with disabilities.

***Decide on Business Size*:** Care must be taken in deciding the size of the business.

- *If too small, the business may not be feasible.*
- *If too big, it becomes too difficult to manage properly and may require extra help, which adds to costs.*
- *If too big, the market may not be capable of absorbing the produce.*

It is usually better to start small and expand the business slowly once the market has been tested and income starts coming in. Initially, self-sufficiency and the capability of handling the business by oneself is the best indicator of the right size of the enterprise.

Several questions need to be answered before determining the size of the enterprise:

1. Who are the clients?
2. Where are the clients?

3. How many clients are there?
4. How much produce or services can each client use?
5. Are there seasons or days of the week when the produce or service is more in demand?
6. Who else is offering the same service or produce?
7. What percentage of the business share can I expect to take?
8. How much money do I have to start the business?
9. How much can I manage by myself?
10. How can I ensure quality?

Identify the Location: Location plays a crucial role in starting a small-scale enterprise. While a farming or farm-related enterprise need not be accessible to the buyers, the micro-entrepreneur will have to travel to the market to sell the produce. When the business involves fresh produce, timely sale is crucial. For example, fruits, vegetables and flowers are highly perishable and have to be sold quickly. Easy access to markets is important. It is necessary for a micro-entrepreneur with a disability to be able to reach the market or to have easy contact with potential buyers. In some cases, it may be necessary to hire someone to help in the delivery of the produce. In the case of services, micro-enterprise location should encourage people from the village to come to the entrepreneur's workplace, which must be easily accessible to clients, and be somewhat attractive. Low-cost decorations can be used to attract clients while good service will ensure their return.

Land and Premises

Land and premises are needed for the establishment of any enterprise. In case these have to be acquired, the start-up costs will increase. If the new micro-entrepreneur already owns these, he or she may have to spend on renovation. The following questions should serve as guidelines:

1. How much space do I need?
2. Do I have a piece of land or building I can use?
3. What will be the cost of the land?
4. Do I need to rent the premises?
5. Does a new building need to be built?
6. Can the existing building (s) be renovated?
7. Do I need decoration? (Decoration may be needed to attract customers.)

Write down your project ideas so you will not forget

Check Availability of Raw Material: Raw material for making the produce should be readily available. Import of the material should be avoided because this will make it difficult to ensure a steady supply.

A Number of Suppliers Should be Identified.

It is important to avoid reliance on a single supplier as this will give the supplier a monopoly and is most likely to lead to an increase in prices over time. Because the profit margin in a micro-enterprise is generally small, it is necessary to keep production costs under close control. It is important to ensure constant quality.

Alternative sources of raw material may also be considered such as forest products that are readily available and free of charge. Recycling and re-use is another way of reducing costs.

The steady availability of water is another important consideration while selecting the enterprise and identifying the raw material. This is especially important for farming activities.

Identify Funding

A disabled person wanting to start a micro-enterprise may obtain a loan for this from family or community members. However, the start-up funds often have to be sought externally. It must be kept in mind that loans have to be repaid and, therefore, one must borrow the minimum amount needed for start-up and running expenses until the venture starts generating income.

In some countries, government loans or institutional micro-credit are offered to small-scale entrepreneurs - whether disabled or not - who have a viable business proposal. Rural persons with disabilities often lack the education and skills needed for preparing a formal proposal and may need the help of family or community members.

Several countries also have disability funds offering loans at low or no interest rates to individuals with disabilities who are registered with the responsible government authority. The loan can be repaid over a period of several years. The loan sometimes requires endorsement by a family or community member in case of non-repayment.

Disabled persons seeking a loan must contact either local government authorities or government ministries that are most likely to offer loans, such as the Ministries of Labour, Social Welfare, Health or Invalids; the ministry may differ from one country to another. Disabled persons may also obtain loans from cooperatives, agricultural organizations, women's groups or farmers' organizations, although such loan facilities are not specifically available for persons with disabilities.

Review the Market

Marketing is very important since competition can be fierce. The following factors must be taken into consideration:

Packaging:	Packaging may or may not be required depending on the product. For the sale of fresh fruits, vegetables or other agricultural produce, there is generally no need for packaging. A simple plastic or paper bag is sufficient.
Presentation:	Presentation can play a role even in the sale of fresh food products. Neatness, cleanliness and organization make the sales outlet attractive and appealing to customers.
Market test:	It is sometimes interesting to test different types of presentation or packaging to find the one that appeals most to customers.
Competition:	Competitors offering the same or similar product must never be ignored as they already have clients and may be more experienced. Check their presentation, price and sales technique. As a new micro-entrepreneur, you can learn from the experience of others and adapt it to your personality. A lot can be learned by looking at the competition. The following are some of the things that need to be checked against.

The Competition

1. Who are my customers?
2. Is there growing demand for my product?
3. Who are my competitors?
4. How are other businesses doing: are they growing? Steady? Decreasing?
5. What are their strengths? Their weaknesses?
6. How does their product differ from mine?
7. If it is the same, why do I think I can take a share of the market?

What is the Right Sales Price for the Product or Service?

Sales price, quality and service ensure that new customers become regular clients.

1. What are the current sales prices?
2. What is the quality of the product sold by the competition?

3. How does the quality of my product compare to that of others?
4. What is my estimated cost price?

If the sales price is too high, customers will go to the competition even if the entrepreneur is a person with disabilities. Clients may buy once to encourage the micro-entrepreneur who is a disabled person but will buy the lower priced product if it is of equal quality. If the price is too low, customers will think that the product quality is also low and continue buying from their regular supplier. The right price should be similar to that of the competition while offering better service and same or better quality.

Check Feasibility Before Starting the Enterprise

Too many people start a new small-scale business, blinded by the attractiveness of the product or by what seems to be an attractive market. However, many micro-enterprises close down after a few months or years of operation, shattering the small-scale entrepreneur's dreams of what appeared to be the perfect way of making a decent living. In order to avoid this, a pre-feasibility study should be conducted. Although this may be based on estimates, it helps to prepare for the future and, in some cases, shows that another activity may be better.

Start-up expenses generally include:

- *Legal professional fees*
- *Licenses / permits*
- *Rent and/or construction*
- *Equipment and tools*
- *Assistive devices (when required)*
- *Raw material*
- *Salaries / wages*
- *Utilities*

Example of Calculation

Purchase of tools	***6 000 baht***
Number of usage years	3 years or 36 months
Cost per month	6 000 baht/ 36 months = 167 baht per month
Quantity of items produced per month	200 units
Cost of tools per unit	*167 baht / 200 units = 0.84 baht per unit*

Calculating Sales Price

Total monthly cost	
Divided by	÷
Quantity of items produced	
Plus	+
20% Profit margin	
Equals	=
SALES PRICE PER UNIT	

Calculating Monthly Income:

Estimated sales price of product	
Multiplied by	x
Estimated quantity sold per month	
Equals	=
TOTAL MONTHLY INCOME	

Calculate the Monthly Gross Profit

Total income	
Minus	-
Total costs	
Equals	=
GROSS PROFIT	

- *If the estimated profit margin appears good, then it is time to go ahead with the investment.*
- *If the profit margin is low, all numbers should be reviewed carefully before investing.*
- *If the profit margin is negative, the micro-entrepreneur should consider another activity.*

Avoid Common Mistakes

Numerous factors may jeopardize the success of an enterprise.

The following are some common mistakes:

Insufficient know-how	The micro-entrepreneur does not sufficiently understand the process and therefore cannot easily find alternatives or solutions to problems encountered (e.g. Pest control, disease, mechanical problems...)
Lack of marketing strategies	Competition may be healthy but too much competition may destroy the market unless creative marketing strategies are developed. Although a person with a disability may

Contd...

	receive special consideration, it is necessary to compete with sometimes powerful and wealthy groups. The issue of disability is not a marketing strategy.
Insufficient cash flow	Cash flow is often what destroys most companies. Careful forecasting of start-up and running expenses is necessary.
Too large start-up	It is always better to start small with a minimum investment and to grow slowly with the market.
Poor record-keeping	Income, profits and losses need to be closely monitored. This helps decide whether the market is good, whether the new small-scale enterprise should be expanded, reduced or halted because of losses.
Giving samples and presents	Generosity needs to be controlled. A certain amount of gratuities should be established but it is always dangerous in a personal business to give small amounts of the product or free service to members of the family and neighbours. This could equal or surpass the profit margin.
Management	Management of the business is, and will always be the key to success. Not all people are good managers and therefore management skills may need to be developed or acquired through training.
Maintenance	Maintaining the equipment and the keeping the business premises clean and in good running condition certainly contributes to reducing operating expenses.

Preparing to Start the Business

Basic and unavoidable steps

There are ELEVEN basic and unavoidable steps in preparing to start a business.

1. Secure funding
2. Open bank account
3. Identify precise location for the enterprise
4. Build or renovate the structure or building required

5. Arrange necessary infrastructure (water, electricity, communication and others)
6. Request permits (if necessary)
7. Purchase and adapt necessary tools, equipment and assistive devices (when required)
8. Identify suppliers of raw materials and consumables
9. Start production
10. Control quality
11. Devise marketing and sales strategies

Secure Funding: Various sources of funding may be considered when starting a small-scale enterprise for a person with disabilities. The major source, obviously, is the family. However, many countries have special programmes to help micro-entrepreneurs with disabilities. For example, a Disability Fund set up by the Government of Thailand offers interest-free loans to persons with disabilities who can make a feasible business proposal. Some international organizations and NGOs also provide financing facilities for different projects and target groups. Documents to confirm the loan or grant must be processed at this stage.

Open Bank Account: Once funding has been identified and confirmed, the money must be deposited in a bank account. To ensure clear accounting, a special bank account should be opened for the business. The loan money can then be deposited in that bank account and withdrawn for the purchase of equipment and raw material. The income from sales is also deposited in this bank account. All transactions should be done through the bank and not directly in cash. This ensures clear understanding and follow-up of money movement for both income and expenses.

***Identify Precise Location for the Enterprise*:** It is then time to choose the precise location for the construction of the facilities. If using an existing building, renovation or modification may be necessary. It may also be necessary to arrange for landfill, excavation, irrigation or other modification. This can often be done manually with the help of family and friends.

Build or Renovate the Needed Structure or Building: Renovation and building may require substantial investments. Nevertheless, these can be greatly reduced by using readily available forest produce, grass, tree leaves and rice straw or used construction material. For example, tree branches can be used as poles; roofing can be made of corrugated steel, rice straw or grass; and walls can be made of dried leaves. The weather is also decisive for the type of material to be used. Decoration should be kept to a minimum, at least in the beginning. However, if the structure is also to serve as a retail outlet, it may be necessary to be creative and use simple yet attractive decorations.

Arrange Necessary Infrastructure: A steady supply of water is vital for an agriculture-based enterprise and a well may be dug or water may have to be transported or channelled to the site. In some cases, electricity may also be needed. Roads must be accessible for smooth delivery of raw material and transport of the produce to the market.

Request Permits (If Necessary): It is very important to confirm if a permit is needed to operate the business. It is costly to set up a business and then learn that it will take a few months to get the required operating permit. Verification should be done at the very beginning so that permits can be processed during preparation for starting the enterprise.

Purchase and Adapt Necessary Tools, Equipment and Assistive Devices: Purchase of equipment should be kept to the absolute minimum. Instruments that are not needed regularly may be borrowed or rented. It is important to verify if a person with a disability can use the equipment. Certain adaptations or modifications may be necessary. The use of prosthesis and orthotics by physically disabled persons would surely help in any type of enterprise. The manual *Adaptive tools for persons with disabilities*, published by the UN Economic and Social Commission for Asia and the Pacific (ESCAP) offers some ideas and suggestions on what is readily available. Although electrical equipment may facilitate certain tasks for persons with disabilities, electricity charges add to production costs and consequently, the sales price. Any equipment or machinery should be purchased after careful consideration.

Identify Suppliers of Raw Material and Consumables: The quality of raw material and reliability of suppliers are crucial, especially in the case of consumer products. Delivery must be punctual to ensure continuous production. Suppliers should be carefully selected by requesting quotations and terms of delivery from several parties. It is better to select a supplier situated close to the enterprise even if the price is slightly higher because it is easier to keep check on a nearby supplier. Prices should always be negotiated and in case of regular purchase, better prices, terms and conditions should be sought.

Start Production: It is time to verify the actual costs of production. Some things may have been forgotten or put aside under the impression that these are not important. The micro-entrepreneur with a disability must start the production and apply his or her know-how to the best of his or her ability. However, some problems may need to be solved such as pests, diseases, breakdown of machinery and shortage of clients. A resource person should be available to support and guide the new disabled person micro-entrepreneur in solving these problems. The total amount of production must be closely monitored. Provincial and district offices sometimes have specialists in various agricultural sectors who can be useful as resource persons. Cooperatives also offer advice to their members.

Control Quality: Quality and reliability of supply are crucial for ensuring steady sales and a good price. Raw material quality must be controlled for good product quality and must be done on a continuous basis to reduce loss and damage. The new micro-entrepreneur's clients will find him or her reliable if the quality is maintained constantly.

Devise Marketing and Sales Strategies: Although competition may make market penetration more difficult, it also proves that there is a market. A new micro-entrepreneur, whether disabled or not, needs creativity and sales strategies to establish his or her product or service in the market. Politeness, friendliness and a neat personal appearance help in selling a product. Developing a relationship with the buyers by providing a regular supply of quality products will convert clients into regular customers. This will also establish a good reputation for his or her product or service and bring more customers

A successful micro-entrepreneur must also be flexible and capable of reducing or increasing prices according to demand and shortages. For products or services sold from his or her home, an accessible location will encourage villagers to go to the micro-entrepreneur. In the case of agricultural produce, the disabled person micro-entrepreneur can sell from home or may send someone to the market with the produce.

The entrepreneur must always check and review the market for the following:

1. Who are the buyers?
2. What quantity of production can the market absorb?
3. Where are the selling points?
4. What is the distance that needs to be travelled to sell the product?

5. What means of transportation are available?
6. How much time is needed to sell the product, including travel?

Packaging may be needed for some products. This adds to the cost and must be carefully selected since it may increase the price of the product to a level that is no longer competitive. Same or similar products must be carefully reviewed for how and whether they should be packaged. Innovative packaging or presentation, however, may allow a new micro-entrepreneur to corner part of a market.

Managing the Business

A Profit-making Business: Running a small-scale business is not only buying, producing and selling. It also means:

- *Keeping clear records*
- *Verifying profit and loss*
- *Managing cash flow*
- *Maintaining tools, equipment and buildings*
- *Reviewing the market regularly*
- *Expanding the business wisely*

Although setting up the micro-enterprise may have its difficulties, making it a profitable venture is the biggest challenge. It is therefore necessary to closely monitor each investment and purchase cost to know the exact profit.

Keep Clear Records

Small-scale entrepreneurs should always keep clear records of their purchase and sales. The records must be simple.

Make a list of all items bought every week.

Purchased item	Quantity	Price per unit	Total price

Make a similar chart of all items sold

Sold item	Quantity	Price per unit	Total price

Verify Profit and Loss

Finding out whether the enterprise is making money or not is crucial for the venture. Sometimes it seems that there is a lot of money coming in but when compared to the costs, there is little profit left. This is called feasibility.

It is necessary to review the feasibility by asking the following questions:

1. Am I making money?
2. Is it worth continuing?
3. What can be changed to increase profit?

It is especially important to verify the profit margin. More production does not necessarily generate more income. It depends on the profit margin, which is calculated by subtracting the production cost from the income as follows:

Income - (Minus) Production costs = (Equals) Profit margin

Manage Cash Flow: Cash flow is the money moving in and out of the enterprise. It is the total amount of money coming in and going out of the business. If all the money received is put in the bank and all expenses are paid from the money in the bank, the cash flow is the total amount of money moving in the bankbook. However, care must be taken not to spend what appears to be profit before reviewing future investment needs. These needs can include:

- Purchase of raw material
- Payment for utilities (electricity, water, etc.)
- Repair of broken equipment
- Payment for extra labour
- Repayment of the loan
- Replacement of tools and material.

Note: *An emergency fund should be set up for the replacement of broken equipment and tools and for purchasing other necessary inputs.*

Maintain Tools, Equipment and Buildings

Tools and Equipment: The life of tools and equipment can be extended by proper maintenance. Metal tools should be protected from rust while wooden tools have to be protected from termites and decay. Mechanical tools must be lubricated regularly.

Building(s), Structure, Environment: The type of structure used for the business determines the maintenance required. In Asian rural areas, many buildings are made of thatch, bamboo, rice straw, grass, dried leaves and other material. These must be checked for pests, especially in cases where production is food-related or stored inside this structure. The building or premises must be kept clean and tidy at all times, whether used as a sales outlet or not. Cleanliness not only makes the place more attractive, it also reduces the threat from rodents and other pests. It further makes the place more enjoyable

in 1991, beyond that year literacy statistics in India is not available. However, the same on household sample basis is available from a semi-government organization, namely the *National Sample Survey Organization*. The literacy rate (7+ Population) increased from 52 per cent in 1991 to 62 per cent in 1998, thus showing an impressive increase of 10 percentage points in a short period of about seven years. However, no significant improvement is noticed in male/female differential in literacy rate, which has declined from 25 to 23 per cent during the same period. It may however be noted that during 1991 to 1998, the increase in female literacy (11 per cent) was higher than the increase in male literacy (9 per cent). In addition, many states have lower literacy rates than at the all-India level and among weaker sections (SC, 37 and ST, 30 per cent), it is very poor.

The rural/urban distribution of literacy rates reveal that increase was higher in rural areas than in urban areas and the difference was of the tune of four percentage points. The rural/urban differential in literacy during the period 1991 to 1998 declined from 28 to 24 per cent but the male/female differential in rural areas continues to be significantly high at 25 percentage points. Despite all these significant achievements, a large number of people in rural areas are still illiterate (44 per cent) compared to which only 20 per cent urban population is illiterate. Not only the literacy rates improved significantly but also the number of illiterates declined considerably during the period 1991 to 1998 and is expected to further decline by the year 2001 (MHRD, 2000d). From 329 million illiterates (7+ population) in 1991, it has declined to 294 million in 1998 and is further likely to decline to 258 million in the year 2001.

Following the general pattern, the adult literacy rate (15+ population) also increased significantly from 49 per cent in 1991 to 57 per cent in 1998, thus showing an increase of 8 percentage points in a short span of about seven years. However, male/female differential in literacy remained high at 27 percentage points, which shows that, both the male and female literacy rates between 1991 and 1998 have increased by equal percentage points. Unless all the females are made literate, the goal of universal literacy will continue to remain a distant dream. The other major concern is that many of the literates are simply literate and have not completed formal schooling. The NSSO data for year 1995-96 reveals that about 10 per cent of the total literates (15+ Population) are either literate without formal schooling or below primary level. About 28 per cent of the total literates have completed either primary or upper primary schooling. The rest of the literates have completed other higher levels of education.

The significant improvement in literacy rates during 1991 to 1998 is because of the measures that have been initiated during this period. The literacy programmes in India are managed by the *National Literacy Mission* (NLM) launched in 1992 with an aim to make 100 million literates of the age group 15-35 years by the turn of the century i.e. 1999. Based on the Ernakulam experience in mobilizing society in the affairs of literacy programmes, the NLM launched *Total Literacy Campaigns* in a large number of districts. Since then a number of districts have become total literate districts. The achievement is also because of the fact that during 1990's, a number of innovative projects and programmes were initiated, which is quite visible in enrolment and drop out trends .

Early Childhood Care and Education (Ecce) Programmes

The National Policy on Education (1987 & 1992) recommended strengthening of ECCE programme as an essential component of human development and UEE. Only a limited statistics is available on ECCE related programmes and whatever is available from the official sources is total number of pre-primary (recognized) centres and their enrolment. In fact, a large number of unrecognized centres are also engaged in ECCE related activities. The *Integrated Child Development Service* (ICDS) is one of the major programmes under ECCE. The scheme is funded by the Central Government and children below age '6' are its clientele. Since the health input at lower ages is more as compared to the educational input, the ICDS and the *Anganwadis/Balw*adis is considered more as welfare activity and is part of the activities performed by the *Welfare Department* and not under the *Department of Education* (Thakur & Mehta, 1999). Since its inception, the ICDS has covered all the community development blocks (5,320) of the country. More than 11 million children of age group 3-6 years were enrolled in these centres most of which are from the disadvantage section of the society. A perusal of *Gross Enrolment Ratio* (GER) during the period 1990 to 1998 reveals that the same has increased from 10 per cent in 1990 to about 17 per cent in 1998. But a few of the 32 States & UTs have GER even less than 10 per cent. However, it may be noted that ECCE programmes are not a pre-requisite condition for obtaining admission in Grade I. Further, it is noticed that the boys/girls differential in GER is almost negligible both at the state and all-India level.

Elementary Education

As mentioned above that free and compulsory education to all children up to the age fourteen is constitutional commitment. In 1993, the Supreme Court of India declared education up to fourteen years of age to be a fundamental right of children in India. The entire school education can be divided in to four parts, namely, primary, upper primary, secondary and higher secondary levels. The National Policy of Education (1968 & 1986) and its revised formulation (1992) envisaged a uniform pattern of school education (10+2 pattern, 12 years of schooling) across the states. Since education is on the concurrent list, i.e. state subject; the States & UTs are free to evolve their own pattern of school education. Eight years of primary education is envisaged in two stages: a junior stage covering a period of five years and a senior stage covering a period of 3 years. It needs to be mentioned that 8 years of compulsory education was envisaged as one integrated unit, although there were two stages in the cycle. Hence elementary education became the compulsory component of education in India (Varghese and Mehta, 1999a). It is this compulsory stage that has been incorporated as a direc-tive principle in the constitution in 1950. The official age (entry) to obtain admission in Grade I is 6 years but a few States & UTs have 5 years as entry-age. The Government has recently decided to re-introduce the Constitutional Amendment Bill, which will make elementary education a fundamental right. This will be implemented as a part of the *Sarva Shiksha Abhiyan*. It may however be noted that about 10-12 states have already made elementary education compulsory. But the situation in most of these states is not different than other states with regards to enrolment and retention.

Primary Education

Primary education is the first stage of compulsory education. It is preceded by pre-school or nursery education and is followed by secondary education. In North America, this stage of education is usually known as elementary education and is generally followed by middle school.

In most countries, it is compulsory for children to receive primary education although it is permissible for parents to provide it. The major goals of primary education are achieving basic literacy and numeracy amongst all pupils, as well as establishing foundations in science, mathematics, geography, history and other social sciences. The relative priority of various areas, and the methods used to teach them, are an area of considerable political debate.

Typically, primary education is provided in schools, where the child will stay in steadily advancing classes until they complete it and move on to high school/secondary school. Children are usually placed in classes with one teacher who will be primarily responsible for their education and welfare for that year. This teacher may be assisted to varying degrees by specialist teachers in certain subject areas, often music or physical education. The continuity with a single teacher and the opportunity to build up a close relationship with the class is a notable feature of the primary education system.

Traditionally, various forms of corporal punishment have been an integral part of early education. Recently this practice has come under scrutiny, and in many cases been outlawed, especially in Western countries.

Australia

In Australia, students undertake preschool then 13 years of schooling before moving to vocational or higher education. Primary schooling for most children starts after they turn 5 years old. In most states, children can be enrolled earlier at the discretion of individual school principals on the basis of intellectual giftedness. In Victoria, New South Wales, Northern Territory, ACT and Tasmania students then move through Kindergarten/Preparatory School/Reception and Years 1 to 6 before starting high school. In Queensland, South Australia and Western Australia students do Year 7 while still enrolled at primary school, although most governmental primary schools are moving to a K to 6 structure to line up with the other states in order to ensure that Year 7 students are able to undertake laboratory practical components of the national syllabus.

- Pre-School/Kindergarten: 4-5 year olds
- Prep./Reception/Kindergarten: 5-6 year olds
- Grade/Year 1: 6–7 years of age
- Grade/Year 2: 7-8 year olds
- Grade/Year 3: 8-9 year olds
- Grade/Year 4: 9-10 year olds
- Grade/Year 5: 10-11 year olds
- Grade/Year 6: 11-12 year olds
- Grade/Year 7: 12-13 year olds (WA, SA, QLD)

Brazil

Main article Education in Brazil

- Year 1: 6 year olds (former pre-school)

- Year 2: 7 year olds
- Year 3: 8 year olds
- Year 4: 9 year olds
- Year 5: 10 year olds
- Year 6: 11 year olds
- Year 7: 12 year olds
- Year 8: 13 year olds
- Year 9: 14 year olds
- Year 10: 15 year olds (optional)
- Year 11: 16 year olds (optional)
- Year 12: 17 year olds (optional)

Burma

Canada: Primary (Kindergarten) (Ages 4–5) students in the Prairie Provinces are not required by statute to attend kindergarten.

- Grade 1 (Ages 5–7)
- Grade 2 (Ages 6–8)
- Grade 3 (Ages 7–9)
- Grade 4 (Ages 8–10)
- Grade 5 (Ages 9–11)
- Grade 6 (Ages 10–12)
- Grade 7 (Ages 12–13) * Quebec, 1e secondaire
- Grade 8 (Ages 13–14) * Quebec, 2e secondaire
- Grade 9 (Ages 14–15) * Quebec, 3e secondaire
- Grade 10 (Ages 15–16) * Quebec, 4e secondaire
- Grade 11 (Ages 16–17) * Quebec, 5e secondaire
- Grade 12 (Ages 17–18) (except Quebec) *

* Quebec only goes up to grade 11 then students are required to go to Cegep before University

Denmark

In Denmark, 9 years of primary school (*Folkeskole*) are compulsory.

Kindergarten (optional): 5–6 years

- 0th grade: 5–7 years
- 1st grade: 6–8 years
- 2nd grade: 7–9 years

- 3rd grade: 8–10 years
- 4th grade: 9–11 years
- 5th grade: 10–12 years
- 6th grade: 11–13 years
- 7th grade: 12–14 years
- 8th grade: 13–15 years
- 9th grade: 14–16 years

10th grade (optional): 15–18 years

Estonia

In Estonia, 9 years of primary school (*Põhikool* or "basic school") are compulsory. The first three grades of primary school are called *Algkool* which can be translated as "beginning school" and can be confused with primary school. In some low density population areas Algkool is the only school available and students enter primary school in bigger towns.

- 1st grade: 7–8 years
- 2nd grade: 8–9 years
- 3rd grade: 9–10 years
- 4th grade: 10–11 years
- 5th grade: 11–12 years
- 6th grade: 12–13 years
- 7th grade: 13–14 years
- 8th grade: 14–15 years
- 9th grade: 15–16 years

Finland

9 years of primary school (Peruskoulu) are compulsory.

- Kindergarten (optional): 6–7 years
- 1st grade: 7–8 years
- 2nd grade: 8–9 years
- 3rd grade: 9–10 years
- 4th grade: 10–11 years
- 5th grade: 11–12 years
- 6th grade: 12–13 years
- 7th grade: 13–14 years

- 8th grade: 14–15 years
- 9th grade: 15–16 years
- 10th grade (optional): 16–17 years

France

Education is mandatory from 6 years old to 16 years old. Grade is determined by the age on September 1 (year ends around July 5th). Free public and free private education is offered from 3 years old (sometimes 2 years old). Home education is allowed. Occasionally classes are of a double level to make up the number of pupil per class, usually to 29.

Pré-élémentaire (day care)

- garderie (day care)
- crèche (0–4 years old)
- Élémentaire

École maternelle (pre-school)

- très petite section (2 years old) (rare)
- Cycle I

petite section (3 years old)

moyenne section (4 years old)

grande section (5 years old) (September - January)

- Cycle II

grande section (5 years old) (February - July)

École primaire (primary/elementary)

- CP (cours préparatoire) (6 years old) (may be tried a second time (7 years old) if reading and writing are not learned the first time)
- CE1 (cours élémentaire 1) (7 years old)

Cycle III

- CE2 (cours élémentaire 2) (8 years old)
- CM1 (cours moyen 1) (9 years old)
- CM2 (cours moyen 2) (10 years old)

Secondary

- Collège (11 - 15/16 years old - junior high school) *Brevet* diploma
- Lycèe (15/16 – 19 years old - senior high school) *Baccalauréat* diploma supérieur

Premier cycle (17-... years old) - Second cycle (20-... years old) - Troisième cycle (22-... years old)

Collège and *Lycée* are usually separate establishments, with large communes having a *collège*, while the *Lycée* are usually in the larger towns and cities.

Germany

The first school for German children is called Grundschule. It takes usually four years, the pupils are between six and ten years old. The education consists of learning to read, write, basic math and general knowledge. In some schools, a first foreign language is introduced, usually English. In the final year of primary school, children receive a recommendation as to which further school they can attend.

- Kindergarten: 3–6 years
- Grade 1: 6–7 years
- Grade 2: 7–8 years
- Grade 3: 8–9 years
- Grade 4: 9–10 years
- Grade 5: 10–11 years (Berlin and Brandenburg only)
- Grade 6: 11–12 years (Berlin and Brandenburg only)

Depending on the recommendation they received from their teacher, children proceed to their mandatory secondary education in either Hauptschule (Grades 5-9, sometimes 10th grade is added which is then called "Werkrealschule"), Realschule (Grades 5-10), or Gymnasium (Grades 5-12). Upon the successful completion of Grades 11 and 12 in the Gymnasium, students receive the Abitur, a diploma with the permission to enter post-secondary education (similar to the A-level or High School Diploma). The Abitur will not be received at the end of Haupt- and Realschule, but graduating students are eligible to enter the 11th Grade of the Gymnasium if they wish to obtain the Abitur.

Hungary

Primary School education for children in Hungary takes 8 years.

- 1st grade: 6–7 years
- 2nd grade: 7–8 years
- 3rd grade: 8–9 years
- 4th grade: 9–10 years
- 5th grade: 10–11 years

- 6th grade: 11–12 years
- 7th grade: 12–13 years
- 8th grade: 13–14 years

Iceland

In Iceland, 10 years of primary school (*Grunnskóli*) are compulsory.

Primary school teaching in Iceland consists of 10 grade levels. These are:

- 1st grade: 6–7 years
- 2nd grade: 7–8 years
- 3rd grade: 8–9 years
- 4th grade: 9–10 years
- 5th grade: 10–11 years
- 6th grade: 11–12 years
- 7th grade: 12–13 years
- 8th grade: 13–14 years
- 9th grade: 14–15 years
- 10th grade: 15–16 years

India

The National Council of Educational Research and Training (NCERT) is the apex body for school education in India. The NCERT provides support and technical assistance to a number of schools in India and oversees many aspects of enforcement of education policies. In India, the various bodies governing school education system are:

- The state government boards, in which the majority of Indian children are enrolled.
- The Central Board of Secondary Education (CBSE) board.
- The Council for the Indian School Certificate Examinations (CISCE) board.
- The National Institute of Open Schooling.
- International schools affiliated to the International Baccalaureate Programme and/or the Cambridge International Examinations.
- Islamic Madrasah schools, whose boards are controlled by local state governments, or autonomous, or affiliated with Darul Uloom Deoband.

- Autonomous schools like Woodstock School, Auroville, Patha Bhavan and Ananda Marga Gurukula.

Primary school teaching in India consists of 12 grade (Standard) levels. These are:

- Kindergarten: nursery - 3 years, Lower Kindergarten (LKG) -4 years, Upper Kindergarten (UKG) - 5 years.
- 1st Standard: 6 years
- 2nd Standard: 7 years
- 3rd Standard: 8 years
- 4th Standard: 9 years
- 5th Standard: 10 years
- 6th Standard: 11 years
- 7th Standard: 12 years
- 8th Standard: 13 years
- 9th Standard: 14 years
- 10th Standard: 15 years
- 11th Standard: 16 years
- 12th Standard: 17 years

Iran

This section requires expansion. *(June 2008)*

Ireland

Primary school teaching in Ireland consists of 8 class levels. These are:

- Junior Infants (4–5 years)
- Senior Infants (5–6 years)
- 1st class (Rang a haon, 6–7 years)
- 2nd class (Rang a dó, 7–8 years)
- 3rd class (Rang a trí, 8–9 years)
- 4th class (Rang a ceathair, 9–10 years)
- 5th class (Rang a cúig, 10–11 years)
- 6th class (Rang a sé, 11–12 years)

Junior and Senior infants correspond to Kindergarten.

The subjects mainly taught in primary school are:

- English (Béarla, Spellings are taught more in Primary education, not taught in Secondary although if you make a spelling mistake in Secondary English work, you would be corrected)

- Maths (Mata)
- Irish (Gaeilge)
- Modern European language (i.e. French or/and German) (Very rarely)
- History (Stair)
- Geography (Tíreolaíocht/Tír Eolas, direct translation "Country-science/Country information")
- Science (Eolaíocht)
- PE (Physical Education), (Corpoideachas, direct translation "Body education"
- Art (Ealaín)
- Drama (Drámaíocht)
- Music (Ceol)
- SPHE (Social, Personal, Health Education), (OSPS, Oideachas Sóisialta, Pearsanta, Sláintiúil)
- Religion (Reiligiún/Creideamh)

The content of the Religion course taught depends on the management of the school. Many schools are managed and owned by the Roman Catholic Church, with a lesser number belonging to the Church of Ireland and to the Multi Denominational Group Educate Together and a handful run by other religions such as Muslims. Each school body decides on the emphasis of its religious instruction. In Catholic schools 2nd and 6th class prepare children for Holy Communion and Confirmation respectively. In the Church of Ireland this preparation is done when the pupil is aged about 14 years, and is in secondary school.

Children may start at primary school at any age between four and six years of age. Most children finish primary school at or around twelve years of age.

Italy

Primary school teaching in Italy consists of 5 grades. Before the First Grade, there is the kindergarten (*scuola dell'infanzia* in Italian), which is not compulsory.

Elementary

First Grade (6–7 years)

Second Grade (7–8 years)

Third Grade (8–9 years)

Fourth Grade (9–10 years)

Fifth Grade (10–11 years)

Schools used to have a six day school week, Monday to Saturday. Lately, as of 2008, most elementary and middle schools have reduced the school week to five days, with high schools remaining with six.

Israel

Japan: Kindergartens nursery schools are private institutions and attendance is not mandatory.

- Nursery School / Kindergarten (Junior): 3-4 year olds
- Nursery School / Kindergarten (Intermediate): 4-5 year olds
- Nursery School / Kindergarten (Senior): 5-6 year olds
- Elementary School Grade 1: 6-7 year olds
- Elementary School Grade 2: 7-8 year olds
- Elementary School Grade 3: 8-9 year olds
- Elementary School Grade 4: 9-10 year olds
- Elementary School Grade 5: 10-11 year olds
- Elementary School Grade 6: 11-12 year olds
- Middle School Grade 1: 12-13 year olds
- Middle School Grade 2: 13-14 year olds
- Middle School Grade 3: 14-15 year olds
- High School Grade 1: 15-16 year olds
- High School Grade 2: 16-17 year olds
- High School Grade 3: 17-18 year olds

English has become a compulsory subject at primary schools in Japan, since April 2011 in order to compete with other Asian countries in English proficiency; Japanese students have among the lowest English TOEFL scores in Asia.

Malaysia

Primary education is compulsory in Malaysia. Children spend 6 years in primary schools. In 6th year, students sit for a national standardized test known as the Ujian Pencapaian Sekolah Rendah (UPSR, Primary School Achievement Test).

Level One:

- Standard 1 : age 7-8
- Standard 2 : age 8-9

- Standard 3 : age 9-10

Level Two:

- Standard 4 : age 10-11
- Standard 5 : age 11-12
- Standard 6 : age 12-13 (UPSR: Ujian Pencapaian Sekolah Rendah or Primary School Achievement Test)

After completing Standard 6, students will go on to secondary schools.

Lower Secondary

- Form 1 : age 13
- Form 2 : age 14
- Form 3 : age 15 (PMR: Penilaian Menengah Rendah or Lower Secondary Assessment)

Upper Secondary

- Form 4 : age 16
- Form 5 : age 17 (SPM: Sijil Pelajaran Malaysia or Malaysian Certificate of Education)
- Form 6 (Lower): age 18(optional)
- Form 6 (Upper): age 19 (optional)

Next, the students will be moving on into universities or college

Netherlands

Children in the Netherlands must be at least four years old to enter primary education. Almost all 4-year-olds (99.3%) in the Netherlands indeed attend primary school, although this is not *compulsory* until children reach the age of 5. Primary school is free of charge. In most schools, children are grouped by age in mixed ability classes, with one teacher for all subjects. Primary school consists of 8 groups (thus 8 years of schooling). During the first two years (both kindergarten), children receive an average of 22 hours of education, during the last 6 years children receive an average of 25 hours per week. Schools are open 5 days a week, but all children have a half day on Wednesdays (ending at noon). At the end of primary school, in group 8, schools advice on secondary school choice. Most schools use a national test to support this advice, for instance the 'Citotoets', a test developed by the Central Institute for Test development.

- group 1: age 4-5 (kindergarten)
- group 2: age 5-6 (kindergarten)

- group 3: age 6-7 (school curriculum starts with writing, reading, etc.)
- group 4: age 7-8
- group 5: age 8-9
- group 6: age 9-10
- group 7: age 10-11
- group 8: age 11-12 (last school year with advice on secondary school choice)

Poland

Primary School:

- 0th - 6–7 years old
- 1st - 7–8 years old
- 2nd - 8–9 years old
- 3rd - 9–10 years old
- 4th - 10–11 years old
- 5th - 11–12 years old
- 6th - 12–13 years old

Middle School:

- 1st 13–14 years old
- 2nd 14–15 years old
- 3rd 15–16 years old

Secondary School:

- 1st 16–17 years old (Vocational School, Liceum and Technikum)
- 2nd 17–18 years old (Vocational School, Liceum and Technikum)
- 3rd 18–19 years old (Vocational School, Liceum and Technikum)
- 4th 19–20 years old (only in Technikum)

Higher education: 18 and over Children may end their schooling after passing secondary school if desired.

Portugal

In Portugal, the primary education (*ensino primário*) is known as the 1st cycle of the basic education (*1° ciclo do ensino básico*). It includes the first four years of compulsory education (*1ª classe, 2ª classe, 3ª classe* and *4ª classe*), their pupils being children between six and ten years old. After the education reform of 1986, the former primary education became part of the basic education (*educação básica*).

Basic education now includes:

- 1st cycle (*1° ciclo*) - former primary education
  - o 1st year (6–7 years old)
  - o 2nd year (7–8 years old)
  - o 3rd year (8–9 years old)
  - o 4th year (9–10 years old)
- 2nd cycle (*2° ciclo*) - former preparatory education
  - o 5th year (10–11 years old)
  - o 6th year (11–12 years old)
- 3rd cycle (*3° ciclo*) - former preparatory education (continuation)
  - o 7th year (12–13 years old)
  - o 8th year (13–14 years old)
  - o 9th year (14–15 years old)

Singapore

Primary education in Singapore, normally starting at age seven, is a four-year *foundation stage* (Primary 1 to 4) and a two-year *orientation stage* (Primary 5 to 6). Primary education is compulsory and fees are low at public schools, there are also other fees per student to help cover miscellaneous costs.

During the foundation stage, all students are taught English Language as a first language, a mother tongue as a second language and Mathematics. Science is introduced from Primary 3 onwards. In addition to these examinable subjects, lessons in Civics and Moral Education, arts and crafts, music, health education, social studies and physical education are conducted at various levels. Students are also introduced to project work, receive pastoral care and career guidance, and are to participate in Co-Curricular Activities and Community Involvement Programmes. In the orientation stage, weaker students are banded based on their abilities in the four examinable subjects. Known as "Subject-based Banding", they take individual subjects either at the standard or foundation level. Conversely, higher mother tongue is offered for higher ability students.

Sri Lanka

Sweden

- Pre-school class (not compulsory), age 6
- *Grundskola*

- o *Lågstadie*
  - – Year 1, age 7
  - – Year 2, age 8
  - – Year 3, age 9
- o *Mellanstadie*
  - – Year 4, age 10
  - – Year 5, age 11
  - – Year 6, age 12
- o *Högstadie*
  - – Year 7, age 13
  - – Year 8, age 14
  - – Year 9, age 15

- *Gymnasieskola* (not compulsory), age 16-18

Gymnasieskola is not compulsory but most common. What you wish to read is your choice, if you have the right grades for your wanted education. If there are more people who wish to read than spots, the ones with the highest grades are accepted. This is either a preparation for University or for work.

During the year before children start compulsory school, all children are offered a place in a pre-school class (*förskoleklass*), which combines the pedagogical methods of the pre-school with those of compulsory school. Between ages 7 and 15, children attend compulsory comprehensive school (*grundskola*), divided in three stages. The vast majority of schools in Sweden are municipally run, but there are also independent schools. The education in independent schools has many objectives in common with the municipal school, but it can have an orientation that differs from that of the municipal schools.

Syria

9 years of primary school are compulsory.

Kindergarten (optional): 5–6 years

- 1st grade: 6–7 years
- 2nd grade: 7–8 years
- 3rd grade: 8–9 years
- 4th grade: 9–10 years
- 5th grade: 10–11 years
- 6th grade: 11–12 years

- 7th grade: 12–13 years
- 8th grade: 13–14 years
- 9th grade: 14–15 years

Tunisia

In Tunisia pre-school education (3–6 years) is optional and provided primarily in three settings: Kindergartens:socio-educational institutions that come under the supervision of Ministry of culture.

Kouttabs:religious institutions also cater for children between 3 and 5 years of age. Their task is to initiate them into learning the Quran as well as reading, writing, and arithmetic. They are under the supervision of the Ministry of Religious Affairs

Preparatory year: It is also an integral part of basic education but it is not compulsory. It is supervised by the Ministry of Education and is provided in public, private and quasi-public primary schools

9 years of basic education are compulsory.

```
Kindergarten (optional): 5-6 years
1st grade: 6-7 years
2nd grade: 7-8 years
3rd grade: 8-9 years
4th grade: 9-10 years
5th grade: 10-11 years
6th grade: 11-12 years
7th grade: 12-13 years
8th grade: 13-14 years
9th grade: 14-15 years
```

United Kingdom

Primary education is provided by state schools run by the government and by independent fee-paying schools. In the state system children are either educated in separate infant and junior schools or in a combined primary school. Schools in the private sector providing primary education are generally known as preparatory schools or prep schools. In the private sector the transfer to the final stage of education sometimes takes place at 14.

England

Children start school either in the year or the term in which they reach five depending upon the policy of the Local Education Authority. All state schools are obliged to follow a centralised National Curriculum. The primary school years are split into Key Stages:

- Nursery, age 1 to 4
- Reception, age 4 to 5
- Year 1, age 5 to 6
- Year 2, age 6 to 7
- Year 3, age 7 to 8
- Year 4, age 8 to 9
- Year 5, age 9 to 10
- Year 6, age 10 to 11

At the end of Key Stage 2 in Year 6 all children in state primary schools are required to take National Curriculum tests in reading and mathematics also called SATs. All state primary schools are under the jurisdiction of the Department for Children, Schools and Families and are required to receive regular inspections by the Office for Standards in Education (OFSTED). Private schools are inspected by the Independent Schools Inspectorate.

They then change schools to go to secondary school.

- Year 7, age 11 to 12
- Year 8, age 12 to 13
- Year 9, age 13 to 14
- Year 10, age 14 to 15
- Year 11, age 15 to 16
- Year 12, (6th form) 16 to 17
- Year 13 (6th form) 17 to 18

Northern Ireland

Children start school either in the year or the term in which they reach four. All state schools are obliged to follow a centralised National Curriculum. The primary school years are split into Key Stages:

- Primary education
  - o Primary school
    - Foundation Stage
    - Primary 1, age 4 to 5
    - Primary 2, age 5 to 6
    - Key Stage 1
    - Primary 3, age 6 to 7
    - Primary 4, age 7 to 8

- Key Stage 2
- Primary 5, age 8 to 9
- Primary 6, age 9 to 10
- Primary 7, age 10 to 11 (Transfer procedure exams to determine secondary school placement.)

At the end of Key Stage 2 in P7, all children are offered the voluntary Eleven Plus (also called the *transfer procedure*) examinations, though the parents of thirty percent of children elect not to, and send their kids to secondary schools instead of grammar schools.

All state primary schools are under the jurisdiction of the Department of Education.

Scotland

In Scotland children typically spend seven years in a primary school, whose years are named P1 to P7. Children enter P1 at the age of four or five (according to a combination of birth date and parental choice).

Primary 1 (aged 4–6)

Primary 2 (aged 5–7)

Primary 3 (aged 6–8)

Primary 4 (aged 7–9)

Primary 5 (aged 8–10)

Primary 6 (aged 9–11)

Primary 7 (aged 10–12)

1st year - aged 12 to 13

2nd year - aged 13 to 14

3rd year - aged 14 to 15

4th year - aged 15 to 16

5th year - aged 16 to 17

6th year - aged 17 to 18

Wales: Children in Wales spend 7 years at primary school between the ages of 4 and 11.

United States

In the United States the first stage of compulsory education is generally known as elementary education. It takes place in elementary schools which usually incorporates grades 1-5. Some schools have a kindergarten and some go up to sixth grade. Elementary schools in the US are also known as grade schools or grammar schools. In some schools, teachers utilize a "looping system" where the same teacher teaches the same group of students for two years. For example, a third-grade class may have one teacher who would teach those students for an entire year, then that teacher would teach fourth-grade the next year, and thereby teach the same class again. The teacher would then revert to the third grade the following year to start the process all over again with a different group of students.

Over the past few decades, schools in the USA have been testing various arrangements which break from the one-teacher, one-class model. Multi-age programmes, where children in different grades (e.g. Kindergarten through to second grade) share the same classroom and teachers, is one increasingly popular alternative to traditional elementary instruction. Another alternative is that children might have a main class and go to another teacher's room for one subject, such as science, while the science teacher's main class will go to the other teacher's room for another subject, such as social studies. This could be called a two-teacher, or a rotation. It is similar to the concept of teams in junior high school. Another method is to have the children have one set of classroom teachers in the first half of the year, and a different set of classroom teachers in the second half of the year.

Preschool: Ages 3–4

Pre-K: Ages 4–5

Kindergarten: Ages 5–6

1st Grade: Ages 6–7

2nd Grade: Ages 7–8

3rd Grade: Ages 8–9

4th Grade: Ages 9–10

5th Grade: Ages 10–11

6th Grade: Ages 11–12

7th Grade: Ages 12–13

8th Grade: Ages 13–14

9th Grade: Ages 14–15

10th Grade: Ages 15–16

11th Grade: Ages 16–17

12th Grade: Ages 17–18

Responsive and effective distribution systems are an essential pre-requisite in a knowledge industry. These often are weak. Within the knowledge distribution systems there are leaks. There are information rich and information poor societies and there is a skewed distribution of knowledge. Yet an average person today has more knowledge than his counterpart had a hundred years ago. An average patient today has more medical knowledge, an average individual has more legal knowledge and an employee has more managerial knowledge than his counterpart had say 50 years ago. Thus in the knowledge revolution, knowledge has not remained the monopoly of a few. And yet the distribution system has gaps and leaks and presents a skewed picture.

Knowledge or information revolutions have become a reality because of some outstanding breakthroughs in the human history. Some of them occurred when:

- alphabets were created
- paper was invented
- zero was discovered
- decimal system was invented
- printing press was invented
- telegraph and radio were invented
- telephone, television, fax machines and Xerox were invented
- computers and internet were invented and
- satellites were put into orbit and telecommunication became a common experience.

These breakthroughs have resulted into the present information and knowledge revolution. Fruits of knowledge revolution are available but there is mal-distribution.

This has contributed to development of islands of prosperity and continents of ignorance, poverty, illiteracy, over-population, backwardness and poor health. If knowledge industry and knowledge society is to develop properly then information has to be structured in such a way that it fulfils some basic conditions of inter-activity, mobility, convertibility, connectivity, ubiquity and globalization, as given by Toffler (1990).

Distances have shrunk in time and inter-activity is instantaneous. Inter-activity results when the sender and the receiver both interact and when electronic messages of one medium interact with messages of another medium. Video conferencing is one such example.

Barriers in Inclusive Education Violating Rights of Education

The right to education is universal and must extend to all children, youth, and adults with disabilities. This right is enshrined in the Convention on the Rights of the Child (1989) and addressed in several significant, internationally approved declarations, including the World Declaration for Education for All (1990), the Standard Rules on the Equalization of Opportunities for Persons with Disability (1993), the UNESCO Salamanca Statement and Framework for Action (1994), and the Dakar Framework for Action (2000).

The goal of the Dakar Framework for Action is to achieve "education for all" by 2015. The goal of Dakar will only be achieved when all nations recognize that the universal right to education extends to individuals with disabilities, and when all nations act upon their obligation to establish or reform public education systems that are accessible to, and meet the needs of, individuals with disabilities.

This obligation on the state extends to the governments of developing and industrialized nations, and must engage all government bodies charged with setting and carrying out public education and international development assistance programmes and priorities.

This Flagship on Education for All and the Right to education for Persons with Disabilities: Towards Inclusion, has been established to act as a catalyst to ensure that the right to education, and the goals of the Dakar Framework, are realized for individuals with disabilities.

This Flagship has been formed by an alliance of diverse organizations, including global disability organizations, international development agencies, intergovernmental agencies, and experts in the fields of special and inclusive education from developed and developing nations. The Flagship welcomes as members all those who share its goals.

The Flagship is only one venue, and is comprised of just a small number of entities and individuals working to achieve the goals of Education for All. To be successful, this Flagship must engage the efforts and resources of other EFA actors, including donor and lender organizations and government ministries. This Flagship must also work in partnership with others involved in the EFA effort, including those whose primary focus is on such issues as quality teacher preparation and training, early child development, gender equity, education in rural areas, education monitoring tools, and other areas critical to the availability of quality and equitable education for all.

Meijer, C.W., Pijl, S.J, and Hegarty, S.: New Perspectives in Special Education, Routledge, London, 1994.

Mittler, P.: *Working Towards Inclusive Education,* David Fulton, London, 2000.

O'Hanlon, C.: *Special Education Integration in Europe,* David Fulton, London, 1993.

Pijl, S.J., Meijer, C.W, and Hegarty, S.: *Inclusive Education A Global Agenda,* Routledge, London, 1997.

Rose, R, and Howley, M.: *Entitlement or Denial? The Curriculum and its Influence upon Inclusion Processes,* The Stationery Office, London, 2001 .

Rouse, M, and Florian, L.: *School Reform and Special Educational Needs: Anglo American Perspectives,* University of Cambridge Institute of Education, Cambridge, 1996.

Sebba, J, and Sachdev, D.: *What Works in Inclusive Education?* Barnardos, Barkingside, 1997.

Slee, R.: *The Inclusive School,* Routledge, London, 2000.

Stainback, S, and Stainback, W.: *Curriculum Considerations in Inclusive Classrooms: Facilitating Learning for All Students,* Paul Brooks, Baltimore, 1992.

Thomas, G, and Webb, J.: *From Exclusion to Inclusion: Promoting Education for All,* Barnardos, Barkingside, 1997.

Tilstone, C., Florian, L, and Rose, R.: *Promoting Inclusive Practice,* Routledge, London, 1998.

Vitello, S. J, and Mithaug, D. E.: *Inclusive Schooling,* Lawrence Erlbaum, Mahwah, New Jersey, 1998.

Vlachou, A. D.: *Struggles for Inclusive Education,* Open University Press, Buckingham, 1997.

Wolfensberger, W.: *The Principle of Normalization in Human Services,* National Institute on Mental Retardation, Toronto, 1972.

Index

❑❑❑